SEARCHING
FOR THE TRUE
BOTTOM LINE

The Normal Christian Life
According to the Epistles

CARL MCCONCHIE

WESTBOW
PRESS®
A DIVISION OF THOMAS NELSON
& ZONDERVAN

WestBow Press books may be ordered through booksellers or by contacting:

WestBow Press
A Division of Thomas Nelson & Zondervan
1663 Liberty Drive
Bloomington, IN 47403
www.westbowpress.com
844-714-3454

Unless otherwise indicated, all Scripture quotations taken from the (NASB®) New American Standard Bible®, Copyright © 1960, 1971, 1977, 1995, 2020 by The Lockman Foundation. Used by permission. All rights reserved. www.lockman.org

Scripture marked (KJV) taken from the King James Version of the Bible.

ISBN: 978-1-6642-1679-2 (sc)
ISBN: 978-1-6642-1678-5 (e)

Print information available on the last page.

WestBow Press rev. date: 01/27/2021

I dedicate this effort to my wife Phyllis, who has been the love of my life for the past 65 years, who has patiently encouraged me along the way.

ACKNOWLEDGMENTS

I want to gratefully acknowledge all the people who assisted me along the way in the formation of this writing. My good friend, Sally Imhoff, was there at the beginning discussing with me the idea for the book and encouraging me to embark on the project. Pamela Williams graciously agreed to read and review the writing with regard to grammar and spelling. Pastor Michael Lacy was there to encourage me and read through the pages with regard to theology and Biblical content. Sandy Samaniego read it for content and readability and to encourage me with regard to the project. Dell and Lois Bailey proof- read it for wording and typing errors. Other willing readers included Pastor Robert McIntyre, Mary Dumas, Don and Sara Robinson and my daughter, Janice Abbott. I am so grateful for all. A word of thanks goes to Nancy Scott and Mike MacMartin for their help with computer issues.

C O N T E N T S

CHAPTER ONE

WHY NOT?

Introductory Argument - part one

In his early thirties, with a wife and two kids, he was repairing the tail light on the back of a dump truck. Somehow, someone in the truck hit the starter pedal and because it had been parked in reverse gear the huge vehicle lurched backward and in doing so crushed the repairman against a wall killing him instantly. Our little church, located in northern New Jersey, was in a state of shock. It was a devastating tragedy for the family, of course, but it was also something that deeply affected everyone in the church family.

A day or two after the accident a young man came into my study at the church. It took me a few minutes to understand what he wanted me, the pastor, to do. He, along with a group of young adults, had been involved in an evangelistic outreach program. They were very excited about the enabling power of the Holy Spirit with respect to bringing people to Christ and seeing lives changed. Finally, after some delay, the young man before me came to the point. He wanted me to lead a group of people down to the funeral home. There, we would stand around the coffin and ask God to raise back to life the one who had been tragically taken from us.

TABITHA AND EUTYCHUS

The question is: Why not? Jesus raised the dead during His earthly ministry. In fact, He did so on three occasions. Of significance is the fact that, as recorded in the book of Acts, Peter and Paul were enabled to raise the dead. A passage in Acts 9 relates the wonderful story of a believer named Tabitha. Luke (the author of Acts) tells us that she was a woman "abounding with deeds of kindness and charity which she continually did" (Acts 9:36). The account is powerful, rivaling in beauty and drama the stories of Jesus raising the dead as found in Matthew 9:25, Luke 7:11-17, and John 11:1-44. We read in verses 37- 42 of Acts 9:

> And it happened at that time that she fell sick and died; and when they had washed her body, they laid it in an upper room. Since Lydda was near Joppa, the disciples, having heard that Peter was there, sent two men to him, imploring him, "Do not delay in coming to us." So Peter arose and went with them. When he arrived, they brought him into the upper room; and all the widows stood beside42 him, weeping and showing all the tunics and garments that Dorcas used to make while she was with them. But Peter sent them all out and knelt down and prayed, and turning to the body, he said, "Tabitha, arise." And she opened her eyes, and when she saw Peter, she sat up. And he gave her his hand and raised her up; and calling the saints and widows, he presented her alive. It became known all over Joppa, and many believed in the Lord. (Acts 9:36-42)

After sending the grieving widows out of the room, Peter did something that Jesus, according to the Gospel accounts, did not do. He "knelt down and prayed" (Acts 9: 40). Peter had seen Jesus raise the dead. According to the record he was there on those three occasions when Jesus brought back the dead.[1] Now it is his turn to attempt the impossible. He does the logical thing; he knelt down and prayed. Should we then attempt, what would seem to be, the impossible?

The story of Paul raising Eutychus is found in Acts 20:7-12. One

---

[1] The NIV Study Bible, (Grand Rapids, Michigan: Zondervan Bible Publishers, 1985) p. 1662.

evening in Troas, Paul is behaving like the proverbial long-winded preacher. He "prolonged his message until midnight." Verses 9 –12 relate:

> And there was a young man named Eutychus sitting on the window sill, sinking into a deep sleep; and as Paul kept on talking, he was overcome by sleep and fell down from the third floor and was picked up dead. But Paul went down and fell upon him, and after embracing him, he said, "Do not be troubled, for his life is in him." … They took away the boy alive, and were greatly comforted. (Acts 20:9-12)

As far as we know, Paul had not seen Jesus raise the dead. He did not hesitate, nevertheless, to attempt the impossible. Again, the question is, should we? If it was given to mortal men such as Peter and Paul to bring back the dead, shouldn't we expect to realize such activity of the Holy Spirit in our day? Furthermore, Jesus promised in John 14:12:

> Truly, truly I say to you, he who believes in Me, the works that I do, he will do also and greater *works* than these he will do; because I go to the Father. (John 14:12)

It is our intention to take up the meaning of this verse later on. But we ask again, "Why not?" Well, on the common- sense level, we could ask in response, "If the man has departed into the presence of Christ, which according to Paul is 'very much better' (Philippians 1:23), why should we think about bringing him back?" Someone might point out, though, that he was very much needed by those left behind.

There is a much better answer to the question and that is what this book is all about. The larger question is: How do we know what is *normative* for the believer in the twenty-first century? What Biblical examples are we to follow? What Biblical instructions, exhortations, admonitions or commandments are meant for us today? If Jesus raised the dead, why shouldn't we? If Jesus cast out demons, why shouldn't we? If Jesus fasted forty days in the wilderness, should we try to do the same? If Jesus overturned the money changers' tables in the temple, should we?

James M. Boice, in a book entitled "Power Religion," argues the following:

> One great principle of hermeneutics (the science of Bible interpretation) is that narrative events are to be interpreted by didactic or teaching events rather than the other way around. In other words, that some-thing has happened once or even more than once does not mean that it is to be taken as normative for us. For instance, we do not repeat annual crossings of the Red Sea. Such miraculous events are redemptive events and are not presented as normative Christian experience. They are to be *remembered*, not *repeated*. What is normative is explicit teaching, and, as we have seen, the New Testament does not teach that evangelism is to be done by cultivating miracles.[2]

THE BOTTOM LINE OF SCRIPTURE

In this writing I intend to take the above statement one step further. I want to be more specific about what is "normative" for today. The answer is to be found in what I call *The Bottom Line*.

I hear that expression or read it just about every day. In fact, if you are listening for it, you might hear it several times a day. Someone is discussing an issue in an interview on a cable news program. Very often you will hear them refer to the *bottom line*. I walk into a pharmacy and see there a brochure. It is entitled *Generic Drugs--The Bottom Line*. Recently I listened to a pastor who was teaching on II Timothy. In pointing out that the epistle contained the final words of the Apostle Paul. He referred to it as "the bottom line." He said that Paul was writing about what really mattered to him as he approached the end of his earthly journey.

The terminology was first used in reference to financial statements. Every year while reading my income tax return I take note of the

---

[2] James M. Boice, "A Better Way: The Power of The Word and Spirit," *Power Religion, The Selling of the Evangelical Church*, Ed. Michael Scott Hortorn, (Chicago: Moody Press, 1982), p. 128.

exemptions, the deductions, the credits, and the net taxable income. But I am most interested in that which is at the bottom of the page -- How much tax am I required to pay? What is the *bottom line*? Today, in conversation or writing, the term is used to refer to the essence of a matter, or the main thing. What does it all add up to? After all the particulars have been considered, what does it all bring us down to

As I have entitled this book, "Searching For The True Bottom Line," I have the following in view: After the history and commands of the Old Testament are presented, after the four Gospels record for us the life and teachings of Jesus, after the book of Acts relates the activities of the early church, and after all that has gone before, coming to the book of Romans and the other New Testament epistles, we come to what I call *The Bottom Line*. After all the commands, teachings, exhortations, encouragements and examples of those who have gone before, we ask, "What then is *normative* for us today?" I believe that what we find in the Epistles by way of instruction, commands and admonitions, presents to us what matters most with regard to Christian life and service. It may seem to be a radical view, but I am suggesting that if something is not found in the Epistles it probably should not be a matter of emphasis in the life of the believer.

For example, in The Letters to The Churches (the Epistles) we have nothing that encourages us to endeavor to bring people back from the dead. Needless to say, *raising the dead* is not among the spiritual gifts listed in Romans twelve or among those found in I Corinthians twelve. However, please note: I am not saying concerning this, or the other matters to be considered in this book, that such things cannot happen today. I certainly do not wish to put a limit on our perception of or acceptance of what our sovereign God might do. Rather the question is -- What does the normal Christian life consist of today? What is to be a matter of emphasis in the Christian life and what is not?

PREACHING THE ENTIRE WORD

Finally, in this introductory chapter I want to share the fact that as the pastor of two churches over the course of forty-six years I have enjoyed preaching from every part of the Bible. Week after week in my preparation of expository messages, the truth and wonder of the Word of

God have been confirmed in my heart and mind over and over again. I deeply love it all -- drawing lessons from the life of Abraham in Genesis, or teaching the books of Ruth, Esther, Job, or studying prophetic books like Daniel and Ezekiel, or presenting series on the Sermon on the Mount, the Upper Room Discourse and the Olivet Discourse. I exult in observing the systematic consistency of the Scriptures -- how it all hangs together in wonderful harmony. I have continued to learn and to appreciate the Bible as the inspired Word of God.

It is my hope that this writing might be helpful to new believers who find themselves somewhat bewildered by the plethora of beliefs and practices of modern day Christendom as well as help for Christians further along the way who desire clarification on certain issues, or help with certain seemingly awkward passages of Scripture.

CHAPTER TWO

SOME THINGS NEVER CHANGE, BUT SOME THINGS DO

Introductory Argument - part two

They were not to pack bags. They were not to buy Travelers Checks. They were not to take cash or credit-cards or any other means of financial security. Food, extra clothing, luggage were items not permitted- not even a carry-on is allowed. These, in essence, are the instructions that Jesus gave the twelve disciples as he sent them out on a mission as recorded in Luke chapter 9:1-5:

> And He called the twelve together, and gave them power and authority over all the demons and to heal diseases. And He sent them out to proclaim the kingdom of God and to perform healing. And He said to them, "Take nothing for your journey, neither a staff, nor a bag, nor bread, nor money; and don't even have two tunics apiece. Whatever house you enter, stay there until you leave the city. And as for those who do not receive you, as you go out from that city, shake the dust off your feet as a testimony against them." (Luke 9: -12)

Now the question is: How many mission boards take this passage seriously as they prepare to send men and women out to the mission fields of the world? I do not know of any who do, but I suspect that there are some who do try to follow the instructions of this passage. Generally, we see missionaries making elaborate preparations, not only raising money and carefully packing much luggage, but sometimes shipping many boxes of goods well in advance of their journey.

How then do we handle this awkward passage? In chapter ten of Luke we find almost the same instructions given to the seventy disciples who are being sent out. That passage even contains a familiar verse that is often heard in sermons about missions. "And He was saying to them, 'The harvest is plentiful, but the laborers are few, therefore beseech the Lord of the harvest to send out laborers into His harvest'" (Luke 10:2). We read in verse one that he sent them out in pairs. That makes a good deal of sense to us, but then we read again that they were to "carry no money belt, no bag, nor shoes; and greet no one on the way" (Luke 10:4).

THE KING MAKES REQUSITION

There is, however, a key sentence that is repeated twice in the passage. It is found in verse 9 and also in verse 11 of chapter ten. They were to proclaim that, "The kingdom of God has come near to you...yet be sure of this, that the kingdom of God has come near." (Luke 10:9-11)

This then is how I understand these passages: Jesus is presenting Himself as the promised Messiah, the long-awaited King of Israel. He is offering His people the promised kingdom of peace and glory. We would expect such a king to claim a right to make requisition of His subjects. Here, it seems, He is telling his ambassadors to depend upon the provision of the subjects of the kingdom. If the people are receiving Him as their king, they will then be pleased to extend hospitality to the servants of the king.

We take note of verse 2 of Luke chapter 9, "And He sent them out to proclaim the kingdom of God and to perform healing." I assume that miracles of healing would not only speak to the compassion of their king, but are meant also to authenticate the message of His emissaries. As we have noted, we twice read in chapter ten, "The kingdom of God has come near to you" (Luke 10:9,10). I am suggesting that the instructions of Jesus as found in Luke nine and ten are not meant to apply to missionaries sent out in our day. Rather, the words had to do with Jesus' offer of His kingdom during His earthly ministry.

HOW DO WE DELINEATE?

This brings us back to the main question presented in this book: How do we know what examples of Scripture, what commandments, instructions, and admonitions are meant for us in our day? We intend in these pages to demonstrate that the New Testament Epistles are to be taken as the *bottom line* in the matter. What we find in the Epistles, we assume, are for us today. If something is not found there, it is then questionable as to whether or not it is normative for us today.

SOME THINGS NEVER CHANGE

Of course, there is a great deal of content in the Epistles that corresponds to what we have previously in Scripture. The teachings of Jesus found in the Sermon on the Mount are also found in the Epistles. The things which He declares in The Upper Room Discourse are carried forth into the Epistles. His teaching there on the ministry of the Holy Spirit is found throughout the Epistles. The moral teachings of the Ten Commandments are repeated in the Epistles. But the instructions of Jesus to His disciples in Luke nine and ten concerning their mission are not found in the Epistles. And as we pointed out in the previous chapter, there is no command or encouragement to raise the dead, though we read of it in the Gospels and in the book of Acts.

The eternal moral law of God as reflected in the content of the Ten Commandments and further interpreted in "The Sermon on The Mount" does not change. That which is based upon the very character of God never changes. So then, we can expect to find and do find such absolutes set forth in the New Testament Epistles. For example, the primacy of love in human relations is a matter of major emphasis in the letters to the churches. John the Apostle writes, "Beloved, let us love one another, for love is from God; and everyone who loves is born of God; and everyone who loves is born of God and knows God. The one who does not love does not know God, for God is love" (I John 4:7-8). Jesus had said in the Upper Room Discourse, "A new commandment I give to you, that you love one another, even as I have loved you, that you also love one another" (John 13:34). And so, Paul admonishes in Galatians five that we should "through love serve one another." He writes, "For the whole Law is fulfilled in one word, in the statement, "YOU SHALL LOVE YOUR NEIGHBOR AS YOURSELF" (Galatians 5:13-14).

BUT SOME THINGS DO

Some things never change and those things are <u>restated</u> in the Epistles. But then again, *some things do change.* A clear example of this is found in the Gospel of Luke, chapter 22. On the night of His betrayal, in the shadow of the Cross, immediately after His prediction that Peter would deny Him three times, we have the words of verses 35-37:

> And He said to them, "When I sent you out without money belt and bag and sandals, you did not lack anything, did you? 'They said, 'Nothing.' And He said to them, 'But now, whoever has a money belt is to take it along, likewise also a bag, and whoever has no sword is to sell his coat and buy one. For I tell you that this which is written must be fulfilled in Me, 'And He WAS NUMBERED WITH TRANSGRESSORS'; for that which refers to me has its fulfillment" (Luke 22:35-37)

As seen in the above passage, we have presented a very clear change in marching orders; and these are in accord with a dramatic change in circumstances. The King is about to be officially rejected as Israel's Messiah. His disciples cannot now expect to receive provision from the subjects of the King. Rather, they can now expect hardship and in fact, spiritual warfare. Peter, taking the words of Jesus literally says, "Lord, look, here are two swords." But Jesus replied, "It is enough" (Luke 22:38). It is implied that the coming warfare will be spiritual in nature, rather than physical. The words of Jesus as found in Luke 10:4-9 are quite different when we come to chapter 22:35,36. So then, we see that some things do change.

There is sometimes a change in God's program for His people. In view of the fact that there is sometimes a change of circumstances and a change of program in accordance with God's sovereignty and purposes, we come back to our original question; How do we know what marching orders, what instructions, admonitions and commandments are meant for us to follow in our day? Again, we suggest that the *bottom line* is to be found in the Letters to the churches. That which is *normative* with respect to our life and service today can be found in that portion of Scripture that begins with Romans and extends through the book of Revelation.

In the chapters that follow we shall consider some of the specific issues that are in question. What about the matter of *fasting*? What about the practice of *exorcism*? What about the emphasis on healing ministries? What about an emphasis on speaking in *tongues*? What about the matter of *Sabbath observance*? There are a number of Christian leaders who currently specialize in such matters. They write books on the subject. They hold special meetings. They single out certain issues and elevate them to a place of central importance. In this writing we will evaluate how much emphasis is given in the Epistles to certain matters which some say are all-important and even key to successful Christian life and service.

The latter part of this book consists of a series of outlines which divide the exhortations and admonitions of the Epistles into categories. An outline for each epistle shows the number of verses devoted to each category.

CHECK OUT MY PREMISE

I invite the reader to consider the validity of my premise. The major premise of an argument is always assumed. The Bible nowhere states that the Epistles present to us *the bottom line*. Bear with me for a while and note as to whether or not my argument is full of contradictions and whether or not the premise matches the facts as they are presented in Scripture. Are there too many problems with the premise? Am I being too radical in my approach to the Word of God? You decide. Again, I want to emphasize that the focus of this writing is not upon doctrine, or historical information, or lessons to be learned from examining Scripture -- although some of that will be touched upon -- but rather upon what is exhorted in the Epistles and what is not. In connection with statements made as to whether or not certain matters are indeed exhorted in the Epistles. I intend to explore why such is the case by discussing passages of Scripture that relate to the matter in question.

CHAPTER THREE

EXORCISM

CASE IN POINT

Once, in a dinner meeting with a small group of pastors, I took part in a discussion concerning the matter of *exorcism*. Our guest was a man whose special ministry was exorcism. He had been invited to speak on this subject at a nearby university. I took this opportunity to ask him about the fact that *exorcism* is not listed among the Spiritual Gifts. After hesitating a moment, he suggested that it is not singled out as one of the Charismata because all believers have the authority to do it when necessary. He did not address the fact that nowhere in the Epistles are all believers said to have such authority, nor are they encouraged to practice *exorcism*. Nevertheless, this man and a number of others like him have made it their specialty.

IT JUST ISN'T THERE

We come now to a prime example of that which pertains to my thesis. Very often emphasis is given to matters that are not supported by the New Testament epistles. There is no mention of *exorcism* in the epistles. Neither Paul, nor Peter, or John or James, or the writer of the book of Hebrews admonishes, or instructs, or encourages anyone to cast out demons. Yes, Satan and his demons are referred to in a number of passages. Spiritual warfare is presented as a matter that deserves serious attention. Believers are admonished to be vigilant with respect to the temptations that come from our adversary, whether subtle or blatant. But nowhere is there any encouragement to cast out demons

The subject is not found where we might expect to find it-- among the lists of Spiritual Gifts. It is not listed in Romans 12:6-8 or in I Corinthians chapters 12-14 or in Ephesians 4:7-13. Yes, in verse 10 of I Corinthians 12 reference is made to the *"effecting of miracles."* There are some who suggest that *exorcism* might be included in that category.

There is also reference made to gifts of healings in I Corinthians 12 verses 9, 28 and 30. The plural forms, *gifts* and *healings* perhaps indicate healing with regard to different kinds of ailments. The casting out of demons might be considered to be a kind of healing. That is a possibility, but the fact remains that *exorcism* is not singled out as one of the gifts. It also should be noted that the gift of *effecting miracles* and *gifts of healings* are not included in the list of spiritual gifts found in Romans twelve. More attention will be given to that fact later on.

The truth of the observation just made is very remarkable, considering the fact that exorcism is so prevalent in the Gospel accounts. Demonic possession is presented as very real with respect to the life and ministry of Jesus on earth. Demonic opposition is seen to be everywhere. Undoubtedly the disciples of Jesus were instructed to make exorcism a part of their ministry, and with some success:

> The seventy returned with joy, saying, "Lord, even the demons are subject to us in Your name." And He said to them, "I was watching Satan fall from heaven like lightning. Behold, I have given you authority to tread on serpents and scorpions, and over all the power of the enemy, and nothing will injure you" (Luke 10:17-19).

But, we ask, has Jesus given such authority to believers in our day? I am suggesting that there is no evidence that He has. We note the last phrase of verse 19, "and nothing will injure you" (Luke10:19). But missionaries in our day have been murdered. Many believers have suffered a great deal at the hands of their enemies down through the years. I am led to believe that neither the authority nor the protection is guaranteed with respect to the power of the enemy to work in the hearts of men against us.

Some might question as to what kind of injury, physical or spiritual, is in view here, arguing that "...nothing can separate us from the love of God" (Romans 8:37-39). The latter promise is certainly true, but I am speaking in reference to the authority and protection that is specifically stated in Luke ten.

At this point some may object, pointing to the content of Mark chapter sixteen, noting in particular the words of verses 15-18:

> And He said to them, "Go into all the world and preach the gospel to all creation. He who has believed and has been baptized shall be saved; but he who has disbelieved shall be condemned. These signs will accompany those who have believed: in My name they will cast out demons, they will speak with new tongues; they will pick up serpents, and if they drink any deadly poison, it will not hurt them; they will lay hands on the sick, and they will recover" (Mark 16:15-18).

Do not these words of Jesus take us from His time into our day as the Gospel is being preached throughout the world (vs.15)? Shouldn't we infer from this that exorcism and other special signs are to be practiced today by His people?

OLDER IS BETTER

Perhaps, but as indicated in the foot-notes of many versions of the Bible, there is a textual problem with regard to verses 9-20 of Mark sixteen. As the reader may know, there is a major controversy in the area of textual criticism (the study of ancient manuscripts). This, perhaps, is a good point at which to get into this matter, because it will also come up in some of the following chapters of this writing.

There is, on the one hand, that which is referred to as "The Majority Text," which relates to an ancient version called "The Textus Receptus." The King James Version of the Bible, as well as the New King James Version, is based upon this text, partly because of the great quantity of manuscripts that support it.

There is, on the other hand, that which is referred to as the "Westcott and Hort text," the designation being based on the names of two scholars, Brooke Foss Westcott and Fenton John Anthony Hort. They put together a Greek version which is based upon fewer, but significantly older manuscripts; these have been discovered since the King James version was first published.[3] The American Standard version of the Bible published in 1901, as well as more modern versions such as the New American Standard Bible, The English Standard Version and the New International version are based on the Westcott and Hort text. There seems to be more support, at least from my perspective, for this latter text among scholars and professors who have served in our evangelical seminaries in recent years. I found this to be true during my college and seminary days.

This consensus of Bible scholars, therefore, does not regard Mark 16:9-20 as part of the original writing of the New Testament because it does not have the support of the older and, thus, better manuscripts. The earliest extant manuscripts do not support the reading. Indeed, the latter part of Mark chapter sixteen is problematic in many respects. So, the matters of *casting out demons, drinking deadly poisons*, and picking up *serpents* as found in Mark 16:9-20 are not, in my opinion, supported in Scripture. Although, some of these things were experienced by Paul, these matters are not exhorted for us today according to the Epistles.

MY ARGUMENT-- BASED ON INTERNAL EVIDENCE

Let me now take the space to share with the reader my take on the matter from another perspective -- that of the theological content of passages in question. Not being by any means a student of textual criticism, I am somewhat able, I believe, to evaluate the content of some of the passages involved in the controversy.

We have, for example, the case of alleged angelic intervention at the pool of Bethesda as recorded in John chapter five:

---

[3] Fenton John Anthony Hort, and Brooke Foss Westcott, *The New Testament in the Original Greek, Vol.1,* (New York: Macmillan Co., 1881.

Now there is in Jerusalem by the sheep gate a pool, which is called in Hebrew Bethesda, having five porticoes. In these lay a multitude of those who were sick, blind, lame, and withered, [waiting for the moving of the waters; for an angel of the Lord went down at certain seasons into the pool and stirred up the water; whoever then first, after the stirring up of the water, stepped in was made well from whatever disease with which he was afflicted] (John 5:2-4).

The words found in brackets, as shown in the New American Standard Version, are those that are in question. They are not found in the oldest Greek manuscripts, rightly so, I believe. The theology would seem to be all wrong. The Bible, as I see it, does not support the idea of healing being offered to the strongest. One version of the story is that after an angel stirred the waters, the one who was able to get into the water first was the one that was healed. That does not seem to correspond well with the Bible's picture of a loving, merciful and gracious God. We might understand an evil angel doing that sort of thing, but we would not expect "an angel of the Lord" (John 5;:4) to be offering healing to the strongest. So, for theological reasons, I believe the later manuscripts to be in error and that the words in question have been wrongly added to the original text.

It is likely that the people waiting by the pool had the mistaken belief that an angel occasionally stirred the waters, but I do not believe that the Bible says so. I intend to use a similar argument in a following chapter on another matter. I have used this passage in John to illustrate the matter of theological content supporting the reading of the older Greek manuscripts. Coming back then to Mark sixteen, I suggest to you that those verses in Mark sixteen do not support the practice of exorcism in our day. Furthermore, even if those verses are accepted as having been in the original text, that does not necessarily mean that the practice is normative for our day. We could say that the predicted practice was fulfilled in the book of Acts; and many do interpret the verses that way.

THE REALITY OF DEMON POSSESSION

The reality of demon possession with respect to its terrible and formidable nature is presented to us in the 17th chapter of Matthew's gospel. Interestingly, there is a manuscript problem, similar to that described above, found in the account. A boy (we don't know how old he was) is possessed with a sinister force that causes him to fall "into the fire and often into the water" (Matthew 17:15). It's a case that the disciples just can't handle. The story is found in Matthew 17:14-21:

> When they came to the crowd, a man came up to Jesus, falling on his knees before Him and saying, "Lord, have mercy on my son, for he is a lunatic and is very ill; for he often falls into the fire and often into the water. I brought him to your disciples and they could not cure him." And Jesus answered and said, "You unbelieving and perverted generation, how long shall I be with you? How long shall I put up with you? Bring him here to me." And Jesus rebuked him, and the demon came out of him, and the boy was cured at once. Then the disciples came to Jesus privately and said, "Why could we not drive it out?" And He said to them, "Because of the littleness of your faith; for truly I say to you, if you have faith the size of a mustard seed, you will say to this mountain, 'Move from here to there,' and it will move; and nothing will be impossible to you. [But this kind does not go out except by prayer and fasting."] (Matthew 17:14-21)

The New American Standard Bible has placed Matthew 17:21 in brackets, with a footnote at the bottom of the page stating that the reading is not supported by the early manuscripts. The New International Version of the Bible does not include the verse in the text. Again, there is an explanatory note at the bottom of the page.

The words of verse Matthew 17:21, which are included in the King James Bible, suggest, on the one hand, that *fasting*, along with prayer, is the secret to successfully casting out a powerful demon. Once again, I find myself disagreeing with that reading for theological reasons. It suggests that we must add works to our faith in order to obtain answers to our prayers. It implies also that Jesus Himself used the method and that we should follow His example. It implies that *fasting* as a discipline was a regular practice in the prayer life of Jesus. All of the above is suggested by a verse that, probably, does not belong in the text.

However, aside from verse 21 of Matthew 17, the passage does present to us the fearsome reality of demon possession. Referring to the difficulty that the disciples had, Jesus speaks of their faith as being too small for the occasion. What they needed was faith which He likens to a mustard seed; though being very small it has the capacity for phenomenal growth. Jesus speaks of a faith that can move mountains. Casting out such a demon is analogous to moving a mountain.

We must not say that Jesus is mistaken concerning the cause of the boy's illness. Neither should we say that Jesus is just going along with the beliefs of that culture in that day. Nor should we say that Jesus is misleading us about the phenomenon of demon possession. There is only one good alternative. We have to believe that Jesus is speaking truthfully. In the Gospel accounts demon possession is seen to be a prevalent and fearsome reality.

A REMARKABLE OMMISSION

It seems quite remarkable, at least to me, that the matter of *exorcism* is not even mentioned in any of the New Testament epistles. Let me say quite plainly that I am not saying that *exorcism* never takes place in our day. I would not limit what God might do at any time or anywhere (on the mission field for example). Rather, we are writing about what is to be emphasized in our day, what is normative as based upon what the Letters to the Churches say or do not say.

It is quite possible that the matter of demon possession and the need for exorcism will be more critical just prior to the return of Christ. Again, I am not denying the reality of demon possession. In the Gospel accounts Jesus recognizes that reality and we cannot say that He was simply naïve about the matter or, on the other hand, simply accommodating His teaching to the beliefs of the day.

This chapter has been entitled "Exorcism--Case in Point" because the matter of *exorcism* illustrates the thesis of this writing. Here we have a matter that is not even mentioned in the New Testament epistles and yet there are Christian leaders who specialize in it. I have observed that there are issues which are lifted up to a place of central importance in Christian life and service when, according to the writers of the Epistles, they are not meant to be. The same is true of other matters that we shall consider. Christian leaders write books, hold meetings and teach on matters that are not encouraged and sometimes not even mentioned in the Epistles.

As Paul, Peter, John and the other New Testament authors wrote letters to those early churches (and to some people who did not as yet have the Gospel accounts in writing, and to a great many who were Gentiles who knew little about the values and lessons presented in the Old Testament), wouldn't we expect them to have included in their writings the things that are really important, that are meant to be normative for Christian life and service? I believe they did.

CHAPTER FOUR

TO FAST OR NOT TO FAST

That is the question

She was a rather attractive middle-age mother of two children who possessed the kind of loving and winsome personality that made her special in the eyes of her husband and many others, including members of our church family. She was also a new believer in Christ. However, she had cancer which eventually took her life. I have often wondered why the Lord in His wisdom often takes home to Himself some very special people. She was one of those.

As I recall she had endured five operations over a period of several years. The church family prayed faithfully, asking the Lord to intervene and turn back her illness. We prayed that the Lord would give the physicians wisdom and skill in their treatment. We asked for a miracle, not only her sake but also for that of her family.

Eventually a man, who was a prominent leader in the church, came to me with a suggestion. In so many words he stated that there was a reason as to why the Lord was not answering our prayers. *We were not fasting.* If we wanted the Lord to respond to our prayers, we should spend some time as a church family in corporate fasting. Well, we did set aside a day of fasting and I have to say that it was a good experience. It was good to just focus on the Lord, putting aside other distractions and spending the time in His presence.

EARNING POINTS WITH THE CREATOR?

However, the theology that brought us to that day is not valid. I do not find anywhere in Scripture teaching that supports the idea that we somehow earn points with God by practicing the spiritual discipline of fasting. Nevertheless, it seems to be the kind of thinking that is entertained in the minds of many of God's people.

Patrick Morley has written a book entitled, "A Man's Guide to the Spiritual Disciplines." The Men's Sunday School class in my last church recently went through the book and found it to be a profitable study. However, he does devote a chapter in the book to fasting as one of the *Spiritual Disciplines*. To his credit he does issue this word of caution on page 118:

> As we have noted with other disciplines, fasting does not "buy" more love or attention from God. It does not earn His favor. It does not improve a person's place in some Christian pecking order. Fasting is simply a tool to help us remove distractions and focus more clearly on relating to God and pursuing His will. When you slow down your physiological life, there can be an expansion on the physiological life, there can be an expansion on the spiritual side of your life. In fact, the acuity, the sharpness of our mental faculties goes up when the blood is not focusing on the digestive process.[4]

He makes a similar comment on page 125 of his book:

> And remember—the point of all this isn't to earn a pat on the back from God. The point is to tangibly demonstrate our love for Him and our desire to lead a more holy life. Again, if we never sacrifice anything for Jesus, how is He going to know that we love Him? How are we going to know that we love Him? Fasting is a wonderful discipline to make such a sacrifice. Fasting gives us opportunity to satisfy our spiritual appetite by sacrificing our physical appetite.[5]

---

[4] Patrick Morley, A Man's guide to The Spiritual Disciplines, (Chicago: Moody Press), page 125
[5] Ibid., p. 125

All of this is well written and certainly has appeal for anyone who desires a closer relationship with the Lord. Morley also states on page 118 that "fasting was common during the era when Jesus lived on earth." But he is misleading when he gives us a list of persons in the Bible who fasted (mostly Old Testament) and then declares that "fasting is an integral part of the Bible."[6]

OUR PREMISE RESTATED

This brings me now to a restatement of that which is my premise in this writing.

Exhortations, admonitions and instructions for the Christian life today are found in the New Testament Epistles (the books of Romans through Revelation). The Epistles present to us the *bottom Line*, that which is normative for our day. If something is not found there, then it is questionable as to whether it should be emphasized in the believer's life and service.

IT'S JUST NOT THERE

Here now is the *bottom line* on the subject of fasting in the Epistles. Fasting as a spiritual discipline is simply not found there. "Hold on now," someone may be saying. "I can think of a couple of places where fasting is mentioned." In fact, Patrick Morley refers to one such passage stating that, indeed, the Apostle Paul fasted.[7] Concerning the matter of apparent references to fasting in the Epistles, they can be divided into two categories:

CASES OF MISTAKEN IDENTITY

First of all, there are the cases of mistaken identity. There are two passages in the book of II Corinthians where the word fasting is found in the Authorized Version (KJV), in which it's a matter of older vocabulary usage as opposed to new. Here is the passage that Morley cites in his statement that Paul fasted:

---

[6] Ibid., p. 118
[7] Ibid., p. 118

I *have been* on frequent journeys, in dangers from rivers, dangers from robbers, dangers from *my* countrymen, dangers from the Gentiles, dangers in the city, dangers in the wilderness, dangers on the sea, dangers among false brethren: I *have been* in labor and hardship, through many sleepless nights, in hunger and thirst, often without food, in cold exposure (II Corinthians 11:26-27).

It seems obvious, taking these two verses together to establish the context, that Paul is not giving us a list of spiritual disciplines. Rather, he is giving us a list of the hardships that he went through and "going without food" is one of them. Yes, the King James Version calls it "fasting" (II Corinthians 11:27). But the difference in translation is simply due to the use of words in the day when the King James Version was published in contrast to the way that we would use those words today. In this case it is not a manuscript problem, the kind we discussed previously. What Paul refers to in this passage is involuntary fasting, or going "without food."

There is a similar passage in II Corinthians 6:4-5:

but in everything commending ourselves as servants of God, in much endurance, in afflictions, in hardships, in distresses, in beatings, in imprisonments, in tumults, in labors, in sleeplessness, in hunger… (II Corinthians 6:4-5)

Once again, it's a case of mistaken identity in the perception of some proponents of fasting today. The context clearly indicates that Paul is giving us a list of hardships that he endured, as opposed to spiritual disciplines that he practiced. That last word in verse 5 of II Corinthians 6 is correctly translated "hunger," as opposed to "fasting."

MANUSCRIPTS MATTER

The second category of passages, used to defend the occurrence of fasting in the Epistles, relates to the manuscript debate that we mentioned in the previous chapter. There is, for example, the apparent reference to fasting in I Corinthians 7:5 as found in the King James Version. However, the word *fasting* is not found in the New American Standard Bible or in the New International Version of the Bible. We have in this verse another instance of that which we referred to in our last chapter -- the conflict between two traditions of Greek manuscript evidence. The older, and in my opinion better, Greek manuscripts do not include the Greek word for *fasting*, while those upon which the King James Bible is based does.

In I Corinthians 7:5, as Paul is admonishing husbands and wives to fulfill their marital duties to one another, he instructs them not to deprive one another he writes: "except by agreement for a time, so that you may devote yourselves to prayer, [The KJV adds "and fasting"] and come together again so that Satan will not tempt you because of your lack of self-control" (I Corinthians 7:5). I have used this passage many times through the years in pre-marriage counseling sessions. Many couples are astounded to realize that the Bible actually commands husbands and wives to fulfill their sexual duties to one another. But now we want to point out that the word "fasting" has been apparently added somewhere along the line in the copying process. Based upon my view that the older manuscripts are better, I do not believe that the word *fasting* belongs in our English versions. I concur with the NIV, the ESV and the NASB versions of the New Testament.

We can also note here that, even if the word *fasting* is accepted as truly belonging in the text and thus correctly included in the King James Version, we still do not have a direct exhortation or even encouragement to practice fasting as a spiritual discipline. Paul would be simply acknowledging it, along with prayer, as a legitimate reason as to why a husband and wife might be separated for a time.

THE SECRET OF SUCCESS?

There comes to mind two other passages where a reference to fasting is found in the King James Version but is not found in the NAS or NIV versions of the New Testament. One of these we mentioned in the previous chapter. In Matthew 17 we find that the Disciples had been trying to drive a demon out of a man's son. When they could not accomplish that feat, they came to Jesus and said, "Why could we not drive it out" (Matthew 17:19)? Jesus replies in verses 20-21 of Matthew 17:

...because of the littleness of your faith; for truly I say to you, If you have faith the size of a mustard seed, you will say to this mountain, 'Move from here to there,' and it will move; and nothing will be impossible to you. [But this kind does not go out except by prayer and fasting]. (Matthew 17:20-21)

As noted before the NASB has put verse 21 in brackets and added a foot-note at the bottom of the page, indicating that the early manuscripts do not contain the verse. The reference to fasting is not found in the older and better Greek texts. This is an important passage, upon which to focus, because of the fact that proponents of fasting point to it as indicating that Jesus must have practiced fasting with respect to such exorcisms; it therefore suggests that fasting is a key to success with regard to answered prayer in difficult cases. They suggest to us, basing their entire argument upon this passage, that Jesus must have known from experience that "this kind does not go out except by prayer and fasting" (Matt 17:21, KJV)—except that the whole sentence is not found in the better manuscripts.

Then again, we have a similar phenomenon in Acts 10:30. "Cornelius said, 'Four days ago to this hour, I was praying in my house...'" The King James Version adds "and fasting." In this case there is no foot-note explaining the matter. The word "fasting" is simply omitted in the NASB and NIV translations.

I find this kind of phenomenon curious. Could it be that certain scribes, copying the scriptures, had the same kind of misguided notion that we referred to at the beginning of this chapter, thinking that fasting adds merit to the discipline of prayer? Did they therefore add "fasting" to the text believing that it ought to be there? We cannot know.

THE CENTRAL PASSAGE

We come now to that which may be regarded as the *central passage* on the matter of Jesus and fasting. (I have devoted a separate chapter to His forty day fast in the wilderness, so as to consider in detail that significant event.) The central passage concerning the question of Jesus and fasting is Matthew 9:14-17:

Then the disciples of John came to Him, asking, "Why do we and the Pharisees fast, but Your disciples do not fast?" And Jesus said to them, "The attendants of the bridegroom cannot mourn as long as the bridegroom is with them, can they? But the days will come when the bridegroom is taken away from them, and then they will fast. But no one puts a patch of unshrunk cloth on an old garment; for the patch pulls away from the garment, and a worse tear results. Nor do *people* put new wine into old wineskins; otherwise the wineskins burst, and the wine pours out and the wineskins are ruined; but they put new wine into fresh wineskins, and both are preserved." (Matthew 9:14-17)

IT'S ABOUT MOURNING

As Jesus responds to the question as to why His disciples did not seem to be fasting, He refers to the basic meaning of the practice as recorded in the Old Testament; "The attendants of the bridegroom cannot mourn...." Fasting in the Old Testament is an expression of sadness, as was the application of sackcloth and ashes. A prominent example of this is found in the book of Daniel, chapters nine and ten. As Daniel discerns that the predicted seventy- year Babylonian Captivity is soon to end he prays for the nation Israel. "So, I gave my attention to the Lord God to *seek Him* with fasting, sackcloth and ashes. ...we have sinned, committed iniquity, acted wicked and rebelled, even turning aside from Your commandments and ordinances" (Daniel 9:3, 5).

We have a similar passage in chapter ten at verse two: "In those days, I, Daniel had been mourning for three entire weeks. I did not eat any tasty food, nor did I use any ointment at all until the entire three weeks were completed" (Daniel 10:2-3). Some would take verse three as supporting the idea of a *partial fast*. Daniel says that he did not eat any "tasty food" by way of contrast to ordinary food.) We take note there of the word "mourning" in the phrase, "mourning for three entire weeks." The concept of sadness and very often contrite acknowledgement of sin is central to the practice of fasting in the Old Testament. In Daniel nine, the prophet is confessing sin on behalf of the nation Israel. In II Samuel chapter 12 we find King

David mourning with respect to the illness of his child, a child that was conceived in sin. We read in verses 15-17 of II Samuel 12:

> Then the LORD struck the child that Uriah's widow bore to David, so that he was very sick. David therefore inquired of God for the child; and David fasted and went and lay on the ground. The elders of his household stood beside him in order to raise him up from the ground, but he was unwilling and would not eat food with them.

Another example of the Old Testament practice is found in Nehemiah chapter 1. When Nehemiah heard that the people of Israel who had survived the Babylonian captivity were in "great distress" and that the wall of Jerusalem was "broken down" and the gates "burned with fire," He said, "When I heard these words, I sat down and wept and mourned for days; and I was fasting and praying before the God of heaven" (Nehemiah 1:3-4).

The meaning of the Old Testament practice is quite clear. Fasting and prayer took place in the context of mourning. So then, in response to the question posed to Him by the Pharisees, as to why His disciples did not fast, Jesus centers upon the concept of *mourning*. In doing so He draws a vivid contrast between the joy of a wedding, when the bridegroom is present, and the sadness of that time when the bridegroom is taken from them. He refers to Himself as the bridegroom and His disciples as the attendants. There will come a day when He is taken away by force and put on a cross. That will be a time for sadness.

However, I do not believe that He is saying that the whole succeeding Gospel age will be a time for mourning and therefore a time for fasting. In the Upper Room Discourse Jesus makes this promise to His disciples, "I will not leave you as orphans; I will come to you. After a little while the world will no longer see Me, but you will see Me; because I live, you will live also. In that day you will know that I am in My Father, and you in Me, and I in you" (John 14:18-20). Considering the context of that promise we understand that Jesus is referring to the coming of the Holy Spirit and His ministry to them. By means of that indwelling Spirit Jesus would be present with His people. The bridegroom is not truly absent from us today.

We have in mind also the emphasis in the Epistles on Christian joy.

For example, the subject of joy is thematic in the book of Philippians: "Rejoice in the Lord always; again, I will say, rejoice!" (Philippians 4:4) It is very important to note at this point that *our joyful fellowship* with the Bridegroom is based upon the truth that He has perfectly conquered the matter of our sin upon Calvary's Cross and given us new life in Him.

WHAT DO WE DO WITH THE NEW WINE?

Now we come to verses 16 and 17 of Matthew nine, verses which seem to receive little attention from many proponents of *fasting*. Jesus now draws a contrast between the new and the old. He is saying, "You don't put new wine (a symbol of joy) into old skins." The NIV Study Bible makes this comment concerning Matthew 9:16-17:

> In ancient times goatskins were used to hold wine. As the fresh grape juice fermented, the wine would expand, and the new wineskin would stretch. But a used skin, already stretched, would break. Jesus brings a newness that cannot be confined within the old forms.[8]

These two verses should not be ignored. Taking note of the grammatical structure we observe that there is a very clear connection between the end of verse 15 and the beginning of verse 16 of Matthew 9. Verse 16 begins with "but." The verse reads, "But no one puts a patch of unshrunk cloth on an old garment; for the patch pulls away from the garment, and a worse tear results" (Matthew 9:16). Taking note of this connection, we must now ask the question: "Why?" Why does Jesus use these two illustrations (new cloth and new wine) contrasting the new and the old? It would seem to be obvious that he is still speaking about the subject of fasting. What else can these verses mean, but that fasting is a practice more appropriately connected to the old than the new? Yes, when the Savior is taken from the disciples to die on a cross and then buried in the garden tomb, there is unspeakable sadness. "But" (Matt 9:16) there is a new age on the way. After

---

[8] The NIV Study Bible, (Grand Rapids, Michigan: Zondervan Corporation, 1985), p. 1455.

the Resurrection and His Ascension into Heaven, the Holy Spirit comes upon His church. It's a new day and that new day is not a continuing day of mourning whereby fasting is the norm. There is a brief time of sadness when the bridegroom is taken from the disciples, but after that, there is the joy of continued fellowship with the risen Savior by means of the Holy Spirit of God. So, don't insist on putting the new into the old skins.

Indeed, there are times of great sadness that come into the lives of all believers. There are times of sorrow when fasting might seem to be appropriate. Jesus Himself stood beside the grave and wept with Mary and Martha concerning the death of Lazarus (John 11:35). But then again, with regard to a deeper spiritual level, we have these words of James, "Consider it all joy, my brethren, when you encounter various trials, knowing that the testing of your faith produces endurance" (James 1:2-3).

RECOGNIZED, BUT NOT ENCOURAGED

Examining the gospel accounts, we find that Jesus gives very little attention to the subject of fasting. In Matthew 6:16-18 He does mention it, not so much as to encourage it, but rather to address the matter of attitude of heart and mind as exemplified by the Pharisees and with respect to anyone involved in the practice. He says, "Whenever you fast, do not put on a gloomy face as the hypocrites *do*,…but you, when you fast, anoint your head and wash your face so that your fasting will not be noticed by men, but by your Father who is in secret; and your Father who sees *what is done in secret* will reward you" (Matthew 6:16-18).

Jesus seems to recognize that fasting can be an indication of genuine piety in the prayer life of a child of God. We see examples of such piety in several passages in the book of Acts. Acts 14:23 is such a passage. "When they had appointed elders for them in every church, having prayed with fasting, they commended them to the Lord in whom they had believed." We keep in mind that the book of Acts is a book of transition, a bridge between the previous age and the new.

By the time of Christ fasting had become, it seems, common practice in connection with the everyday prayer life of many devout people It was a spiritual discipline practiced in addition to the fasting observed during those special times in one's life when mourning called for it. Jesus does not pointedly encourage the practice of fasting, nor does He forbid it. But here in Matthew nine verse 16 He seems to identify it with the "old wineskins." One does not put new wine into old skins. We stated by way of introduction that, "Some things never change, but then again some things do." Perhaps that is why Jesus does not give much attention to it as a spiritual discipline and why it is not even mentioned in the New Testament Epistles. That, of course, is our main point. It is not mentioned in the Epistles. Again, we note that His forty day fast is discussed in the next chapter.

MODERN TEACHING

And yet, a great many books and articles continue to be written about fasting as a spiritual discipline that has great value. It is presented as the key to successful or break-through prayer. You might find writings like "Fifteen Great Reasons to Fast" or "Ten Secrets of Successful Fasting" (Fictitious titles). I came across an online article entitled "Prayer and Fasting for Evangelism" by Helene Nsin Oum. In it she describes four kinds of fasting. There is:

1. The Absolute Fast- no food or drink for a maximum of three days.
2. The Supernatural Fast-forty days and forty nights, as with Moses and Christ. This must be especially enabled by God.
3. The Normal Fast- from sunrise to sunset. Only liquids are taken in during these hours.
4. The Partial Fast- refraining from certain foods during the time period.[9]

The above may reflect the beliefs and practice of some in our day as gleaned from what is thought to be Biblical examples, but in reality, has no real basis whatsoever in Biblical teaching or exhortation.

Another example of modern teaching on the subject is seen in the writings of Jentezen Franklin. In a book, which is stated as being a New York Times Best Seller and is entitled "Fasting," he has written the

---

[9] NSIN OUM, Helene, *Prayer and Fasting for Evangelism,* online article, (Lausanne World Pulse,) p. all.

following sub-title: "Opening the door to a deeper, more intimate, more powerful relationship with God."[10] In an early chapter he states that "the three duties of every Christian are giving, praying, and fasting." Arguing from Matthew chapter six he writes:

> In the Beatitudes, specifically in Matthew 6, Jesus provided the pattern by which each of us is to live as a child of God. That pattern addressed three specific duties of a Christian: giving, praying, and fasting. Jesus said, "*When* you give…" "and "*When* you pray…" and *When* you fast." He made it clear that fasting, like giving and praying, was a normal part of Christian life. As much attention should be given to fasting as is given to giving and to praying.[11]

However, as we said earlier in this chapter, as Jesus is recognizing the practice of many pious people of the day, He gives them instruction concerning their practice. He tells them not to make a show of it, but he does not instruct them to fast. The word "when" when used of people in that day does not constitute specific instruction on the matter. He is rather saying that if you are fasting as a spiritual discipline than you should hide the matter – "anoint your head and wash your face" (Matthew 6:17). It seems outlandish to state that the above-mentioned threesome - fasting, praying, giving - constitute successful Christian living. Franklin says, "When you faithfully follow the three duties of a Christian, God rewards you openly."[12]

Later in his chapter entitled "Fasting for Your Breakthrough," he refers to the passage in Matthew 17 where Jesus heals a demon-possessed boy and then declares that "this kind does not go out except by prayer and fasting" (Matthew 17:21). Mr. Franklin seems to be unaware that Matthew 17:21 is not found in the better manuscripts, as we stated earlier. Never-the-less, later in the chapter he says the following:

---

[10] Jentezen Franklin, *Fasting*, (Lake Mary, FL, Charisma House, 2006) cover.

[11] Ibid., page 11.

[12] Ibid., page 14.

Do you desire to know God's will for your life, who you should marry, or what you should do in a critical situation? I'll show you how fasting brings you to a place of being able to clearly hear God's will. … Whether you desire to be closer to God or are in need of great breakthroughs in your life, remember that nothing shall be impossible to you. Fasting is truly a secret source of power![13]

Again. we state, in accordance with our premise, there is no mention of fasting in the New Testament Epistles. There is nothing there to in anyway support his *three duties* of the Christian life formula. Paul has much to say about praying and giving, but he has nothing to say about fasting. If fasting is one of those three special duties, how do we account for such a great omission as perpetrated by Peter, Paul, John, and the other writers of the Epistles?

BUT JESUS DID FAST – at least on one occasion.

As stated earlier, there is no record of Jesus fasting in the Gospel accounts, except on one very important occasion. He prayed often. He prayed in the matter of choosing the twelve disciples. He took them away from the crowds and taught them how to pray. But it is never said that he fasted when praying, except for that which is recorded in Matthew chapter four and in Luke chapter four. We examine that one time in the next chapter.

---

[13] Ibid., page 16.

CHAPTER FIVE

CRITCAL FAST

Forty Days with The Wild Beasts

We come now to the most important fast of all time and eternity. There has never been, nor will there ever be a more critical fast than that which we read of in the Gospel of Matthew, chapter four, and in the Gospel of Luke, chapter four. We therefore have decided to devote a separate chapter to the matter of Jesus fasting in the wilderness for forty days and forty nights. We want to address the significance of it and ask why He went through this extraordinary experience. Why did He fast for forty days and forty nights in the wilderness? What does it mean?

Gathering information from the Gospel accounts, this is what we know: Jesus fasted for forty days and forty nights (not simply in the daytime, which is the practice of some and seems to have been the practice of many in Jesus' day). Luke says at the beginning of this passage that, Jesus was "full of the Holy Spirit ...and was led around by the Spirit in the wilderness for forty days" (Luke 4:1-2). We observe that, chronologically, this took place immediately following His baptism in the Jordan River by John the Baptist. Mark states, "Immediately coming up out of the water, He saw the heavens opening, and the Spirit like a dove descending upon Him; and a voice came out of the heavens: 'You are My beloved Son, in You I am well pleased.' Immediately the Spirit impelled Him *to go* out into the wilderness" (Mark 1:10-12).

Matthew tells us that "Then the devil left Him; and behold, angels came and *began* to minister to Him" (Matt. 4:11). Matthew also tells us that it was not until after the forty-day period that Jesus became hungry, "And after He had fasted forty days and forty nights, He then became hungry" (Matt. 4: 2). Mark records that He was tempted in the wilderness for forty days and was "with the wild beasts," but he does not mention the fast (Mark 1:13). We observe also that there is no mention of thirst or drinking in any of the Gospel accounts.

THIS IS THE ONLY TIME

There is one intriguing matter to be observed with regard to all that is recorded in the Gospels. *This is the only time.* It is never stated that He fasted other than during this period of forty days. We often read that He went off, sometimes to a mountain, to pray, (Luke 6:12), but we do not read that He fasted during such times of prayer. When His disciples asked Him for teaching on prayer, as recorded in Luke chapter eleven, He has much to say, but does not mention fasting.

For example, when it was time to choose the twelve disciples, the scripture reads as follows:

> It was at this time that He went off to the mountain to pray, and He spent the whole night in prayer to God. And when day came, He called His disciples to Him and chose twelve of them, whom He also called apostles (Luke 6:12-13):

We might expect to find a reference to *fasting* in connection with such an important decision, but that is not the case. Of interest is the fact that this same writer, Luke, writes in Acts 13:2 of the early church *fasting* with regard to the commissioning of Paul and Barnabas, "Then when they had fasted and prayed and laid their hands on them, they sent them away" (Acts 13:2). We might surmise that the early church followed that which had been the tradition of pious people in those days -- serious prayer called for fasting. But again, we point out, it is not recorded that Jesus *fasted*, except with regard to those forty days and forty nights in the wilderness.

But the question now is: Why did He *fast* during that time and what did it mean to Him? We suggest to you that it was most essentially a time of *mourning*. At a time of unspeakable mourning, when, it would seem, He was extremely vulnerable, He was tempted by the devil. I suggest to you that He was, among other things, *mourning the loss of a loved one*. I hope to explain to you in this chapter what I mean by that.

WAS THAT BAPTISM NECESSARY?

Before we address the question as to why He fasted for forty days and nights, we want to consider the matter of His baptism. Why did He insist on being baptized? The one experience follows the other in the Gospel accounts. The two events would seem to be tied together by that proximity in the text. The last verse of Matthew three reads: "and behold, a voice out of the heavens said, 'This is my beloved Son, in whom I am well-pleased'" (Matthew 3:17). The first verse of chapter four reads: "Then Jesus was led up by the Spirit into the wilderness to be tempted by the devil" (Matthew 4:1). In Mark we have these words, "Immediately the Spirit impelled Him *to go* out into the wilderness. And He was in the wilderness forty days being tempted by Satan; and He was with the wild beasts, and the angels were ministering to Him" (Mark 1:12-13).

ANOTHER ASSUMPTION

I ask the reader to grant me, for the sake of argument, another assumption. And that is this: The meaning of the Christian ordinance of baptism is dramatized by the act of immersion. The word for baptism in the Greek text is "*baptizo*" (first person singular verb- "I baptize."). That word evolved from an old verb, "*bapto*", which had to do with the dyer's trade. The dyer would take a piece of cloth and dip it into a colored solution so as to add color to a piece of material. Looking up the word in a Greek lexicon, the first English word to be seen is "*dip.*" For example, Zondervan's, *The Analytical Greek Lexicon* renders it:

> 1) pr. to *dip, immerse; to purify or cleanse by washing; to administer the rite of baptism, to baptize;* met. With various

references to the ideas associated with Christian baptism
as an act of dedication, devotion, … [14]

If you look up the noun, "*baptismos*", it is rendered: "…pr. *an act of dipping or immersion; a baptism,* Heb. 6:2; an ablution…".[15] Abbott and Smith in their "Manuel Lexicon of The New Testament lists "*bapto*" as meaning, "to dip…to dip in dye, to dye...". "*Baptizo"* is rendered: "to dip, immerse, sink…".[16] Look up these words in any Greek lexicon and you will find the above to be the case. The primary meaning is: *to dip, immerse.*

THE CENTRAL PASSAGE ON BAPTISM

The central passage with regard to the theology of baptism is found in the sixth chapter of Paul's letter to the Romans. We read in Romans 6: 3-5:

> …or do you not know that all of us who have been
> baptized into Christ Jesus have been baptized into His
> death? There-fore we have been buried with Him through
> baptism into death, so that as Christ was raised from the
> dead through the glory of the Father, so we too might
> walk in newness of life. For if we have become united with
> *Him in the likeness* of His death, certainly, we shall also be
> *in the likeness* of His resurrection, …

We have in this passage a picture of our salvation experience. My understanding of it all is this: When we trust in Jesus Christ as our Savior who died on the cross for our sins and was raised from the grave, we are identified with Him in that experience. In the mind of God, we are united with Him on the cross. God sees us as being on the cross with Him, in the grave with Him, and then risen with Him. Paul says in Galatians 2:20, "I have been crucified with Christ; and it is no longer I who live, but Christ

---

[14] *The Analytical Greek Lexicon,* (Grand Rapids, Michigan: Zondervan Publishing House, 1970), p. 65

[15] Ibid., p. 65

[16] Abbott-Smith, G., *A Manuel Greek Lexicon of the New Testament,* T. & T. Clark, Edinburg, 1956. P. 74

lives in me and the *life* which I now live in the flesh I live by faith in the Son of God, who loved me and gave Himself up for me" (Gal. 2:20).

We would ask, "When Paul? When were you crucified with Him?" I think Paul would say, "When I first believed, I was identified with Him, united with Him on the cross, in the grave and in His resurrection."

Water baptism then is a picture of or a dramatization of that spiritual reality. The dipping into water is a symbolic picture of what happened to us when we first believed. We died and were buried with Him. That means that our sins were atoned for. But then we were raised with Him. That means that we now have *newness of life*. There has been imparted to us a new nature, by way of which and in conjunction with the Holy Spirit, we are able to live for Him. And that is precisely Paul's point in Romans six. We don't need to continue in a life of sin because we have been raised with Him in *newness of life*.

Let me suggest to you that the rite of baptism has for us two meanings:

1.) Cleansing- the waters of baptism symbolize the washing away of our sins. Acts 2:38
2.) Identification with Christ- It is a picture of our death, burial and resurrection with Him. We are "united with Him" in death and resurrection (Romans 6:5).

However, when Jesus was baptized in the Jordan, the first matter listed above did not apply. "He made Him who knew no sin *to be* sin on our behalf…". (II Cor. 5:21) When He insisted on being baptized by John "to fulfill all righteousness" (Matt. 3:15), He did not have in mind the washing away of His own personal sins. Rather, it had to do with the picture of His own death, burial and resurrection.

We can imagine it this way: When Jesus visited that scene by the Jordan and saw John baptizing multitudes of people, when He saw men and women being lowered into those muddy waters and then lifted back to their feet, He knew exactly what the dipping process meant. It was a picture of death, burial and resurrection and more specifically, His own death, burial and resurrection. So then, His insistence on being baptized was an act of submission to the Father's will for Him. He thereby was submitting Himself to the Father's plan, which meant a horrible death on the cross, upon which He would bear the sins of the world. He would then be buried in the ground and finally, on the third day raised again.

This was for Him an act of dedication and signaled the beginning of His earthly ministry. He knew exactly what lay ahead and in perfect submission to His Father in Heaven He dedicated Himself to the task. We understand then, why the Father's voice was heard from Heaven saying, "This is my beloved Son in whom I am well pleased" (Matthew 3:17).

Why did Jesus insist on being baptized? Theologians and Bible scholars have debated this question through the years. I suggest that the answer that carries the deepest meaning and which makes the most sense is the one stated above. It was for Him an act of commitment to the Father's will; and a plan that would culminate in death, burial and resurrection.

This brings us back to the former question: Why does He now fast for forty days and forty nights in the wilderness? Let me present to you a theory. I suggest to the reader that His fast is indicative of a heart that is in a state of sorrow, a state of mourning if you please. We remember from our discussion of Matthew 9:15 in the previous chapter, that Jesus connects the act of fasting with the state of mourning. Let me also suggest that His mournful heart has to do with the commitment that He has just expressed at His baptism, a commitment to die on a cross for the sins of the world.

We read in Matthew 27 these words concerning His time on that cross:

> Now from the sixth hour darkness fell upon all the land until the ninth hour. About the ninth hour Jesus cried out with a loud voice saying, "ELI, ELI, LAMA SABACHTHANI?" that is, "MY GOD, MY GOD, WHY HAVE YOU FORSAKEN ME" (Matthew 27:45-46)?

My question for the reader is this: *Was Jesus mistaken?* In the extremity of the moment, when He had been on the cross almost six hours, was He simply wrong when, due to extreme weakness or pain, He cried out with a loud voice, "My God, My God, why have you forsaken me?" Or did He know perfectly well the nature of His situation?

Indeed, there was at that moment a very real separation between God the Father and God the Son. The Apostle Paul declares this: "He [That is God the Father] made Him who knew no sin [God the Son] *to be* sin on our behalf, so that we might become the righteousness of God in Him" (II Corinthians 5:21). The sins of the world are laid on Him, all kinds of sin. All the sins that human beings are capable of -- theft, rape, murder, etc., but the most universal of all is idolatry, worshipping other gods, things, people or oneself, more than the one true God. The Bible classifies that as *spiritual adultery,* a theme that runs through several of the prophetic books of the Old Testament.

Now, think through this with me. God is love (I John 4:8,16). Historical, orthodox theology has concluded that all the members of the Trinity share equally in all the attributes of the divine essence. From eternity past, Father, Son and Spirit have existed in a relationship of perfect love. But now, for the first and only time, the cords of love and trust between Father and Son are broken. The Father looks down upon His Son and sees *spiritual adultery.* And since a holy and just God cannot accept the reality of sin, He must turn His face away. At that moment (we don't know how long that moment was; the darkness lasted three hours.), Jesus, in perfect awareness of the shame of it all and the separation that has now occurred, cries out with a loud voice, in spiritual suffering, "My God, My God, why have you forsaken me" (Matt. 27:46?) It is an emotional response of One who is suffering beyond measure, literally. Of course, He knows why. It is because He has become the sin bearer. His cry is an emotional response to the enormous pain of the separation.

One of my professors in seminary, visiting Bible lecturer, John G Mitchell, used to put it this way: "Can anyone possibly comprehend what happened during those three hours of darkness? Does anyone really know?"[17] We cannot plumb the depths of those three hours of darkness. On that cross, during that time, He endured spiritual suffering that mere human beings cannot hope to understand. Perfect love between infinite persons was torn asunder. Hollywood movies that depict the great physical suffering of our Savior miss the main point. That which caused Him to sweat, as it were, drops of blood in Gethsemane (Luke 22:44), was not so much an anticipation of the physical-suffering, as it was an anticipation of spiritual suffering, when Jesus would lose that intimate love relationship with His Father.

---

[17] John G. Mitchell, *The Gospel of John,* (Dallas, Texas: Lecture series delivered at Dallas Theological Seminary, 1961.

Return with me to the Garden of Gethsemane and the anticipation of the Savior of those hours of darkness at the cross. His suffering in the Garden is recorded in the Gospels of Matthew, Mark and Luke. We read that He said, "My soul is deeply grieved, to the point of death; remain here [to His disciples] and keep watch with Me" (Matt. 26:38). Then we read, "And He went a little beyond *them*, and fell on His face and prayed, saying, 'My Father, if it is possible, let this cup pass from Me, yet not as I will, but as You will.'" (Matthew 26:39) The petition is almost the same in all three Gospels. "And He was saying, 'Abba! Father! All things are possible for You; remove this cup from Me; yet not what I will, but what You will'" (Mark 14:36). And as noted, we read in Luke, "And being in agony He was praying fervently; and His sweat became like drops of blood, falling down upon the ground" (Luke 2244).

The question now is: What does He mean by *the cup*? Merrill F. Unger, in his Bible dictionary, states that the *cup* "is employed in both Testaments in some curious metaphorical phrases:" He speaks of it being used as the natural type of sensual allurement as well as "a general expression for the condition of life, prosperous or miserable." He refers to a number of different usages: "cup of consolation," "cup of salvation," "cup of blessing," and finally, the "cup of trembling," literally, "cup of reeling, intoxication . . .cup of fury." In this final category he refers us to Isaiah 51:17, 22 where it is "the cup of His anger" and "the chalice of reeling" (Isaiah 51:17), "the cup of reeling," and "the chalice of My anger" (Isaiah 51:22). He refers us also to Jeremiah 25:15, where there is a warning for anyone "who worships the beast and his image:" "...he also will drink of the wine of the wrath of God, which is mixed in full strength in the cup of His anger; ...."[18]

We suggest to the reader that Jesus uses the word *cup* in a figurative sense and is referring to the *cup of God's wrath*. In a form of spiritual suffering that we cannot begin to understand, He is anticipating that moment when the *cup of God's wrath* will be poured out upon Him during those three hours of darkness. Again, we say that during that time, the bonds of love and relationship between Father and Son were severed and in an emotional response Jesus cries out, "My God, my God, why have You forsaken Me" (Matt. 27:46)?

---

[18] Merrill F. Unger, *Unger's Bible Dictionary,* (Chicago: Moody Press, 1957), p. 236.

Thinking again of His Baptism, we believe that at that time, Jesus was committing Himself to go through with the divine plan. Just as He foreknew the time and manner of His death, He also foreknew the separation between Father and Son that was forthcoming three years later.

Shortly thereafter, we find Him fasting in the wilderness. I believe that His extended fast is an expression of a sorrowful heart. He is mourning the loss of a loved One, His Father in Heaven. Why only forty days? Considering the magnitude of the sorrow, we could imagine it as lasting much longer, except that He is now participating in every aspect of genuine humanity, and as such a human body that has limitations.

It is notable that the attack from the enemy takes place at the time of His sorrowful fasting, when it would seem that He was the most vulnerable. His burden was heavy *beyond measure*, yet He remained steadfast in His commitment to the task that lay ahead. He was to be the sin-bearer, with respect to the sins of the entire world (I John 2:2).

All of the above discussion is to suggest that His fasting in the wilderness was of a very special and unique nature, not something to be held up as an example for the believer to follow today.

By way of review, concerning all that we have said about *fasting*, we set forth the following:

1) There is no reference in the Epistles to the matter of fasting as a spiritual discipline. On the one hand, Paul is simply referring to fasting as a hardship that he endured—going without food. (II Corinthians 11:27). There is, on the other hand, the verse in I Corinthians 7:5 where there is a textual problem. The older and better manuscripts do not support the reading of "fasting."

2) There is a *central passage* in the Gospel account concerning Jesus and *fasting*. In response to the question as to why the disciples of Jesus are not fasting, He declares that you do not put "new wine" into "old skins." The coming age was not to be a time of mourning and fasting, but a time of joyful fellowship with the risen Christ (Matthew 9:14-17).

3) Jesus gives very little attention to the matter of *fasting* during the time of His teaching ministry. He never suggests that fasting is a key to successful prayer. (There is a textual problem with regard to Matthew 17:21. The better manuscripts do not support the words, "and fasting.") He does rebuke the Pharisees for their hypocrisy and admonishes that there be a humble heart and mind that chooses to fast in secret (Matthew 6:16-18).

4) Concerning the matter of His forty day *fast* in the wilderness, we have suggested that in accordance with the basic idea of fasting--it has to do with mourning—Jesus is mourning the forthcoming loss of fellowship with His Father during those three hours of darkness on the Cross. His was a redemptive experience that is not to be held up as a discipline that we should try and follow.

We ask the reader at this point to understand that we are not declaring that believers today should never fast in connection with their prayers. If it is a means of putting all else aside and focusing on fellowship with our God, we can imagine it as being a good thing in the prayer life of the believer. However, we should take care lest we think that we are earning the answers to our prayers by the practice—that it is somehow the secret of breaking-through to Him.

CHAPTER SIX

THE BAPTISM OF THE SPIRIT

And the gift of tongues

ARE THERE TWO BAPTISMS?

There are some people who declare that there are two Baptisms of the Spirit. They acknowledge that there is a Baptism of the Spirit mentioned in I Corinthians 12:13, but they say that that Baptism of the Spirit is not the same as that which we have in the book of Acts, chapter two. We will suggest, by way of our analysis of Scripture, that such is not the case. There is only one *Baptism of the Spirit* and it is found in a context that perfectly matches the argument set forth in chapters 1-11 of the book of Acts.

BACK TO OUR PREMISE

In our study thus far and in accordance with the premise of this writing, we have been calling attention to certain matters which are not found in the New Testament Epistles. In some of the cases we have considered there is not even mention made of the subject, let alone admonitions or exhortations whereby we are enjoined to apply them to the Christian life. As we have stated previously, there is no mention of *exorcism* or *fasting*, at least with regard to the better Greek manuscripts. The gift of *tongues* is found in one section of one Epistle. We find there one exhortation concerning the gift, "forbid not to speak in tongues." But we hardly interpret what we have there as an encouragement to seek or practice the gift. Considering the Epistles as a whole, we have to say that the gift of *tongues* is conspicuous by its absence.

Concerning now the *Baptism of the Spirit,* we observe that in the Epistles we find no exhortation or instruction that anyone is to seek that Baptism. Rather, we have these words in I Corinthians 12:13, "For by one Spirit we were all baptized into one body, whether Jews or Greeks, whether slaves or free, and we were all made to drink of one Spirit." Paul, speaking to the church at Corinth-- which was hardly an example of what a church should be-- declares that this spiritual blessing has already taken place in the lives of those who are true believers in Christ. It is not something to be sought; it is a reality that has already taken place.

IT WAS PREDICTED

It all begins with an announcement made by John the Baptist, one that is recorded in all four Gospels. As John is preaching beyond the Jordan, calling the nation of Israel to repentance, he makes this prediction, "As for me, I baptize with water for repentance, but He who is coming after me is mightier than I, and I am not fit to remove His sandals; He will baptize you with the Holy Spirit and fire" (Matthew 3:11). Similar wording is found in Mark and Luke, although Mark mentions the *Spirit*, but not the *fire.* The wording in the Gospel of John is somewhat different, "I did not recognize Him, but He who sent me to baptize in water said to me, 'He upon whom you see the Spirit descending and remaining upon Him, this is the One who baptizes in the Holy Spirit.' I myself have seen, and have testified that this is the Son of God" (John 1:33-34). The difference in wording would seem to be no problem, in that we can imagine that John makes the announcement more than once and alters the wording somewhat each time. We notice that the reference to *fire* is omitted in this passage as well.

The Baptism of the Holy Spirit is also predicted by Jesus shortly before His ascension back to Heaven, "Gathering them together, He commanded them not to leave Jerusalem, but to wait for what the Father had promised, 'Which,' *He said,* 'you heard of from Me; for John baptized with water, but you will be baptized with the Holy Spirit not many days from now' " (Acts 1:4-5).

THE PROMISE IS FULFILLED

That which is recorded in the second chapter of Acts appears to be the fulfillment of the promise. There is the "noise like a violent rushing wind." There are the "tongues as of fire...resting on each one of them." We read, "And they were all filled with the Holy Spirit" (Acts 2:2-4). We note at this point that the Greek word translated *tongues* is the plural of the word that sometimes refers to "the human tongue," sometimes to "a particular language or dialect spoken by any particular people," and sometimes, "figuratively, for speech in general." The Greek word is *glossa,* from which we get the English word, *glossary.* A natural understanding of the text as presented would seem to indicate that the disciples were enabled by the Holy Spirit to speak in languages other than their own, languages not learned in the normal way. And so, we read "...the crowd came together and were bewildered because each one of them was hearing them speak in his own language" (Acts 2:6). The last word is that verse, "language," is a translation of the Greek word *dialecto*—from which we get the English word, *dialect.* Perhaps it is not necessary to ask, but is that which we have in Acts two the fulfillment of the promise? The term, *Baptism of the Spirit,* is not found in the passage.

The answer to that question, however, is found plainly stated in Acts chapter eleven. As Peter reports back to Jerusalem as to what had happened at the house of the Roman centurion, Cornelius, he says this, "And as I began to speak, the Holy Spirit fell upon them just as *He did* upon us at the beginning. And I remembered the word of the Lord, how he used to say, 'John baptized with water, but you will be baptized with the Holy Spirit'" (Acts 11:15-16). Therefore, we can see plainly that the promise concerning the Baptism of the Holy Spirit was fulfilled on the day of Pentecost, as recorded in Acts chapter two. That, however, is not the end of the story. That work of the Spirit is seen also in chapters 8, 10 and 19 of Acts and, I believe, in I Corinthians 12:13.

GETTING A LITTLE TECHNICAL

In the verses quoted from the Gospels (Mark 1:8, Luke 3:16), there is the repeated contrast between water and Spirit. John's ministry was characterized by "water," but the ministry of the Christ would be characterized by "the Holy Spirit." Before the terms "water" and "the Holy Spirit," there is, in the Greek text, a little preposition that can be transliterated as "in." There is a difference of opinion as to whether that word should be translated into English as "with," or "in." The Greek word is "en." Greek scholar, A.T. Robertson, insists that the case is locative and that it means *in the sphere of.*[19] The American Standard Bible (published in 1901) agrees and translates, "I baptize in water, but He shall baptize you in the Holy Spirit" (Luke 3:16)."[20]

We might look at it this way: When people were baptized by John, they got wet with water, but when people are baptized by the Messiah, they get wet with the Spirit. On the one hand believers are immersed in the sphere of water, while on the other they are immersed in the sphere of the Spirit. Some Bible versions, however, translate the Greek word, *"en"* as instrumental--baptized *with* water and *with* the spirit.

Turning again to I Corinthians 12:13 we find an additional Greek preposition used: Paul says, "For by one Spirit we were all baptized into one body, whether Jews or Greeks, whether slaves or free, and were all made to drink of one Spirit" (I Cor. 12:13). First there is the preposition *"en"* and then there is the preposition *"eis."* The word *"eis"* is usually translated "into." And so, the New American Version translates, "For in one Spirit we were all baptized into one body" (I Corinthians 1 Cor. 12:13). In this chapter also we find, I believe, a verse which is parallel and explanatory of I Cor. 12:13. We read, "But now God has placed the members, each of them, in the body, just as He desired" (I Cor. 12:18). Taken in the context of I Corinthians 12 we can define and describe that which is referred to as *the Baptism of The Holy Spirit.* When we put our trust in Christ and what He has done for us on the Cross, God places us within the Body of Christ, makes us drink of His Holy Spirit, and grants to each one of us, at least one Spiritual Gift. That is the Baptism of the Spirit.

Let us now consider what we have in the book of Acts. The diagram below depicts how different groups of believers were placed into or baptized

---

[19] Robertson, A.T., *Word Pictures in the New Testament, (From CD-ROM, E-Sword, Rick Meyers, 2008)*
[20] *The American Standard Bible, 1901*

into the Body of Christ. The first ones in are from among the Jews who were gathered together at Pentecost.

THE BAPTISM OF THE HOLY SPIRIT

All who believe, whether Jews or Gentiles (I Cor. 12:13)

Gentiles—Acts 10 -- third group into the Body

Samaritans –Acts 8 --second group into the Body

Jews—Acts 2 --first ones into the Body

THE BODY OF CHRIST

X X X X XX X X X X X X X X X X X X

X   X

X   The Holy Spirit   X

X   X

X X X X X X X X X X X X X X X X X

Spiritual Gifts

THE PRIMARY PURPOSE OF TONGUES

Keeping in mind the above diagram, let us scan through the first eleven chapters of the book of Acts, noting, first of all, three key verses in Acts one:

> Gathering them together, He commanded them not to leave Jerusalem, but to wait for what the Father had promised, "Which," *He said,* "you heard of from Me; for John baptized with water, but you will be baptized with the Holy Spirit not many days from now. But you will receive power when the Holy has come upon you; and you will be My witnesses both in Jerusalem and in all Judea and Samaria, and even to the remotest part of the earth (Acts 1:5,8).

THE BAPTISM OF THE SPIRIT

THE FIRST ONES IN ARE JEWS

It all begins on the Day of Pentecost when, as recorded in chapter two, the Holy Spirit falls upon those who had been waiting for the fulfillment of the promise. They are in Jerusalem and they are Jewish believers. They are there granted the Gift of *Tongues,*

a phenomenon readily observed by all present. It was very important that the gift be manifested prominently, as we shall see later on. The ability of these Jewish believers to speak in many different languages would seem to be significant with respect to symbolism. The Gospel of Jesus Christ is to be proclaimed to the many peoples of the world. Though the phenomena would seem to be appropriate, that is not, as I see it, the primary purpose of the Gift of *Tongues* in the book of Acts.

We note, first of all, that the Jews are the first ones in the water, so to speak. They are the first ones to be immersed in the Spirit and placed into the newly formed Body of Christ.

Following the general outline of Acts as presented in Acts 1:8; (both in Jerusalem, and in all Judea, and to the uttermost parts of the earth,) we now move on to Samaria. We find in chapter 8 that Philip is having a great deal of success as he proclaims Christ in Samaria and so we read, beginning in verse 14 of Acts 8, "Now when the apostles in Jerusalem heard that Samaria had received the word of God, they sent them Peter and John, who came down and prayed for them that they might receive the Holy Spirit. For He had not yet fallen upon any of them; they had simply been baptized in the name of the Lord Jesus. They began laying their hands on them, and they were receiving the Holy Spirit" (Acts 8:14-17).

It is not stated in this passage that the Samaritan believers were enabled to speak in *tongues.* We can assume, I think, that they did. We can safely assume that these Samaritans--who were half Jews, half Gentiles—are the second group established within the Body of Christ. They are the second people-group to receive the Baptism of the Holy Spirit. They are the second group into the water, so to speak.

Next, we come to the all-important story of Cornelius, a Roman Centurion, "a devout man and one who feared God with all his household, and gave many alms to the *Jewish* people and prayed to God continually" (Acts 10:2). Peter has his profound vision of a great sheet being lowered from heaven, in which there are all kinds of animals, clean and unclean. Peter is commanded to eat, even that which under the law, was deemed unclean. The great lesson, of course, is that the Gospel is to be preached to the Gentiles, who had been regarded as unclean.

The event is quite dramatic, in more ways than one. As Peter is delivering his sermon at the house of Cornelius, before he can finish his message, "the Holy Spirit fell upon all who were listening to the message" (Acts 10:44). The next three verses are very significant:

> All the circumcised believers who came with Peter, were amazed, because the gift of the Holy Spirit had been poured out on the Gentiles also. For they were hearing them speaking with tongues and exalting God. Then, Peter answered, "Surely no one can refuse the water for these to be baptized who have received the Holy Spirit just as we did can he." (Acts 10:45-47)?

However, the story does not end there; it is continued in chapter eleven, Peter now reports back to Jerusalem concerning the remarkable event that had just taken place. It's important to take note of these verses in chapter eleven. Peter says:

> And I remembered the word of the Lord, how He used to say, 'John baptized with water, but you will be baptized with the Holy Spirit.' Therefore, if God gave to them the same gift as *He gave* us also after believing in the Lord Jesus Christ, who was I that I could stand in God's way." When they heard this, they quieted down and glorified God saying, "Well then, God has granted to the Gentiles also the repentance that *leads to* life (Acts 11:16-18).

We notice then, that Gentiles are the next and final people-group to be baptized into the Body of Christ. The Gospel will now be proclaimed, "even to the remotest part of the earth" (Acts 1:8).

THE PRIMARY PURPOSE

There is an interesting and, I believe, significant statement found in verse 18 of Acts eleven, "they quieted down...." That seems to imply that the Jewish believers in Jerusalem, to whom Peter is reporting, are not at all happy about the possibility of Gentiles being welcomed into the Church of Christ. But that which made the difference was the report that the obvious and manifest gift of *tongues* had been observed, not only by Peter, but by the Jewish believers from Jerusalem who were there and saw and heard it all. The gift of speaking in *tongues* was designed to be very convincing. How do you convince the Jews of those days that Gentiles, inherently unclean in their minds, are to be included in the fellowship of Christ? It would have to be accomplished by something very evident and very powerful. The powerful event that took place in the house of Cornelius was exactly the same in nature as that which had taken place in Jerusalem. And so, we read, "... 'Well then, God has granted to the Gentiles also the repentance *that leads* to life'" (Acts 11:18). That which we have just considered would seem to have been the primary purpose of the gift, at least as presented in the book of Acts.

WHAT ABOUT TWO BAPTISMS?

The answer to that seems to be obvious. It is found in the very wording of I Corinthians 12:13. "For by one Spirit we were all baptized into one body, *whether Jews or Greeks*, whether slaves or free, and *we were all made to drink of one Spirit* [Emphasis mine]." Isn't that analogous to the theme which we have just considered in Acts? Paul's emphasis on unity in I Corinthians twelve is parallel to that which we have in Acts 2, 8, 10 and 11. The Baptism of the Spirit set forth in I Corinthians 12:13 is the same as that which we have in Acts 2.

SPIRIT BAPTISM IN EPHESIANS FOUR

Additional support for maintaining that there is but one Baptism of the Spirit is found in Ephesians 4. The apostle Paul exhorts us to be "diligent to preserve the unity of the Spirit in the bond of peace" (Eph.4:3). In verses 4 and 5 of Ephesians 4 he declares that there is "one body and one Spirit, just as you were called in one hope of your calling; one Lord, one faith, one baptism, one God and Father of all who is over all and through all and in all" (Ephesians 4:4,5).

Commentators differ as to whether the term "one baptism" refers to water baptism or the Baptism of the Spirit. The context would seem to support the latter. The words "one body" and "one Spirit" are analogous with much of what Paul says in I Corinthians 12. When Paul speaks of "one God and Father of all" we are reminded of the emphasis presented in I Corinthians 12:13 where he declares that "we were all baptized into one body, whether *Jews or Greeks, whether slaves or free,* and were all made to drink of one Spirit" [emphasis mine]. Finally, the subsequent verses in chapter four speak of gifts being given to men when "He ascended on high" (Ephesians 4: 7-13.)

SUMMING UP

In the New Testament Epistles, we are never exhorted or encouraged to seek the Baptism of the Holy Spirit, because, according to Paul, we already have it. All believers in Christ today have been placed into the Body of Christ. We have all been made to "drink of one Spirit," receiving gifts for the purpose of moving the Church forward (I Corinthians 12:13). We may not have the gift of *tongues,* but we have all been gifted to serve in some way.

WHAT ABOUT THE GIFT OF TONGUES?

That question has been directed to me a number of times during my years of pastoral ministry. Someone comes to me and asks a question that goes something like this: "Pastor, what do you think about speaking in tongues?" My response has often been as follows: I suggested that we look at the table of contents in her Bible. After scanning the books of the Old Testament, noting that there we find books of history, poetry and prophecy, we turn to the New Testament. I mention that we have the four gospels presenting to us the life and ministry of Jesus Christ. After that, I point out that we have the book of Acts, which has recorded the activities of the early church. "Now we come," I say to the letters to the churches, beginning with Romans and extending to the end of the Bible. After all that has gone before, the question is: what is the bottom line? How then are we to live today? What specific instructions do we find in the Epistles as to how to serve and live for Christ in our day?"

I then proceed to take them through the Epistles, one by one giving a brief synopsis of each book as we go along. I suggest that the book of Romans is the most definitive and most complete of Paul's letters with respect to all that we need to know about Christian living. After devoting several chapters to the subject of our salvation in Christ, Paul comes to the matter of living victoriously, now that we have received new life in Christ. Chapter eight is one of the more beloved chapters in the Bible. In that chapter Paul refers to the Holy Spirit eighteen times in declaring to his readers that the enabling power of the Holy Spirit is the key to successful Christian living. There is, however, no mention of speaking in tongues in the eighth chapter of Romans.

In chapter twelve of Romans, we find a list of the Spiritual Gifts. In verse six Paul says, "Since we have gifts that differ according to the grace given to us, each of us is to exercise them accordingly: if prophecy, according to the proportion of his faith; ..." (Rom. 12:6). Reading on down through verse thirteen of Romans 12 we find that reference to the gift of tongues is not found here or in the sixteen long chapters of the book of Romans.

Let me now continue to scan the Epistles with you, the reader, as I have done with individuals personally. We will skip over, for the moment, the book of I Corinthians. We will come back to it. Moving on to the book of II Corinthians we find no reference to the gift of tongues throughout its thirteen long chapters. Life in the Spirit is central to Paul's theme in the book of Galatians. He exhorts them in verse 16 of chapter five, "But I say, walk by the Spirit, and you will not carry out the desire of the flesh," Again, in verse 25 of Galatians 5 he says, "If we live by the Spirit, let us also walk by the Spirit." However, we find no reference to the gift of tongues in the book of Galatians.

In his letter to the Ephesians, Paul writes of the wonderful riches of grace that are found in the believer's relationship with Christ. There are two profound prayers in this Epistle, one in chapter one and another in chapter three, in which Paul prays that we might know, experientially, the blessings of those riches. In chapter one he writes, "I pray that the eyes of your heart may be enlightened, so that you will know what is the hope of His calling, what are the riches of the glory of His inheritance in the saints, and what is the surpassing greatness of His power toward us who believe." (Ephesians 1:18-19)

In all of these eloquent words, there is no expressed desire of Paul that there should be the realization of the gift of tongues in the life of the believer. The gift of tongues is not found at all in the wonderful book of Ephesians – somewhat surprising in view of the fact that many suggest to us that the gift is something of the epitome of spiritual experience.

Moving on now chronologically through the New Testament Epistles. We find no mention of tongues in Colossians, or I and II Thessalonians, or I and II Timothy, or Titus, or Philemon or Hebrews or James, or I and II Peter, or I, II and III John, or Jude or in the letters to the seven churches in the book of Revelation, chapters 2 and 3.

How is it possible that something seemingly so important can be omitted by all these New Testament writers? I speak facetiously. Are we therefore able to say that the subject is conspicuous by its absence?

As promised, we come back now to I Corinthians, chapter twelve through fourteen. In the one section of Scripture where the matter of tongues is set forth, it is presented as a problem that Paul needs to address. Many words have been written; many books have been published on this subject. In accordance with the theme of this writing there is just one important point that needs to be made. There is almost nothing by way of encouragement for anyone who desires to practice the gift. Rather, the gift of speaking in tongues is devalued – presented as the least to be desired.

Towards the end of chapter 12 of I Corinthians we find a listing of the Spiritual Gifts in verses 27-31. In verse 28 of that passage Paul sets forth the gifts in the order of greatness, "And God has appointed in the church, first apostles, second prophets, third teachers, then gifts of miracles..." It seems fair to connect verse 31 with verse 28 of I Cor. 12 and to thereby know which gifts he considers to be the greater. There are two things that we might notice from Paul's words in I Cor. 12. First of all, the gift of tongues is not meant for everyone – the opinion of many in our day to the contrary. "All do not speak with tongues, do they?" (I Cor.12:30)

Secondly, we observe that the gift of tongues is at the bottom of the totem pole – excuse the figure. It's at the bottom of the list: least of all to be desired among those listed.

Next, we observe, reading on into chapter 13, that Paul mentions the matter of tongues first as he shows us "a still more excellent way, "(I Cor. 12:31 the way of love. We may assume that he begins with the "tongues of men and of angels" (I Cor.13:1) first of all because the gift of tongues was problematic in the church at Corinth

At this point we take the space to suggest that, in presenting to us the wonderful *love* chapter of the Bible, Paul is writing rhetorically; he uses lofty-poetic language to depict the glories of God's love, the love which is reproduced in us by means of His Holy Spirit. It is not likely that we shall ever mountains – in the literal sense. (I Cor 13:2), Likewise, this verse does not give us declarative truth that we are able to speak with the language of angels (I Cor. 13:1).

At the beginning of chapter 14 we find Paul exhorting the believer to "Pursue love, while desiring spiritual gifts" (I Cor. 14:1); but especially that you may prophesy" (I Cor.14:1). It seems obvious that the *love* chapter is presented as a parenthesis in his argument. He then picks up where he left off at the end of chapter 12. The gift of prophecy is at the top of the list, just under the gift of being an apostle, which gift is not available to us today. We observe that the gift of prophecy is at the top of the list, while the gift of speaking in tongues is at the bottom.

Reading on down through I Corinthians 14 we find Paul devaluing the gift in a number of ways. It would seem obvious that most of what he says in this long chapter is not complimentary with regard to this gift. When it seems as if he may be speaking well of its exercise, he then qualifies it. He says in verse 5 of I Cor.14, "Now I wish that you all spoke in tongues..." but then he says, "but even more that you would prophesy; ..."

Likewise, is verse 18 of I Corinthians 14, "I thank God, I speak in tongues more than you all:" but then he adds, "however, in the church I desire to speak five words with my mind so that I may instruct others, rather than ten thousand words in a tongue." It would seem that in all of Paul's treatment of the subject in I Corinthians 12-14, it is presented as a relative matter. We see this in his concluding statement in verse 39 of I Cor. 12, Therefore, my brethren, desire earnestly to prophesy, and do not forbid to speak in tongues."

That last exhortation, "do not forbid to speak in tongues" (I Cor. 14:39), represents to some degree my position on the matter. I am not inclined to say dogmatically that the gift is inoperative in our day, but I am pointing out that the gift is not even mentioned in all of the Epistles, except for this one place in I Corinthians 12-14 and there it is dealt with as a problem. Paul's solution to the problem is to devalue it on the one hand and regulate it on the other.

With respect to the Baptism of the Spirit we have pointed out that New Testament Epistles do not contain any exhortation or encouragement to seek that work of the Holy Spirit. Rather, it is stated that those who have trusted in Christ as Savior have already received it (I Cor. 12:13).

The gift of speaking in tongues is listed among others in I Corinthians chapters 12-14. However, as Paul writes to that church, he deals with it as a problem to be regulated. It is not even mentioned once in the other Epistles, Significant is the fact that it is not found among the gifts listed by Paul in Romans 12.

By way of review, we have pointed out with respect to the matter of exorcism that it is not mentioned in the New Testament Epistles. Likewise, we have shown that the subject of fasting as a spiritual discipline is not found in the Epistles. In this chapter we have set forth the matter of the gift of tongues as not being found the in Epistles, except in one place, where it is treated as a problem.

CHAPTER SEVEN

THE PRIMACY OF PROPHECY

A Gift for Today?

We begin this chapter with a positive. *The Gift of Prophecy* is set forth in two major portions of Scripture as a gift to be earnestly desired and exercised. The Apostle Paul begins chapter twelve of Romans by urging us to "present" our "bodies a living and holy sacrifice, acceptable to God, *which is*" our "spiritual service of worship" (Romans 12:10.) Then after warning us not "to be conformed to this world" and "not to think more highly of" ourselves "than he ought to think:" and reminding us of the unity of the Body of Christ, he admonishes us to exercise our spiritual gifts (Romans 12:1-6):

> Since then we have gifts that differ according to the grace given to us, *each of us is to exercise them accordingly*: if prophecy, according to the proportion of his faith; if service, in his serving; or he who teaches, in his teaching; or he who exhorts, in his exhortation; he who gives, with liberality; he who leads, with diligence; he who shows mercy, with cheerfulness (Romans 12:6-8).

Some initial observations can be made concerning the above list of spiritual gifts:

First, the gift of being an Apostle is not included -- by way of contrast to that which we find in the lists that Paul gives us in I Corinthians 12 and Ephesians 4. We would expect the gift of being an Apostle to be listed first of all.

Secondly, with the exception of the gift of *prophecy*, the gifts mentioned seem to be quite within the realm of the ordinary. The more spectacular gifts, or gifts that appear to be more dramatic in their presentation, such as *miracles, healings, tongues* and *interpretation of tongues,* are not included here in Romans twelve.

Thirdly, the gift of prophecy is included in the Romans twelve passage. The gift, that we might think of as being a foundational gift of the first century and similar in kind to *miracles, healings,* and *tongues,* is included and is at the top of the list. I find that to be most interesting. After all, don't we read in Ephesians 2: 20 that the Church of Christ is "built on the foundation of the apostles and prophets…?" We might think of those two gifts as belonging together; so why is the gift of being a prophet included in the Romans twelve list and that of being an Apostle not included? -- to be discussed later.

PROPHECY RULES

Turning to I Corinthians twelve we find Paul more than once exhorting us to desire the gift of prophecy. We read in verses 28-31:

> And God has appointed in the church, first apostles, second prophets, third teachers, then miracles, then gifts of healings, helps, administrations, *various* kinds of tongues. All are not apostles, are they? All are not prophets, are they? All are not teachers, are they? All are not *workers* of miracles, are they? All do not have the gifts of healings, do they? All do not speak with tongues, do they? All do not interpret, do they? But earnestly desire the greater gifts. And I show you a still more excellent way (I Corinthians 12:28-3).

In these verses Paul seems to be setting forth the gifts in their order of value. He then exhorts us to *earnestly* desire the "greater gifts." The gift of prophecy is listed there as second only in value to that of being an apostle.

After then presenting to us the great "love" chapter of the Bible, (chapter 13). coming to chapter fourteen, he exhorts, "Pursue love, yet desire earnestly spiritual *gifts,* but especially that you may prophesy" (I Corinthians 14:1). In the verses following, Paul argues for the value of the gift of prophecy and contrasts it to that of tongues. He says, "But one who prophesies speaks to men for edification and exhortation and consolation." (I Cor. 14:.3). He declares further, "Now I wish that you all spoke in tongues, but *even* more that you would prophesy; and greater is one who prophesies than one who speaks in tongues, unless he interprets, so that the church may receive edifying" (I Cor.14:5).

So then, without question, we have, in two New Testament Epistles, definite exhortation and encouragement with respect to the gift of prophecy. In fact, we are instructed to "desire earnestly … the gift of prophecy" (I Corinthians 14:1). The question we want to address is: Why are the two major passages that mention the gift of prophecy, written by the same human author, so different in content?

WHAT IS A PROPHET?

Marvin R. Vincent, in his *Word Studies,* gives us a rather technical definition and description of what a prophet is and does:

> The popular conception of a prophet is limited to his foretelling of future events. This is indeed included in the term, but does not cover its meaning entirely. The word is from *phemi-*to speak, and *pro,* before, in front of. This meaning of the preposition may have reference to time, vis., *before, beforehand;* or to place, vis., in *front of,* and so, publicly; and this latter meaning in turn easily runs into that of *in behalf of.* The prophet is, therefore, primarily, one who speaks, standing *before* another, and thus forming a medium between him and the hearer. This sense runs naturally into that of *instead of.* Hence it is the technical term for *the interpreter of a divine message.* The central idea of the word is, one to whom God reveals Himself and through whom He speaks. The revelation

may or may not relate to the future. The prophet is a *forth-teller*, not necessarily, a *foreteller*.[21]

Referring to the Old Testament and the Hebrew word, *nabi*, Merrill Unger states that "a prophet is a declarer, an announcer, one who utters a communication." He says that "the great majority of biblical critics prefer the active sense of *announcing, pouring* forth *the declaration of God*."[22]

Again, Vincent says, "In the New Testament, as in the Old, the prominent idea is not prediction, but the inspired delivery of warning, exhortation, instruction, judging, and making manifest the secrets of the heart."[23]

Graham Houston, in a detailed book on the subject of prophecy, maintains that there are two classes of prophets in the Scriptures. He writes:

> To recapitulate: in the New Testament, prophetic phenomena can be divided into two classes. First, there is the absolutely authoritative prophecy exercised by the apostles and their associates who, like the classical prophets of the Old Testament claimed that their message communicated the actual words of God, to the church and, through the church, to the world. This kind of prophecy, much of which was recorded in the Scriptures of the New Testament, formed a unique and unrepeatable foundation, along with the teachings of Jesus, for the body of Christ.[24]

Houston refers us to Ephesians 2:20 where Paul declares that the church has "been built on the foundation of the apostles and prophets, Christ Jesus Himself being the corner stone. So, on the one hand we have

---

[21] Marvin R. Vincent, *Vincent's Word Studies*, (taken from E-Sword, CD-Rom, Rick Meyers, 2000.)

[22] Merrill Unger, *Unger's Bible Dictionary*, (Chicago: Moody Press, 1957), p. 890.

[23] Vincent, Op. Cit.

[24] Graham Houston, *Prophecy, a Gift for Today*, (Downers Grove, Illinois: Inter Varsity Press, 1989), p.110.

the men of both the Old and New Testaments who received truth from God (Special Revelation) and gave us books of Scripture such as, Isaiah, Jeremiah, Daniel, etc., and the Epistles of Paul, Peter and John.

WHAT PETER THOUGHT ABOUT THE WRITINGS OF PAUL

The Apostle Peter has this to say about Old Testament Prophecy, "But we know this first of all, that no prophecy of Scripture is a matter of one's own interpretation, for no prophecy was ever made by an act of human will, but men moved by the Holy Spirit spoke from God" (II Peter 1:20-21). It is well worth noting what Peter has to say, two chapters later, about the writings of Paul:

> Therefore, beloved, since you look for these things, be diligent to be found by Him in peace, spotless and blameless, and regard the patience of our Lord as salvation; just as also our beloved brother Paul, according to the wisdom given him, wrote to you, as also in all *his* letters, speaking in them of these things hard to understand, which the untaught and unstable distort, as *they* do also the rest of Scripture, to their own destruction (II Peter 3:14-16).

We notice that Peter refers, most significantly, to Paul's writings as "Scripture," on a par with the prophecies of old. These men, such as Peter, Paul, John and others, were prophets of God who received that Special Revelation by which we have received the Holy Scriptures.

A SECOND CLASS OF PROPHETS

Graham Houston proceeds in his book to call our attention to the passage found in I Corinthians 14 and declares that there is another kind of prophet and another kind of prophecy which must be considered. He refers to it as "Christian prophecy."[25] Paul interacts with this kind of prophecy

---

[25] Ibid., p. 110

and endeavors to set in order its manifestation in the local church. Paul writes, "For one who speaks in a tongue does not speak to men but to God; for no one understands, but in his spirit, he speaks mysteries. But one who prophesies speaks to men for edification and exhortation and consolation" (I Corinthians 14:2-3). Later in the chapter Paul says:

> So then tongues are *for a sign*, not to those who believe, but to unbelievers; but prophecy is for a sign, not to unbelievers; but to those who believe...What is *the outcome* then, brethren? When you assemble, each one has a psalm, has a teaching, has a revelation, has a tongue, has an interpretation. Let all things be done for edification... Let two or three prophets speak, and let the others pass judgment. But if a revelation is made to another who is seated, the first one must keep silent. For you can all prophecy one by one, so that all may learn and all may be exhorted; and the spirits of the prophets are subject to the prophets; for God is not a God of confusion, but of peace, as in all the churches of the saints (I Corinthians 14:22-33).

With a view to this passage and other references found in the book of Acts, Houston writes the following concerning a second class of prophets:

> Secondly, there is clear evidence that the early church recognized prophetic activity which made no such claims to being the very Word of God. Such prophecy, which we have in this book called New Testament prophecy or Christian prophecy, did not seek to communicate the logos (word) of God, the apostolic message which focused on the person and work of Jesus Christ and offered a coherent explanation of reality, physical and spiritual, with Jesus at the center of all things. Christian prophecy is not to be confused with the preaching and teaching of

that logos, which was a distinctive ministry which the
Holy Spirit raised up for the upbuilding of the body....[26]

To sum up, Graham Houston, in his book maintains at length that
there are two kinds of prophets found in the Scripture. There are the classic
prophets of Old, many of whom gave us the very words of the Bible, but
there is also the kind of prophet, and prophetess, that Paul writes about in
I Corinthians 14. Houston includes with those in Corinth, prophets such
as Agabus (Acts 11:28,21:10) and prophetesses such as the four daughters
of Phillip mentioned in Acts 21, verse 9. I am inclined to believe that this
kind of prophecy falls within the category of foundational gifts and served
to help meet the needs of God's people living in the first century.

WHY NOT A THIRD CLASS?

If it can be argued that there are two classes of prophecy in the
Scriptures, and I believe it can, then what about the possibility of a third
class of prophecy? Since there are two, why not three? I am inclined to
believe that there is another kind of prophecy, one that is relevant to our
day, one that is listed as a spiritual gift in Romans chapter 12.

It also involves revelation from God and in loving ministry "speaks
to men for edification and exhortation and consolation." (I Corinthians
14:3) The gift of prophecy found in I Corinthians 12 is the same gift as
mentioned in Romans 12, but the function of the gift takes, I believe, a
different form.

In general accordance with that which I have in mind Kenneth L
Chafin has written the following:

> The gift of "prophecy" should probably be translated as the
> gift of preaching or communication. While the popular
> understanding of prophecy is that it is foretelling things
> which will happen, it more often means telling forth the
> word of God. And there continue to be those individuals
> to whom God gives the gift of spiritual communication.

---

[26] Ibid., p. 111.

While I was a student I heard the late great Andrew W. Blackwood, who had already retired as the preaching professor at Princeton Theological Seminary. He was a great student of worship and of preaching and gave much emphasis to the reading of Scripture in worship. He was with us for an entire week, and the high point of the day was when he stood to read from the Word of God. There was a sense in which even though he was reading a passage that I had read many times before, as he read it God spoke in a fresh way to my mind and my heart. It takes nothing away from his study and planning and training to say that God had given him the gift of communication.[27]

A COMPLETED CANON OF SCRIPTURE

In the above quote Kenneth Chafin labels it the "gift of spiritual communication." I would add to that by saying that the gift of prophecy listed in Romans 12:6 is the gift of spiritual communication that is based upon the completed Special Revelation that God has given us in His Word, the Bible. We have today the completed canon of Scripture, something that the church in Corinth did not have when Paul dealt with that problematic body of believers. There is no longer a need for the revelations to individuals of which Paul writes in I Corinthians 14. The operation of the gift of prophecy in apostolic times served to give guidance to individuals and would also, along with miracles and healings, provide confirming signs for the early church. The case of "a prophet named Agabus" as found in Acts 21:10-11 is one of some interest:

> As we were staying there for some days, a prophet named Agabus came down from Judea. And coming to us, he took Paul's belt and bound his own feet and hands, and said, "This is what the Holy Spirit says: 'In this way the

---

[27] Andrew L. Blackwood, "I,2 Corinthians," *The Communicators Commentary*, Ed. Lloyd J. Ogilvie,
(Waco, Texas: Word Books, Publishers, 1985), p. 153.

Jews at Jerusalem will bind the man who owns this belt and deliver him into the hands of the Gentiles.'" (Acts 21:10-11)

What is quite interesting is that in spite of this prophecy and in spite of the fact that his friends were begging him not to go, Paul went anyway. What then, we may ask, was the purpose of this special revelation to Paul? Perhaps it served as a test for Paul and his commitment to suffer hardship for His Savior and perhaps it also was a lesson for all, that the Lord, indeed, knows the end from the beginning. Some call them "foundational gifts,"-spiritual gifts such as miracles, healings, tongues, and this form of prophecy. Many look at it this way: The church was in its infant stage and the canon of Scripture was incomplete. At that time God authenticated the teachings of His servants and confirmed His program to His people through a number of "foundational gifts." There are many who say, however, that these gifts are not just a thing of the past, but continue in their operation today.

THE VERY BREATH OF GOD

Let us not lose sight of the fact that the Word of God is extremely special in nature. In II Timothy 3:16-17 Paul writes, "All Scripture is inspired by God and profitable for teaching, for reproof, for correction, for training in righteousness; so that the man of God may be adequate, equipped for every good work." The significant Greek word here is "theopneustos," which is made up of two words, the word for God and the word to breathe. Paul is declaring that all Scripture is God-breathed -- that the completed canon of Scripture is the very breath of God. The NIV Study Bible puts it this way, "Paul affirms God's active involvement in the writing of Scripture, an involvement so powerful and pervasive that what is written is the infallible and authoritative word of God."[28]

This passage goes on to assert that, because it is the God-breathed Word, it is profitable for teaching. It is profitable for reproof. Vincent

---

[28] *The NIV Study Bible*, New International Version, (Grand Rapids, Mi; 1985), p. 1846.

in his "Word Studies" suggests that this has the idea of conviction.[29] It is profitable for correction. It is profitable for training in righteousness. Vincent indicates that the word for correction means "to stand upright," while the word for training refers to child training or discipline.[30]

All of this means that "the man of God may be adequate, equipped for every good work." (II Timothy 3:17) The King James Version reads, "...that the man of God may be perfect, thoroughly furnished unto every good work." (II Timothy 3:17/KJV). All of this suggests that the inspired and infallible Word of God can be looked upon as supplying our every need when it comes to the above listed ministries of God in our lives. Perhaps there is, therefore, no longer a need for the type of revelations to individuals that are mentioned in I Corinthians 14. We now have the Special Revelation, which is the completed, inspired Word of God. This is not to say dogmatically, however, that class two prophecy is forever gone from God's program.

IS BILLY GRAHAM A PROPHET?

The writer of the book of Hebrews adds to our understanding of the remarkable nature of the completed Word of God. He declares in Hebrews 4:12 that there is the quality of animation about it, "For the word of God is living and active and sharper than any two-edged sword, and piercing a far as the division of soul and spirit, of both joints and marrow, and able to judge the thoughts and intentions of the heart" (Hebrews 4:12).

At this point my question is this: When Billy Graham stands before a great crowd of people and says, "The Bible says...," is he any less a prophet than an Isaiah or Jeremiah declaring, "Thus saith the Lord?" I suggest that he is armed with a greater and more powerful revelation from God than was ever realized by any Old Testament prophet. The same can be said of an Andrew Blackwood simply reading the Scripture (see the above quote by Kenneth Chafin).

---

[29] *Vincent's Word Studies*, (from E-Sword, CD-Rom, Rick Meyers, 2000).
[30] Ibid., E-Sword

THE DISTINCTIVE NATURE OF ROMANS TWELVE

As noted previously, the presentation of the spiritual gifts in Romans 12 differs significantly from that given in I Corinthians 12. The gift of apostleship is not listed, although Paul does refer in verse 3 to his own gift in that regard. The gifts which seem to be more dramatic in their presentation, such as *miracles, healings, tongues* and the *interpretation of tongues,* are not mentioned.

On the other hand, there are similarities with respect to Paul's argument in the two chapters. In both passages Paul speaks about the unity of the Body and the diversity of gifts. In the Corinthians passage Paul interjects the importance of giving proper place to the love of God (chapter 13—the Love Chapter). In Romans 12, after listing spiritual gifts Paul says in verse 9 of Romans 12, "*Let* love be without hypocrisy. Abhor what is evil; cling to what is good. *Be* devoted to one another in brotherly love; give preference to one another in honor" (Romans 12:9-10). He continues in that vein through verse 21 of Romans 12. All of this, however, draws attention to the great difference between the two chapters with respect to the gifts that are listed. Why is the list so different from the lists given in I Corinthians 12? (There are actually three lists in that chapter: one in verses 8-10; another in verse 28; and a third list, slightly different, in verses 29-30 of I Corinthians 12.

My suggestion, in response to that question, is as follows: In I Corinthians Paul is addressing the problems of a local church of the first century. On the other hand, Paul is writing the book of Romans for the ages. Under the influence of the Holy Spirit, Paul writes a great theological treatise which some have called, *The Fifth Gospel,* because it is so profound and complete in presenting to us the *good news* as to the meaning of the life and ministry of Jesus. The major divisions of the book can be set forth as Sin, Salvation, Sanctification, Selection (with regard to the place of the nation Israel) and Service. Just as the theology of the previous sections is to be regarded as definitive and complete, so the section on Service, (living and serving for Christ) can be regarded as normative with regard to the centuries to come.

The gift of being an Apostle is not listed with a view to the fact that in the years to come the Apostolic age will have been gone. Furthermore, the foundational gifts, those which were associated with the Apostolic Age, such as miracles, tongues, etc., are also gone, in the sense of being no longer normative. The gift of prophecy, however, continues, but is now functioning in accordance with the completed canon of Scripture.

A PROBLEMATIC PHRASE

There is a curious phrase found in verse 6 of Romans 12. Verse 6 reads, "Since we have gifts that differ according to the grace given to us, each of us is to exercise them accordingly: if prophecy, according to the proportion of his faith." Commentators writing on the last part of that verse, *"according to the proportion of his faith,"* have struggled to make sense of those words. The Greek word translated "proportion" is "anlogia," from which we get the English word, "analogy." Vincent in his Word Studies points out that in classical Greek the word was a mathematical term. It speaks of proportion or measurement.[31] It can be translated, "according to the measure of faith."

Commentators disagree as to whether the word "faith" in the verse is to be taken in the objective or subjective sense. Many of us today use the phrase, "the analogy of Scripture," which has to do with various portions of Scripture corresponding to one another in meaning or content." We might also speak of the "analogy of the faith." Some then see a reference to *"the* Faith" as the body of Christian doctrine and suggest that Paul is saying that the prophet must be sure that his message corresponds to or is analogous to other portions of the revealed Word. That would seem to make sense, but French commentator, Frederick L. Godet has written the following on this verse:

> ...Others think it possible to give the term faith the objective meaning which it took later in ecclesiastical language, as when we speak of the evangelical faith or the Christian faith; ... The prophet in his addresses should respect the foundations of the faith already laid, the Christian facts and the truths which flow from them.

---

[31] *Vincent's Word Studies*, op., cit

But the word faith never in the N.T. denotes doctrine itself; it has always a reference to the subjective feeling of self-surrender, confidence in God, or in Christ as the revealer of God.[32]

THE PROPHET AND HIS FAITH

Most of the commentators I have consulted believe, along with Godet, that the word "faith" should be taken in the subjective sense. It is a reference to the prophet's own faith. But why do we have this reference to the prophet's faith as being important which respect to the exercise of his gift?

The structure of verses 6-8 of Romans 12 looks this way:

"…if prophecy, according to the proportion of his faith;
if service, in his serving;
or he who exhorts, in this exhortation;
he who gives, with liberality;
he who leads, with diligence;
he who shows mercy, with cheerfulness." (Romans 12:6-8)

The emphasis of the exhortation seems to be on "the doing." "If this is your gift, then do it and do it properly. Focus on the gift that you have. If it's *service*, then serve. If it's *teaching*, then teach. If it's *giving*, then do it with liberality. If it's the gift of *showing mercy*, then do it cheerfully." Each one in the Body of Christ is to focus on his gift and exercise it. But notice, concerning the gift of *prophecy*, Paul says, "Do it in accordance with the faith that God has given you. Do it in faith." The emphasis on the execution of the gift of *prophecy* seems to be in accord with that which is exhorted with respect to the other gifts listed. If *prophecy* is your gift, then do it and do it in accordance with the proportion or measure of faith that God has given you.

---

[32] Frederick L. Godet, *Commentary on the Epistle to the Romans*, translated from the French by Rev. A.
Cusin and Talbot W. Chambers, (Grand Rapids, Mi.: Zondervan Publishing House, American ed. 1956), p. 431.

The question then is; why is faith especially important with respect to the gift of *prophecy*? I suggest the following as a possible interpretation of the phrase used in Romans 12:6, "...in accordance with the proportion of his faith:" While a degree of faith is important with respect to any spiritual gift, it is suggested that the prophet's need for faith is very important. Does this support the idea of a third class of prophecy--that of communicating the mind and will of God as derived from the completed Canon of Scripture? It's not just a matter of sharing a dream of a vision that one has had. It's a matter of laboring over the Word, interpreting the content and deciding how best to communicate it. Preparing messages to be communicated to God's people does require, and certainly should require, the exercise of faith during the process. The prophet should be open by faith to the Spirit's illumination (not revelation) concerning the Scripture (I Corinthians 2:9-13).

A SIGN OF THE SECOND COMING?

We come now to a consideration of one more area with regard to the subject of *prophecy,* the question as to whether or not a renewed exercise of the gift of *prophecy* is an indication or a sign of the soon-coming Second Advent of Christ. In his sermon delivered on the Day of Pentecost, Peter quotes from the second chapter of the Old Testament book of Joel (Joel 2:28,29):

> 'AND IT SHALL BE IN THE LAST DAYS,' God says, 'THAT I WILL POUR FORTH OF MY SPIRIT ON ALL MANKIND; AND YOUR SONS AND YOUR DAUGHTERS WILL PROPHECY, AND YOUR YOUNG MEN WILL SEE VISIONS, AND YOUR OLD MEN SHALL DREAM DREAMS; EVEN ON MY BONDSLAVES, BOTH MEN AND WOMEN, I WILL POUR FORTH OF MY SPIRIT and they shall prophesy (Acts 2:17-18).

In the verses that follow we find unmistakable references to phenomena that will take place just prior to the Second Coming of Christ. In Acts 2:19-21 we read:

> 'AND I WILL GRANT WONDERS IN THE SKY ABOVE AND SIGNS ON THE EARTH BELOW, BLOOD, AND FIRE, AND VAPOR OF SMOKE. THE SUN WILL BE TURNED INTO DARKNESS AND THE MOON INTO BLOOD, BEFORE THE GREAT AND GLORIOUS DAY OF THE LORD SHALL COME. AND IT SHALL BE THAT EVERYONE WHO CALLS ON THE NAME OF THE LORD WILL BE SAVED' (Acts 2:19-21).

At the time of this writing reports are coming out of the Middle East that seem to indicate a great renewal of the phenomena that Peter speaks of in Acts two; dreams, visions and individuals receiving revelations from God. Joel C. Rosenberg, in a book entitled *Inside the Revolution*, writes of "The Big Untold Story." He says, "You rarely even hear about it in churches in the West, in the East, or even in the Middle East. But

the big untold story is that more Muslims are coming to faith in Jesus Christ today than at any other time in history."[33]

Under the subtitle, *Dreams and Visions*, he gives this account:

> Ultimately, I'm told that most Iranian MBBs [Muslim Background Believers] are not coming to Christ primarily through *The Passion of The Christ* or the JESUS film, or through radio and satellite TV ministries, or even through the work of the mushrooming house-church movement. ...They are giving many unbelievers initial exposure to the gospel, and they are certainly strengthening the faith of new believers as well as those who have been following Christ for some time. But they are not enough to

---

[33] Joel C. Rosenberg, *Inside the Revolution*, (Carol Stream, Illinois: Tyndale House Publications, Inc. 2009), p. 379.

bring many Iranians to a point of decision. What is bringing these Iranians to Christ are dreams and visions of Jesus.[34]

Rosenberg goes on to supply us with many, many illustrations of men and woman having dreams and seeing visions that result in finding Jesus Christ as Lord and Savior. He continues page after page in describing the extraordinary happenings that are taking place in Iran and in other Middle Eastern countries. He gives the following example, among many others, of the kind of dreams or visions that are bringing people to Christ:

> One Iranian Muslim woman had a dream in which God told her, "Whatever the two women you are going to meet with tomorrow tell you, listen to them." Startled, she went through the next day curious who she would meet. She had no plans to meet anyone, but sure enough, at one point two Iranian Christian women came up to her and explained the message of salvation to her. She obeyed the Lord's directive from the dream, listened carefully, and then bowed her head and prayed to receive Christ as her Savior.[35]

The stories are both very interesting and uplifting, especially when so much of what we see and hear by way of the main stream media is of a negative nature. We are exposed to so much bad news, day after day, that it is encouraging to realize that God is still calling people to Himself around the world.

However, I do make an observation with respect to all that I read about in Rosenberg's book—and there are several chapters and many pages—that there is no mention of or illustrations given of the kind of prophecy that Peter speaks of in Acts two. The gift of prophecy is exercised when a man or woman of God communicates a message from God to others for the purpose of "edification and exhortation and consolation." (I Corinthians 14:3) It's wonderful to hear of dreams and visions, but the gift of prophecy is not in evidence, at least in the pages of Rosenberg's

---

[34] Ibid., p. 387
[35] Ibid., p. 387

book. The reader may recall that we have before referred to three classes of prophecy. I am not now referring to that which Paul speaks of in Romans 12:6, but rather to what is referred to in I Corinthians 14:39 (Second Class Prophecy). Certainly, pastors and others are preaching the Word of God, but the kind of individual prophecy addressed in I Corinthians 14 is not reported. Again, "never say never." I do not want to say that the gift never happens or limit our perception of what God might do in the lives of His people.

BUT, WHAT ABOUT JOEL TWO?

We come back now to the question raised by Peter's sermon as recorded in Acts 2:17 as he quotes a passage from the Old Testament book of Joel: are the frequent occurrences of dreams, visions and prophecies an indication that the Second Coming of Christ is just around the corner?

Peter, quoting Joel says, "'AND IT SHALL BE IN THE LAST DAYS,' GOD SAYS, 'THAT I WILL POUR FORTH OF MY SPIRIT ON ALL MANKIND; AND YOUR SONS AND YOUR DAUGHTERS SHALL PROPHESY, AND YOUR YOUNG MEN SHALL SEE VISIONS AND YOUR OLD MEN SHALL DREAM DREAMS; (Acts 2:16)... AND THEY SHALL PROPHESY" (Acts 2:17). This is, indeed, a difficult passage to interpret, primarily because Peter goes on in Joel's prophecy to refer to dramatic signs in the "sky above," with "the sun" being "darkened" and "the moon" being turned into blood (Acts 2:19,20). This certainly sounds like events that precede Christ's coming to earth. Opinions advanced by commentators have been many and quite diverse.

Stanley D. Toussaint, writing in The Bible Knowledge Commentary, correctly, I believe, interprets the meaning of "...this is what was spoken of through the prophet Joel" (Acts 2:16): He declares that "this is that" does not mean "this is like that." "It means that "Pentecost fulfilled what Joel had described. However, some of the prophecies of Joel quoted in Acts 2:20 were not fulfilled, such things as "wonders in the sky above and signs on the earth below, ...". The implication is that the remainder would be fulfilled if Israel would repent."[36] It was not revealed to the Old Testament prophets that there would be a period of sometime intervening between the suffering and the reign of the Messiah. On the Day of Pentecost Peter declares that the pouring forth of the Spirit predicted by Joel was being fulfilled. In Acts 2:17-21, Peter seems to be saying that *the rest* would be fulfilled when Israel as a nation was ready to repent and receive their Messiah. In the meantime, individual Israelites could, of course, repent and receive Him as their King.

Therefore, we are inclined to believe that the gift of *prophecy* (class two prophecy) is not necessarily a sign of the Second Coming of Christ. Joel's prophecy was fulfilled on the day of Pentecost. Men and women in apostolic times did dream dreams and have visions and they did prophesy, both men and women. Consider the aforementioned four daughters of Phillip the Evangelist. Again, I do not say that there will not be a resurgence of this kind of prophecy just prior to His coming; but I am saying that Peter's words in Acts 2 do not, necessarily, call for it.

IN REVIEW

We have noted that the exercise of the gift of prophecy is encouraged in the New Testament epistles. We have suggested that we find in Scripture three classes of prophecy. There were the classic prophets of old, through whom God spoke and through whom He gave us the Bible by means of Special Revelation. Secondly, the grace-gift of prophecy as one of the *foundational gifts* is set forth in I Corinthians 14 by Paul and is referred to in the book of Acts—for example, Agabus and the four daughters of Phillip. (Acts 21:8,9 and Acts 21:10-12). Furthermore, I have suggested that there is a third class of prophecy and that that is the kind exhorted in Romans chapter twelve. I base my thinking on the unusual listing of the gifts in that chapter, whereby the sign gifts, or foundational gifts are not included and where special attention is given to the importance of faith as it relates to the exercise of the gift of prophecy. This kind of prophecy

---

[36] Stanley D. Toussaint, "Acts," *The Bible Knowledge Commentary*, editors: John F. Walvoord and Roy B. Zuck, (Wheaton, Illinois: Victor Books,--Scripture Press Publications, 1983), p. 358.

involves the communication of spiritual truth – the truth which is derived from the *special revelation* found in the completed canon of Scripture. The truth is communicated as the Holy Spirit enables the effective functioning of the gift. As to the second type of prophecy, will it be revived in the last days? not necessarily so. But I will not close the door on that possibility.

But prophecy, as the spiritual gift of communicating the written Word of God, continues to be exercised by His servants today. Of all His grace gifts, none could be more important and relevant to our day than that.

JESUS -- THE GREATEST EXPOSITOR

In a post-resurrection appearance, Jesus joins two disciples as they walk toward the village of Emmaus. After they expressed their sadness as to all that had just taken place in Jerusalem Jesus says:

> "O foolish men and slow of heart to believe in all that the prophets have spoken! Was it not necessary for the Christ to suffer these things and to enter into His glory?" Then beginning with Moses and with all the prophets, He explained to them the things concerning Himself in all the Scriptures (Luke 24:25-27).

What a wonderful exposition of Scripture this must have been! And that's what it was. The Old Testament canon of Scripture was complete and available to God's people in that day. Jesus referred to it often throughout His ministry. But here we read that He expounded Scripture, apparently at length. We can only wonder as to how long His message was. We read that, "beginning with Moses and with all the prophets, He explained to them the things concerning Himself in all the Scriptures." That would seem to be a lengthy exposition of Old Testament scripture. This is a wonderful and surely unequaled example of the gift of spiritual communication in action. We do not share in it, except to read that it happened. It was an exposition of Old Testament Scripture. In the process He opens the eyes and hearts of these two men to things in the Word of God, things which they had probably never seen before. Now here is an important point: He is not revealing new truth to them, but is shedding light on truths already there.

To this kind of spiritual communication, we should aspire, whether from the point of view of the pulpit or the pew. Today we have the completed canon of Scripture, both Old Testament and New, and we have the Holy Spirit to lead us into all truth:

> I have many more things to say to you, but you cannot bear *them* now. But when He, the Spirit of truth, comes, He will guide you into all the truth; for He will not speak on His own initiative, but whatever He hears, He will speak; and He will disclose to you what is to come. He will glorify Me, for He will take of Mine and disclose it to you. All things that the Father has are Mine; therefore, I said that He takes of Mine and will disclose it to you (John 16:12-15).

PREACHING OR TEACHING?

At this point some are, no doubt, asking what distinction Paul makes in Romans twelve between the gift of prophecy and the gift of teaching. I am not sure that I can give an answer to that question which will satisfy. But let me share my impression of the matter as based upon my own experience.

After many years of speaking weekly from the pulpit and also teaching adult Sunday school during much of that time, as well as teaching overseas in a Bible college, I perceive a difference in the speaking experience. In the classroom I find myself imparting information, explaining doctrine, making points about the spiritual life, answering questions, and interacting with students in various ways.

But on Sunday morning in the pulpit, standing up before a congregation of God's people, it's a different experience. It is still teaching, but it's a different kind of teaching. Through the process of study, reflection and prayer, I have prepared a message to impart to an assembly of God's people. It's expository in nature. I have the people stand for the reading of the text. Then I endeavor to explain what God is saying to us from the passage. No one is interrupting my presentation. No one is openly asking questions. I am able to complete my line of thinking, and thus in the process answer questions that, perhaps, had come to the minds of people as they might have disagreed with something I said, or wondered where I was going with it all.

And yes, to a greater or lesser degree, I have sensed the presence of the Holy Spirit in it, enabling my continuity of thought and verbalization of the message, and sometimes granting an emotional realization of His blessing. Indeed, I can say from my own experience, there has been a difference between my pulpit experience and that of my teaching experience.

There comes to mind one final observation concerning the definitive listing of spiritual gifts found in Romans twelve. Paul does not list prophecy and teaching one after the other, as he does in I Corinthians twelve. First there is listed *prophecy*, then *serving* and then t*eaching*. I'll let the reader make of that what he or she may.

CHAPTER EIGHT

THE QUESTION OF HEALING—Part One

Call for the Elders

An unforgettable event in my life took place many years ago when I was a Junior Deacon in what was, at that time, a small New England church. Someone's precious little girl was desperately ill and was in the Critical Care Unit of a local hospital. I felt led to call the other members of the board and suggest that we get together that evening and pray for God to intervene and deliver the girl from her illness. The pastor was called and, though it was rather late in the evening, we gathered in his house for an extended time of prayer. The next morning, we learned that the little girl was very much better and well on her way to complete recovery. I share this account to express my long-held belief that God does answer prayer and He does heal the sick when it's in accordance with His good will.

Just a few years ago I was invited to speak at a Sunday afternoon service in a church in Minsk, Belarus. It is one of the larger evangelical churches in the area and on this afternoon, it was packed with people. As one of two men who were to speak that afternoon, I spoke first, my Bible message being interpreted by a woman translator who had come with the man who was to speak after me in the service. I learned later that she did a rather poor job of interpreting what I had to say.

The man who followed me in that service had traveled there from Texas and I soon learned why the church was packed with people, mostly elderly, on that Sunday afternoon. It was to be a healing service and the traveling evangelist wasted no time in getting into it. In fact, near the beginning, the Pastor interrupted to suggest that there ought to be an invitation extended first of all to give opportunity for anyone who might be interested in receiving Jesus as their Lord and Savior. The evangelist agreed to that and proceeded to deliver a Gospel message that lasted for, perhaps, five minutes. An invitation was given and one man came forward. Someone was assigned to speak to him personally about the decision he was making.

After that the healing session began and went on for about two hours. I sat and watched as what seemed to be an unending line of people moved down the center aisle to be prayed over and touched by the woman assistant (the one who had translated for me).

That evening, as I shared my experience of that event with a friend, we wondered as to the extent of healing that had indeed taken place. We also wondered about the aftermath of it all in the minds of those who had come forward. The preacher was heading back to Texas, but how many of that church would be left behind with feelings of dismay and/or guilt with respect to the thought that they did not have enough faith to be healed?

BUT WHAT DOES THE BIBLE SAY?

We now ask the question as to what is taught, or exhorted, or encouraged concerning the subject of *healing* in the New Testament epistles. What do Paul, Peter, John and the other inspired writers of Scripture say in their Letters to the Churches? Again, in accordance with our premise, we emphasize that *The Bottom Line of Scripture* is to be found in the Epistles. If a matter is not encouraged or exhorted, and in some cases not even mentioned in the Epistles; it is therefore questionable as to whether it should be a matter of emphasis in the Christian life today.

We pray for people constantly in Mid-week services across the country. The human condition is such that it is difficult to find any matter that so occupies us week after week. People are always hurting, it seems, and so we pray for upcoming surgeries, for chronic conditions and for those in Critical Care. We pray. It is the loving thing to do and we believe that our God listens to our concerns. It would seem, therefore, that we should not only pray believing in a loving and caring God, but also with knowledge as to what the

Bible actually says about this all-important matter. On the one hand we read in I Corinthians 12:9 of the "gifts of healings." But we also read in I Timothy 5:23 where Paul says to Timothy, "No longer drink water exclusively, but use a little wine for the sake of your stomach and your frequent ailments."

WHY SO MANY ILL?

A number of commentators writing on this passage have suggested that the key phrase is "your frequent ailments." Albert Barnes writes in his commentary on I Timothy that the word translated "ailments" means weaknesses or sicknesses. "The word would include all infirmities of body, but seems to refer here to some attacks of sickness to which Timothy was liable, or to some feebleness of constitution; but beyond this we have no information...." Timothy is exhorted not to be a water-drinker (lit. Greek) exclusively, but to take a little wine for his stomach and his frequent infirmities.

Commentators have struggled with the matter of fitting this verse into the context of what precedes and what follows in the chapter. Barnes suggests the following:

> Paul appears to have been suddenly impressed with the thought which is very likely to have come over a man who is writing on the duties of the ministries—or the arduous nature in regard to the ministerial office. He was giving counsel in regard to an office that required a great amount of care and anxiety. The labors enjoined were such as to demand all the time; the care and anxiety incident to such a charge would be very likely to prostrate the frame, and to injure the health. Then he remembered that Timothy was yet but a youth; he recalled his feebleness of constitution and his frequent attacks of illness; He recollected the very abstemious habits which he had prescribed for himself, and, in this connection, he urges him to a careful regard for his health, and prescribes the use of a small quantity of wine, mingled with his water as a suitable medicine in his case."[37]

---

[37] Ibid., on I Timothy 5:23.

A.T. Robertson goes so far as to suggest that Timothy was a "semi-invalid."[38] Perhaps, we need not go that far, but just to recognize that Timothy was somewhat sickly. Furthermore, we have also these words in II Timothy 4:20 where Paul says,

"Erastus remained at Corinth, but Trophimus I left sick at Miletus." To this is added the case of Paul himself. In II Corinthians 12:7-19 he speaks of his "thorn in the flesh," concerning which he prayed three times. He says, "Concerning this I implored the Lord three times that it might leave me. And He has said to me, 'My grace is sufficient for you, for power is perfected in weakness.' Most gladly, therefore, I will rather boast about my weaknesses, so that the power of Christ may dwell in me" (II Corinthians 12:8-9).

Therefore, as we faithfully pray for those who are ill, we have in mind the fact that in the Epistles we read of some who, apparently, were not immediately healed of their infirmities. Spiros Zodhiates, who is a scholar of New Testament Greek and who is also a native of Greece, has written the following on the subject:

> Does the Christian ever get sick? Of course, he does. The fact that he does, proves to us that accepting Jesus Christ as one's very own Savior does not exempt a person from susceptibility to physical sickness. Unfortunately, there are many ill-informed people who try to preach otherwise, and such people cause a great deal of confusion which may have calamitous results. When a person *believes that he is not supposed to get sick, and he does become ill, he develops guilt complexes which may lead him to utter mental and spiritual ruin.* This subject, therefore, is of extreme and fundamental importance because of the modern exploitation of uninformed consciences on this matter.[39] [Emphasis mine]

---

[38] A.T. Robertson, *Word Pictures*, (E-sword.) on I Timothy 5:23.
[39] Spiros Zodhiates, *The Patience of Hope*, (Grand Rapids, Michigan: WM. B. Eerdmans Publishing Company, 1960), p. 117.

Having taken note of the above scattered passages, we come now to an all- important passage of Scripture which we want to consider in detail.

THE ONE AND ONLY PASSAGE

With regard to the premise of this writing, that the exhortations and admonitions of the New Testament Epistles are all important with regard to the Christian life today, it is interesting to note that there is but one and only one passage to be considered. There is but one passage in all the Epistles where we are enjoined to act with respect to the need for healing ministry. That one passage is found in the book of James, chapter 5, verses 13-18. It is a profound and wonderful passage indeed:

> Is anyone among you suffering? *Then* he must pray. Is anyone cheerful? He is to sing praises. Is anyone among you sick? *Then* he must call for the elders of the church and they are to pray over him, anointing him with oil in the name of the Lord; and the prayer offered in faith will restore the one who is sick, and the Lord will raise him up, and if he has committed sins, they will be forgiven him. Therefore, confess your sins to one another so that you may be healed. The effective prayer of a righteous man can accomplish much. Elijah was a man with a nature like ours, and he prayed earnestly that it would not rain, and it did not rain on the earth for three years and six months. Then he prayed again, and the sky poured rain and the earth produced its fruit. (James 5:13-18)

AN EXHORTATION SELDOM HEEDED

It is interesting to note that with regard to this one passage where we are told what to do with regard to illness, we have an exhortation that goes unheeded. The person who is ill is instructed to do something. He or she is exhorted to call for the elders of the church that they might come and pray for that one. And yet with respect to my ministry in two churches over a period of forty-six years I cannot recall one instance where the one who is ill has actually called for the elders to come. Yes, there have been a number of times when I have been with of a group of men who have gone to someone's home to pray with respect to an illness. Those special prayer meetings have been meaningful, but it has always been at the suggestion of one of us or someone else in the church family, as opposed to a call from someone who is ill. I am sure that some pastors can testify otherwise, but I am under the impression that people, for some reason, are not inclined to heed the specific instruction of James 5:14.

Secondly, we observe in verse 14 that the *elders* are those who are to be called.

The one who is ill is not instructed to call for someone who has a gift of healing. He or she is not instructed to get to some healing service. Rather, "call for the elders."

The Apostle Paul in his pastoral epistles has a great deal to say about what elders are expected to be and do. He must be "able to teach" (I Timothy 3:2). Paul says, He is to "Guard through the Holy Spirit who dwells in us, the treasure which has been entrusted to you" (II Timothy 1:14). He must be "hospitable, loving what is good, sensible, just, devout, self-controlled, holding fast the faithful word which is in accordance with the teaching, so that he will be able to exhort in sound doctrine and to refute those who contradict" (Titus 1:7-9). Peter exhorts elders to "… shepherd the flock of God among you, exercising oversight not under compulsion, but voluntarily, according to *the will of* God; and not for sordid gain, but with eagerness; nor yet as lording it over those allotted to your charge, but proving to be examples to the flock" (I Peter 5:2-3). But nowhere do we read that elders were to have a *gift of healing*. Nevertheless, the elders are to be called to the bedside of the one who is ill.

Next we observe from James 5:15 that the "prayer offered in faith" will restore the one who is sick…" At this point we ask the question: Whose faith? By implication it is the faith of the elders involved; they are the ones who have been called to pray. This would seem to be in contrast to healing ministries today where it is easy to place the blame for failure on the one who needs healing; that is to suggest that he or she did not have enough faith when the healing touch was applied or the prayers said.

THE ANOINTING WITH OIL — A SACRAMENT?

It is thought by many that the elders should carry with them a little bottle of oil and apply it to the forehead of the one who is ill. It is supposed that this is somehow a means of grace, almost a sacrament, if you please.

More common among evangelical commentators is the view that the application of oil is a symbol of the presence of God and/or the Holy Spirit and is therefore an aid to faith. There is, however, another view of that which is exhorted here, a view that is very well expounded by Spiros Zodhiates in his commentary on the book of James.

TWO GREEK WORDS

Zodhiates believes that our English versions have mistranslated this part of verse 14. He renders it, "And let them pray over him, having rubbed him with oil, in the name of the Lord."[40] He points out that there are two very different Greek words found in the New Testament which are translated by just one English word, "anoint." The word used here is *aleiphoo* while the other word, *chrioo*, is used elsewhere in the New Testament.

He writes:

> The *difference between these two Greek words is fundamental* and will provide the real key to the understanding of this difficult verse. The verb used here, aleiphoo, is the mundane and secular word, while the word chrioo is the sacred and religious word. ...In Luke 4:18, we have the Lord Jesus entering the synagogue in Nazareth and reading from the Book of Isaiah as follows: "The Spirit of the Lord is upon me, because he hath anointed me to preach the gospel to the poor." etc. The word used here is not the same as that in James, but the verb chrioo. It is the verb from which the word Christ comes. The Lord Jesus was the Christ because He was anointed by His Father for

---

40 Zodhiates, p. 122.

that particular work of redemption. This word chrioo is therefore exclusively used to denote sacred purposes. ...The words chrisis, chrisma, and chrioo, all referring to the sacred anointing, are the constant and recurring words for all religious and symbolic anointing. The word used by James is never used in the New Testament with the sacred and symbolical meaning of the verb chrioo. It is used in describing the anointing of the dead body of Christ by the women in Mark 16:1. It is also used to describe the anointing of the feet of Jesus by the woman in a Pharisee's house, in Luke 7:38,46. ... In reality in English the word "anoint" has come to have the sacred meaning which the verb chrioo has in Greek, and only this Greek word should be translated by the English "anoint" and not the one used by James. The verb aleiphoo used by James should rather be translated "to oil." It is the equivalent to the expression "rubbing or oiling" that we so commonly use today. We would never use chrioo to mean "to anoint" a piece of machinery or the human body.[41]

In the next chapter of his commentary Zodhiates goes on to say that the anointing spoken of in James 5:14 "is no sacrament, but something done to relieve the physical affliction of the suffering one. It refers to rubbing with olive oil, or to oiling with oil." He says that it "refers rather to the application of physical means for the relief of physical pain."[42] He cites the story of the good Samaritan who found a man by the wayside who was in great need of help. We read that he used two elements so as to minister to the physical needs of the man, oil and wine -- probably wine as a disinfectant because of its alcoholic content, and oil for its soothing effects."[43] Zodhiates maintains that this was the equivalent of medical attention in a day when doctors were scarce and transportation difficult. It was common practice in that day in an effort to provide material relief for the body.

---

[41] Ibid., p. 123
[42] Ibid., p. 125
[43] Ibid., p. 126

As a student of New Testament Greek, Zodhiates is able to suggest to us that the tense of the participle is important in this verse. "Someone is sick among you? Let him invite the elders of the church and let them pray over him, *having rubbed* him with oil in the name of the Lord" (James 5:14). "The first thing which the elders are supposed to do is to rub the patient with oil." But what if the patient is a woman? Zodhiates points out that most churches have designated women who would be well able to serve when needed.[44] In our day we do what we can to make the infirmed person more comfortable, encouraged and assisted physically; this can mean calling the doctor.

Zodhiates is not alone in his view of James 5:14. There are many other commentators who point out the difference between the two Greek words, the secular and the sacred, and believe that the verse supports the idea of God and medicine. We do what we can for people physically and we pray. In still another chapter on the subject Zodhiates refers to the great work of medical missions. He says, "Is it not in these words that medical missions found their impetus? There would hardly be much medicine practiced in the depths of many undeveloped and uncivilized countries if it were not for medical missionaries, who have done a splendid piece of work."[45]

THE IMPORTANCE OF CONFESSION

There is but one passage in the Epistles having to do with the subject of healing. The profound and complete nature of the passage can be seen in the fact that it brings in the importance of the confession of sins as well as the dynamics of effectual prayer. First, in reference to confession, we notice these words, beginning in verse 15, "...and if he has committed sins, they will be forgiven him. Therefore, confess your sins to one another, and pray for one another that you may be healed" (James 5:15-16).

In the Greek text of the quotation cited above, an important little word occurs at the beginning of that portion of James 5:15. The Greek word is "*kan*" and it means "and if." *If* in a particular case of illness, sin is involved,

---

[44] Ibid., p. 127. Zodhiates devotes about three chapters in his commentary to this subject. I recommend these chapters to anyone wishing to pursue the matter.
[45] Ibid., p. 129.

the confession of that sin then becomes relevant. Of course, illness is not necessarily the result of sin. The chronic illness of Timothy, referred to above, was not the result of unconfessed sin. Paul's thorn in the flesh (II Corinthians 12:7) obviously was not the result of sin in his life.

The all too common notion that physical infirmity is the result of some sin was dismissed by the words of Jesus as found in John 9:1-3. With regard to a man who was blind from birth the disciples asked, "Rabbi, who sinned, this man or his parents, that he would be born blind?" In response Jesus said, "*It was* neither *that* this man sinned, nor his parents; but *it was* so that the works of God might be displayed in him" (John 9:2-3). However, the Scripture does teach that sometimes unconfessed sin is involved.

THE ANALOGY OF I CORINTHIANS ELEVEN

In the context of the institution of The Lord's Supper we have these words of Paul as found in I Corinthians 11:27-32:

"Wherefore whosoever shall eat this bread, and drink this cup of the Lord unworthily, shall be guilty of the body and blood of the Lord. But let a man examine himself, and so let him eat of that bread, and drink of that cup. For he that eateth and drinketh unworthily, eateth and drinketh damnation to himself, not discerning the Lord's body. For this cause many are weak and sickly among you, and many sleep. For if we would judge ourselves, we should not be judged. But when we are judged, we are chastened of the Lord, that we should not be condemned with the world" (I Corinthians 11:27-32 /KJV).

Years ago, a pastor-friend of mine shared with me a practice in his church concerning the observance of Communion. He said that they always observed the Lord's Supper during the Evening Service at his church because it was unlikely that non-believers would be in attendance at that time as opposed to a Sunday morning when a number might be present. He believed, based on I Corinthians 11:27-32, that a non-believer could bring damnation upon himself by partaking of the elements of Communion. This idea, no doubt, is based upon the rendering of verse 29 of I Cor. 11 in the King James Version of the Bible, "For he that eateth and drinketh unworthily, eateth and drinketh damnation to himself, not discerning the Lord's body." (1 Corinthians 11: 29 /KJV). I am glad that the New King James Version does not have the word *damnation*, and instead has *judgment.*

Greek scholar, Marvin R. Vincent, writes concerning the use of the word "damnation" in this passage, "This false and horrible rendering has destroyed the peace of mind of more sincere and earnest souls than any other misread passage in the New Testament. It has kept hundreds from the Lord's table."[46] Vincent goes on to comment on the difference between two important Greek words, "Krima is a temporary judgment, and so is distinguished from katakrima condemnation, from which this temporary judgment is intended to save the participant. The distinction appears in I Cor. 11:32. The A.V. of the whole passage is marked by a confusion of the renderings of *krinein* to judge and its compounds [emphasis mine]."[47]

May I suggest to the reader that Paul's warning in this passage has to do with God's discipline, or temporary judgment, upon the believer who continues in unconfessed sin, or fails to consider the Lord's Supper as a sacred opportunity to place his sin under the blood of Christ. When at the Lord's Table, he is not partaking of ordinary food—not that which is to satisfy one's appetite and give pleasure to himself. The bread and the cup symbolize the value of the Lord's death on our behalf. The observance of Communion is a sacred opportunity for self-examination and confession of sin. Paul says, "But if we judged ourselves rightly, we would not be judged" (I Corinthians 11:31). Confession of sin is self-judgment. Failure in this regard can lead to the believer being disciplined by his Heavenly Father, which, according to verse 30, can mean illness.

THE MEANING OF CONFESSION

The classic passage on the matter of fellowship with God and the importance of confession is I John 1:5-10. We read, "If we say that we have no sin, we are deceiving ourselves and the truth is not is us. If we confess our sins, He is faithful and righteous to forgive us our sins and to cleanse us from all unrighteousness" (I John 1:8-9).

---

[46] Marvin R.Vincent, *Vincent's Word Studies in the New Testament*, (CD Rom-E-sword) on I Corinthians 11:29.

[47] Ibid., on I Corinthians ll:29.

At the beginning of this Epistle we find that John wants us to have "fellowship" with the "Father, and with His Son Jesus Christ" (I John 1:3). In verses 5-10 we find the Apostle alternating between the positive and the negative, verse by verse in presenting his argument:

> *Positive* – "This is the message we have heard from Him and announce to you, that God is Light, and in Him there is no darkness at all" (I John 1:5).
>
> *Negative*-- "If we say that we have fellowship with Him and yet walk in darkness, we lie and do not practice the truth."
>
> *Positive* – "but if we walk in the Light as He Himself is in the light, we have fellowship with one another, and the blood of His Son cleanses us from all sin."
>
> *Negative* – "If we say we have no sin, we are deceiving ourselves and the truth is not in us."
>
> *Positive* – "If we confess our sins, He is faithful and righteous to forgive us our sins and to cleanse us from all unrighteousness."
>
> *Negative* – "If we say that we have not sinned, we make Him a liar and His word is not in us." (I John 1:5-10)

In this manner John emphasizes the contrast between light and darkness, fellowship and estrangement, truth and lying, confession and making Him a liar. The English word translated "confession" is made up of two Greek words, *homo* and *legeo*. *Legeo* is a verb that means to "say" while the prefix, *homo*, added to it conveys the idea of "one and the same," as in the word "homosexual." To confess means to "say the same thing," that is to say the same thing about your sins that God says about it.

If we are walking in the light of His Word and are willing to face the truth about ourselves, if we are willing to let His light shine upon some sin, we say, I agree with you Lord. I say the same thing about it that you say about it. As we thus confess our sin, we are involved in the self-judgment that Paul speaks about in I Corinthians 11:27-31. At that moment of confession, the sin is placed under the blood of Jesus His Son and we are perfectly cleansed by the infinite value of His sacrifice.

Bear in mind that the subject of I John as a whole is not salvation, but fellowship. The danger here is not that of the loss of salvation, but the loss of fellowship. At the moment of self-judgment or confession, the slate is wiped perfectly clean and we are restored to fellowship with "the Father, and with His Son Jesus Christ" (I John 1:3). There is now nothing between Father and child and there is no need for some kind of discipline or temporary judgment so as to bring that one to the point of facing what may be wrong in his or her life. We note the following, "These things we write, so that our joy may be made compete" (I John 1:4)

Coming back to consider the warning of I Corinthians 11:9, I suggest to the reader that Communion observance is a unique opportunity for self-examination and self-judgment. But if a believer comes to the Lord's table, perhaps time after time, and does not appreciate its significance, then the Lord, in his wisdom, may allow His child to suffer some weakness or infirmity so as to bring him back into fellowship with Himself.

We have compared the verses in I Corinthians 11 with those in I John 1 so as to better understand what James is saying in his letter about healing and confession of sin. "Therefore, confess your sins to one another, and pray for one another so that you may be healed" (James 5:16). In such a meeting with the elders who have been called to the home there is the "rubbing with oil" (James 5:14), there is, perhaps a discussion of spiritual matters and the need for forgiveness in some matter, and there is the prayer of faith for those who are ill.

HE WASHED THEIR FEET

On the night of His betrayal, in an upper room, Jesus took a towel and a basin of water and began to wash the feet of the twelve disciples (John 13:5). This was in accordance with the practice of the day whereby the host of a home provided that which was a common courtesy of the day, the washing of the feet of guests who had come. Sometimes a servant would carry out the task. Sometimes the host himself would attend to it. At least containers of water were located in the area so that someone, perhaps the guests themselves, could take care of the matter.

On this occasion, in a profound demonstration of humility, Jesus took upon Himself the role of a servant and proceeded to wash their feet.

Coming to Simon Peter the Lord encountered strong resistance. Peter said, "Lord, do you wash my feet"(John 13:6)? Jesus then promised that Peter would understand later on, but Peter replied, with words which in the Greek language convey a very strong negative, "Never shall You wash my feet" (John 13:7-8). In his characteristic dogmatism he is saying, "Never, no way, absolutely not." The words of Jesus which follow, as found in John 13:8-11, are very significant and germane to the subject which we have been discussing, the confession of sins:

> ...Jesus answered him, "If I do not wash you, you have no part with Me.' Simon Peter said to Him, "Lord, then wash not only my feet, but also my hands and my head." Jesus said to him, "He who has bathed needs only to wash his feet, but is completely clean; and you are clean, but not all of you." For He knew the one who was betraying Him; for this reason He said, "Not all of you are clean." (John 13:8-11")

In our previous discussion of I John 1 we made a distinction between the matter of the salvation of the believer and the fellowship of the believer with God. I suggest to the reader that Jesus Himself makes the same distinction as seen in the verses cited above. There is a distinction made between the complete act of cleansing, or the complete bath and the washing of the feet. A person going out for the evening may thoroughly bathe himself before going, but as he walked the dusty streets of Jerusalem toward his destination, shod only in sandals, his feet would become dirty. When he arrived at someone's home, he didn't need another bath; he rather needed to have his feet washed.

A CRUCIAL DISTINCTION

Far too many believers today are not clear in their minds concerning the distinction between eternal salvation and a close walk with their Lord. Jesus informs Peter that he is clean. Not only is Peter clean, but so are the others, with the exception of Judas, who, I believe, never did come to a saving knowledge of Christ. Jesus assures Peter that he does not need the complete bath that he has requested. He is saved for eternity. His sins have been forgiven. Regeneration has taken place. He needs only to have his feet washed so as to be in good fellowship with his Savior. "If I do not wash you, you have no part with Me" (John 13:8). A literal translation might mean that there is nothing between the two persons that can be shared. In other words, there is no fellowship. The spiritual meaning of that which Jesus says relates to the confession of sins and the forgiveness that John speaks of in his first epistle.

John tells us that if we do not acknowledge the sin that occurs in the daily life, we are deceiving ourselves (I John 1:8). We often stumble along the way. We fall short of that which pleases Him. That does not mean that the life of the believer can be characterized by sin. (Note: I John 3:4-10). But we do fall short of any semblance of perfection on a daily basis. But the promise is: "If we confess our sins, He is faithful and just to forgive us our sins and to cleanse us from all unrighteousness" (I John 1:9).

When the born-again child of God commits a sin, he does not lose his salvation; but that sin can hinder his fellowship with his Heavenly Father. He does not need another salvation experience; rather he needs to have his feet washed. He needs the restoration to fellowship as sins are forgiven through the means of confession or self-judgment. It is extremely important that every child of God recognizes the distinction. By God's grace I can say that I have peace of mind concerning my sonship in God's family. Furthermore, there is the blessing of knowing that every day can be a new beginning. I can begin again, white as snow in His sight (because of the great value of the shed of Jesus) as I attend to the regular matter of having my feet washed – that is by confession.

Yes, I understand that in that upper room Jesus is giving his disciples a wonderful example of humble service. But is there also the spiritual lesson there as found in that conversation between Jesus and Peter. The apostle who records the event (John) is the one who speaks about the importance of confession in the first chapter of his first epistle.

Part of my purpose in sharing this passage is to show how very often, and this is especially so with regard to the Upper Room discourse (John 13-17), lasting principles are carried forth into the Epistles. The teaching of the Upper Room Discourse was given in view of His death, resurrection and the age to come and therefore looked ahead to our day. The teachings of that discourse are therefore found throughout the Epistles. The words of John in his first epistle correspond to the lesson that Jesus gives us on the importance of having our feet washed (John 13). Therefore, coming back to the main idea of sin and illness we note that sometimes God's children refuse to acknowledge the need for confession and, thus, He may, in His wisdom, discipline his child with illness (I Corinthians 11:30). All of this we consider with a view to the teaching of James 5 regarding the confession of sin.

CHAPTER NINE

THE QUESTION OF
HEALING—Part Two

Effectual Fervent Prayer

As we continue our consideration of James 5:13-18 we come to a statement in James 5:16 that has been the reason for many long discussions by prominent theologians and Bible students. What is the meaning of the text which is rendered in the familiar King James language, "effectual fervent prayer" (James 5:16 /KJV)? As we are encouraged in the passage to pray for one another, petitioning God for healing we might ask, "Well, how fervently must we pray?" If there seems to be failure with respect to healing, if it seems that God is not hearing our petitions, is it because we are not being sincere enough or not praying hard enough?

Albert Barnes, in his commentary on this passage seems to imply that the above might be true. He points out that the verb form of the Greek word which is translated by the two English words, "effectual fervent" (James 5:16) is *energeo,* from which we get the English word, "energy." He writes, "It is not listless, indifferent, cold, lifeless [prayer], as if there were not vitality in it, or power, but [it is] that which is adapted to be efficient, earnest, sincere, hearty, persevering."[48] But, how do we know if our prayers are energetic enough?

Some of the translations we find in the prominent Bible versions do

---

[48] Albert Barnes, *Albert Barnes' Notes on the Bible,* (CD-Rom, E-Sword, Rick Meyers), on James 5:16

not seem to make much sense. As noted, the King James renders it, "The effectual fervent prayer of a righteous man availeth much"(James 5:16). The Updated New American Standard Version reads, "The effective prayer of a righteous man can accomplish much."

Marvin Vincent says concerning the words, "effectual fervent," "The rendering of the A.V., besides being unwarranted by the text, is almost a truism. An effectual prayer is a prayer that avails."[49] The New American Standard Version has a similar problem, substituting the word "effective" for "effectual fervent"(James 5:16). It is still somewhat of a truism.

This idea is supported by the following reference to Elijah whose prayers were so effective that even the weather was changed. His prayers were, indeed, very effective (James 5:17-18). But the question remains, "How do we make our prayers powerful and effective?" Do we pray more fervently? If so, how fervently must we pray? Do we pray with more faith? Are we righteous enough in His eyes?

Vincent writes of James 5:16 that he prefers the rendering of the Revised Standard Version: "The supplication of a righteous man availeth much in its working."[50] None of the Bible translations seem to be very satisfying or clear. Let me suggest that the text can be clarified and be truly analogous with other passages on the subject of prayer.

ENERGIZING PRAYER OR ENERGIZED PRAYER?

Referred to above is the Literal Translation of the Bible written by Jay P. Green. We notice that he renders the participle in the verse with these words, "…being made effective." He writes, "Very strong is a righteous petition, being made effective." [51] The passive voice is used indicating that someone or something acts upon the prayer, causing it to be effective. It seems to me that this approach to the Greek participle found in James 5:16 moves toward a better understanding of the passage.

I turn once again to the scholarship of Spiros Zodhiates, who states

---

[49] Marvin R.Vincent, *Word Studies in the New Testament*, (CD Rom, E-Sword, Rich Meyers).

[50] Ibid., on James 5:16

[51] Green, (e-sword).

that there have been long discussions on the participle, *energoumenee*, as to whether it is in the middle or passive voice.[52] There is in the Greek language of the New Testament that which is referred to as the *Middle Voice*. In English grammar we have the active and passive voices of the verb. But in Greek there are the active, middle, and passive voices. At this point we should inform anyone who is not familiar with New Testament Greek that the spelling of the Greek participle is the same, whether middle or passive. The voice, whether middle or passive, cannot be determined by the spelling. The meaning must be determined by other factors such as context, usage in other scriptures or by a comparison with the content of other passages.

We can illustrate the function of different voices this way: If I say, "I threw the ball," the verb, "threw" is in the active voice. I acted upon the ball. I threw it. If I were to say, "I was thrown by the horse," that is in the passive voice. Another agent, the horse, acted upon me. It threw me. But in the Greek, I could use the middle voice. I could say, "I threw the ball for myself," or "I myself threw the ball." In some way the interest of the subject in the sentence is emphasized. Zodhiates points out that the participle is *energoumenee*, from which we get the English word, energy. Writing on the question of middle or passive he writes:

> This is important. If it is in the middle voice, that would indicate that the petition makes itself energetic or effective. If it is in the passive voice, that would mean that there is another external agent involved which acts on prayer and makes it effective and resultful. If it is the first, then the slogan used by a preacher, "Pray, and you can put God to work for you," is Scripturally right. If it is passive, however, he is definitely wrong, for even prayer would be subjected to the absolute sovereign will of God. We personally favor the passive voice, as do the ancient Greek commentators. To this conclusion we have come after much study and prayer. We believe that prayer is null and void unless energized by God Himself. God is sovereign

---

[52] Spiros Zodhiates, *The Patience of Hope*, (Grand Rapids, MI: WM. B. Eerdmans Publishing Company, 1960), p. 195.

at all times and our prayers, in order to be effective, must be in accordance with His sovereign will for us. ...If our prayers do not agree with God's sovereign will, they will not be granted. If what we ask of God is not what He intended us to have from the foundation of the world, He will not give it to us. Our petitions must be energized by Him.[53]

Accepting this view of the passage we can translate the verse this way, "The _energized_ prayer of a righteous man is very effective, very strong, accomplishing much." When the Spirit of God acts upon my heart and mind as I pray, when the prayer is energized by Him, when the prayer is, therefore, in accordance with His will, wonderful things can happen. I do not have to work up the energy by myself (middle voice), or try to pray more fervently so as to gain my request. Rather, I pray sincerely, trusting God to energize the petition if it is His sovereign will to do so.

Elijah could not have brought drought or rain by his prayers, _no matter how fervently he prayed_, except it was God's will to so change the weather. Regardless of what His will may be, He wants us to fellowship with Him in our concerns.

GROANINGS TOO DEEP FOR WORDS

The words of Romans 8:26-27 do not address the matter of healing, but they do speak of the Holy Spirit with respect to prayer and human suffering. We read:

> In the same way the Spirit also helps our weakness; for we do not know how to pray as we should, but the Spirit Himself intercedes for *us* with groanings too deep for words; and He who searches the hearts knows what the mind of the Spirit is, be-cause He intercedes for the saints according to *the will of God.* (Romans 8:26-27)

---

[53] Ibid., p. 195

Commenting on the words, "in the same way," the NIV Study Bible says, "As hope sustains the believer in suffering, so the Holy Spirit helps him in prayer, with groans that words cannot express. In Romans 8:23 it is the believer who groans; here it is the Holy Spirit who groans. Whether Paul means words that are unspoken or *words that cannot be expressed in human language* is not clear—probably the former, though v. 27 of Romans 8 seems to suggest the latter."[54]

It is interesting to note that the Greek word here for "weakness" is *asthenia,* which is the same word found in James 5:14, "Is anyone among you sick?" This word includes physical, emotional, and spiritual disability and in those weaknesses "we groan within ourselves" (Romans 8: 23) and very often we groan vocally. The subject of this passage in Romans 8 is the suffering that God's children are allowed to bear in this life as we all wait for the "redemption of our" bodies (Rom. 8:23). And so we read in verse 18 of Romans 8, "For I consider that the sufferings of this present time are not worthy to be compared with the glory that is to be revealed to us" (Romans 8:1 8.)

Three times we read in this passage of "groaning." In verse 22 of Romans 8 we read that "the whole creation groans and suffers the pains of childbirth together until now." In verse 23 of Romans 8 Paul states that "…also we ourselves, having the first fruits of the Spirit, even we ourselves groan within ourselves, waiting eagerly for *our* adoption as sons, the redemption of our body." And then in verse 26 of Romans 8 we learn that "…the Spirit Himself intercedes for *us* with groanings too deep for words." Creation groans. The child of God groans. The Holy Spirit groans. Have you ever found yourself in the presence of a loved one who is groaning in physical suffering? Perhaps you are at the bedside, or perhaps that one is in the next bedroom. It is a very difficult time, indeed!

In verse 26 of Romans 8 we read that the "Spirit also helps our weakness." John A. Witmer points out that the Greek word here for "helps" is a very rich word that pictures someone helping another carry a heavy

---

[54] The NIV Study Bible, (Grand Rapids, Michigan: Zondervan Bible Publishers, 1985), p. 1718.

load.[55] In the weakness of our suffering, whatever it may be, we often do not know how to pray as we should. We may be praying for healing when our God, in His good wisdom, wills that we learn about His grace in the midst of our suffering. But the Spirit within us is there to help. The Holy Spirit groans within us, sharing in our suffering and interceding for us "according to *the will* of God." May I suggest at this point that the Holy Spirit can, in this kind of experience, change the direction of our prayers. I believe that this is the testimony of the Apostle Paul as found in II Corinthians12 concerning his thorn in the flesh (II Corinthians 12:7-10). He learned to rejoice in the inner-working power of Christ in the midst of his suffering.

Of course, it may be God's will to grant healing, as stated in James 5:16. We are there encouraged to pray for healing. In that case the prayer is energized in that direction in accordance with the will of God.

THE TRINITY IN VIEW

Paul tells us in this passage about the relationship of God the Spirit and God the Father in this context of human suffering. He says, "...but the Spirit intercedes for us with groaning too deep for words; and He who searches the hearts knows what the mind of the Spirit is, because He intercedes for the saints according to the will of God" (Romans 8:26-27). John Witmer makes this comment:

> Even though the Spirit's words are not expressed, the Father knows what the Spirit is thinking. This is an interesting statement about the Father's omniscience and the intimacy within the Trinity. The Lord Jesus continually intercedes for believers in God's presence (v. 34: Heb.7:25) and the Holy Spirit also intercedes on their behalf! Though believers are ignorant of what to pray for

---

[55] John A. Witmer, *"Romans"*, *The Bible Knowledge Commentary*, ed. John F. Walvoord and Roy B. Zuck, (Wheaton, Ilinois: Victor books, a division of SP publications, Inc., 1983), p. 473.

and how to voice those requests, the Spirit voices those requests for them.[56]

Having then noted that the Holy Spirit shares the burden of our suffering with respect to prayer, we turn to Jesus' teaching on prayer as found in Luke 11:1-13.

THE IMPORTANCE OF IMPORTUNITY

"Importunity is a King James word. The newer versions use the word "persistence" in verse 8 of Luke chapter eleven. After giving His disciples, what we now call, *The Lord's Prayer* in verses 2-4 of Luke 11 Jesus teaches on the importance of importunity or persistence in prayer by sharing with them the following parable:

> Then He said to them, "Suppose one of you has a friend, and goes to him at midnight and says to him, 'Friend, lend me three loaves; for a friend of mine has come to me from a journey, and I have nothing to set before him'; and from inside he answers and says, 'Do not bother me; the door has already been shut and my children and I are in bed; I cannot get up and give you anything,' "I tell you, even though he will not get up and give him anything because he is his friend, yet because of his persistence he will get up and give him as much as he needs" (Luke 11:5-8).

At first reading of this parable, one might be tempted to think that Jesus is teaching that we must beg concerning our needs, that our Heavenly Father is not inclined to willingly or readily respond when we go to Him. Thoughtful consideration of all that the Bible says about our Father's love and care for us, as well as the verses that follow in this text should assure us that such is not the case. The value of persistence in prayer is to be found in other considerations. Jesus continues His teaching on the subject in the verses that follow:

---

[56] Ibid., p. 473.

> So, I say to you, ask, and it will be given to you; seek,
> and you will find; knock, and it will be opened to you.
> For everyone who asks, receives; and he who seeks, finds;
> and to him who knocks, it will be opened (Luke 11:9-10).

What is not easily seen in our English versions is that Jesus is still teaching on the importance of persistence in our praying. The Greek text makes that clear by the use of the present tense in these verbs. The present tense of the Greek verb speaks of action that is continuous as opposed to that which is completed or takes place in a moment of time. The emphasis is not so much on the time as being present, as upon the kind of action; the action is on-going.

The tense of the Greek verb (present- imperative) seems to suggest that we should keep asking, seeking and knocking. Reading it with a consideration of the Greek text reveals what a large emphasis is being placed on the importance of importunity, of persisting in prayer before His throne of grace. The question is still before us, however, as to the value of such persistence. Why must we keep on praying?

Jesus, I believe, tells us why in the verses that follow:

> Now suppose one of you fathers is asked by his son for
> a fish; he will not give him a snake instead of a fish, will
> he? Or if he is asked for an egg, he will not give him a
> scorpion, will he (Luke 11:11-12)?

Imagine that one day as you are enjoying a peaceful day of fishing at the local creek, you mention to the Lord that you might like to catch a big one that morning. Suddenly, there is something big on the line; you do have a catch. Eagerly you pull it out only to be surprised and repulsed by the sight of a Cotton Mouth Water Moccasin which you accidentally hooked. Watch out for the poisonous bite! Likewise, one evening you reach in to lay hold of an egg that you think might taste good for breakfast, only to find that you have in your hand a white scorpion. I have read that in the Middle East there is a kind of scorpion that is white and, curled up in the grass or a nest, might resemble an egg. Watch out for the deadly sting!

The lesson regarding prayer is obvious. Much of the time we don't really know how to pray. In our limited wisdom we often cannot distinguish between that which will be good for us and that which will be harm us. We ask for a fish, not realizing that, in reality, it is a snake. Jesus assures us in this passage that our Heavenly Father is not about to give us that which will hurt us. Therefore, the text seems to suggest that we do not give up concerning what is on our hearts, but continue *to ask, seek* and *knock*. In due time, our Heavenly Father will answer in accordance with His good will and wisdom.

THE PUNCH LINE

There is one more verse, a most important verse, to be considered on the subject as presented here by Jesus. I refer to the last line of the verse as *the punch line,* not because it is comical, as in a joke, but because it takes us by surprise. It is unexpected. In Matthew 7:7-11 we have a parallel passage which is very much the same as that which we have here. There, as here, the value of persistence in prayer is emphasized, but without the added element that is found at the end of verse here in Luke 11:13. Luke chooses to record more of what Jesus had to say on the matter.

> "If you then, being evil, know how to give good gifts to
> your children, how much more will *your* heavenly Father
> give the Holy Spirit to those who ask Him" (Luke 11:13)?

Suddenly, we encounter something that is unexpected, but which we now know is in harmony with what Paul says in Romans eight and with what James says in the fifth chapter of his epistle, the ministry of the Holy Spirit in the prayer life of the believer. Paul says that we "do not know how to pray as we should, but the Spirit intercedes for us with groaning too deep for words…" (Romans 8:26). James tells us, that when our prayers are energized, great and wonderful things can happen. The message is, I think that we should not give up on a matter, but keep on praying.

At this point, another relevant passage comes to mind. In I John 5:14-15 we read, "This is the confidence which we have before Him, that, if we ask anything according to His will, He hears us. And if we know that He hears us *in* whatever we ask, we know that we have the requests which we have asked from Him." In our consideration of James 5:16 we have suggested that the participle there is in the passive voice, meaning that the *energized* prayer of a righteous man can accomplish great things. We have also suggested that the agent energizing the effective prayer is the Holy Spirit. We then went to Romans chapter eight (verse 23} and Luke chapter eleven (verses 9-13) to observe teaching concerning the ministry of the Holy Spirit in the prayer life of the believer.

Because of the ministry of the Holy Spirit we are enabled to pray in accordance with the will of God. We can also understand that because of the ministry of the Holy Spirit in our prayers, the "prayer offered in faith (James 5:15)" that James speaks of can also be realized. The energizing influence of the Holy Spirit provides the direction and the faith that leads to answered prayer.

Sacred Agreement

To all of this can be added two relevant verses that are found in Matthew eighteen. We read, "Again I say to you, that if two of you agree on earth about anything that they may ask, it shall be done for them by my Father who is in heaven. For where two or three have gathered together in My name, I am there in their midst" (Matthew 18:19-20). Obviously, with regard to verse 19 of Matthew 18 there is a deeper meaning concerning answered prayer than appears on the surface. It's not just a matter of two buddies agreeing to split the money as they pray together to win the lottery. In a serious vein it's not even a matter of two elders agreeing to pray for a certain person who is ill. It has to be more than two persons agreeing on the human level.

Rather, verse 19 of Matthew 18 should be interpreted in connection with Matthew 18:20, where there is a reference to the very presence of Christ in a group, even if it is very small. Jesus says, "For where two or three have gathered together *in My name*, I am in there in their midst" (Matthew 18:19-20-italics mine) Since these believers are gathered in His name, it is implied that they also are praying in His name. The words of Jesus concerning prayer as found in John chapter 16 are analogous:

In that day you will not question Me about anything. Truly, truly, I say to you, if you ask the Father for anything in My name, He will give it to you. Until now you have asked for nothing in My name; Ask and you will receive, so that your joy may be made full. These things I have spoken to you in figurative language; an hour is coming when I will no longer speak to you in figurative language, but will tell you plainly of the Father. In that day you will ask in My name, and I do not say to you that I will request of the Father on your behalf; for the Father Himself loves you, because you have loved Me and have believed that I came forth from the Father (John 16:23-28).

What does it mean to pray in the name of Jesus? It is a much more profound matter than simply that of adding those five words to the end of a prayer, as we commonly do. It should be borne in mind that the big revelation of the Upper Room Discourse (John 13-17) is the soon-coming presence of the Holy Spirit. That truth is found in chapter 14, chapter 15 and here in chapter 16 of John, verses 5-15. It would seem that the expression, "in My name" has to do with that presence and influence of the Holy Spirit acting in the place of the Lord Jesus who has returned to Heaven. I suggest to the reader that to pray *in the name of Jesus* is to pray in union with, and thus under the influence of the Holy Spirit. The two who are praying in Matthew 18:19 are praying in the name of Jesus. They are gathered together in the name of Jesus and they are praying in union with the Holy Spirit. They are involved in *a sacred agreement* that guarantees the answer to their prayer.

The above paragraphs have been an elaboration on the powerful and effective prayer that James speaks of in the fifth chapter of his epistle. In this writing we have devoted two chapters now to an exposition of the one passage on healing that is found in the New Testament epistles. Much more could be said.

BUT SOMETHING IS MISSING

The passage that we have been considering (James 5:13-16) would seem to be very complete. There we find specific instructions as to how the local church should function with regard to the infirmed. The elders are to be called so that they could minister both spiritually and physically. They pray and provide physical comfort and encouragement (the rubbing with oil). Faith is to be an important element of their prayers. The possibility of unconfessed sin is to be considered. By implication, the ministry of the Holy Spirit with respect to energized prayer is presented as an encouragement. But according to some, something is missing:

There is no reference to seeking out someone who has a gift of healing. There is no suggestion that getting the person to a healing service might be the way to go. Yes, we have that wonderful story in the Gospels of the four friends who carried a man to Jesus and lowered him down through a roof so that the man might find miraculous healing at the feet of Jesus (Luke 5:17-26). But may I remind the reader of that which is the premise of this writing. *The Bottom Line of Scripture* is to be found in the Epistles. The question is: How do we know what is normative for our day? After the history of the Old Testament and that of the Gospels and that which is found the book of Acts, how then do we live today with respect to Christian life and service? I hope that it is obvious that I greatly value the teaching of all the Scripture. In these chapters I have brought into consideration passages from Matthew, Luke and John, as well a passage from the book of Romans. With regard to the *specifics* for living and serving in our day, the commandments, exhortations and admonitions which are found in the Epistles are to provide the guidance that we need.

It is acknowledged that "gifts of healing" are referred to in I Corinthians twelve (vs. 9, 28, 30). Also listed there are the gifts of tongues, interpretation of tongues, effecting of miracles, the word of wisdom, the word of knowledge and others. These are sometimes called the *foundational gifts*. They were, no doubt, important in the life of the first century church. But other than being mentioned there in I Corinthians twelve, we do not find the exercise of them exhorted or even mentioned elsewhere throughout the Epistles.

We never read of Paul saying something like this, "I had to leave

Trophimus sick at Miletus. Timothy, would you please send for brother "so and so." He is known to have the gift of healing. Trophimus could really use his help right now."

We never read of anything like this from Paul or Peter or John or anyone writing in the Epistles. No church is ever reprimanded for not giving enough attention to *gifts of healing*. It is never suggested that the preaching of the gospel would be enhanced if there were more emphasis on healing or "the effecting of miracles" (I Corinthians 12:10).

Rather, concerning the ever-present need of healing, we read that we should "confess our sins to one another and pray for one another" so that we may be healed (James 5:16). That sounds like something in which all of us could and should be involved in the normal life of our churches today.

CHAPTER TEN

THE SABBATH DAY
CONTROVERSY

The Question of the Jewish Sabbath

In early September the ocean water at the South Carolina beach was still quite warm. With a gentle breeze coming off the surf and sunny skies overhead it was a very pleasant Sunday morning. At ten o'clock in the morning many people had already left their RV's in this campground and were either at or headed for the beach. My wife and I were located on a lovely site just a few hundred feet from the water's edge. From that vantage point we could see all the appealing activities-- people tossing foot-balls, throwing Frisbees, playing with their dogs in the waves and couples young and old strolling up and down the beach, stooping now and then to pick up shells or other interesting objects. Occasionally there would be someone with a metal detector, looking for hidden treasure. Of course, many chose to spend most of the day reclining under an umbrella or lying out in the sun.

But something quite different caught my attention on this Sunday morning. Exiting from an RV, which was parked in the row just behind us, a couple with their young children got in their car and drove off. As they were dressed up quite nicely and carried Bibles, it was obvious to me that they were going to church. My thought was, "That's great! How appealing that is, to see people go to the trouble and take the time, on a vacation Sunday, to go to church while the great majority just head for the beach!" Of course, I didn't know what church they went to or exactly why they went. The registration plates on their car indicated that they had come from another state. Were they going to visit a church because it was a duty they felt obligated to perform, or was it out of a love for the Lord and a desire to assemble with God's people on the Lord's Day? I didn't really ask myself that question on that Sunday morning; I just appreciated what I saw and assumed that they were Christian people. As for my wife and myself, while on vacation at that location we might go look for a church to visit, or attend the casual service that was offered at the campground. Or, not feeling obligated *under Grace* to so observe the day, we might not go anywhere. Almost always we did, but some of my cherished memories are of sitting in a sand chair at the very waters-edge, early in the morning, reading my Bible. But that could occur on any day of the week, not just on a Sunday.

A CHRISTIAN SABBATH?

My father referred to Sunday as the Sabbath. He was wrong of course. The Sabbath of the Bible was observed on the seventh day of the week, while we faithfully went to church on the first day of the week. He drove us about nine miles through suburban traffic to our place of worship on Sunday mornings. After Sunday School and the Morning Service we rode the nine miles home, with my Dad stopping at a convenience store to pick up the Sunday newspaper. That journey, as well as buying the Sunday paper, was a violation of the fourth commandment as given to the people of Israel some fifteen hundred years before Christ. My mother and grandmother cooked us Sunday dinner. That too was a violation of the commandment. After dinner the adults of the house very often would take a nap. After all, the Sabbath was a day of rest. (This was before the era of Sunday afternoon televised football.) As a kid this was not appealing to me, having too much energy to lie around the house all afternoon. I preferred to be outside shooting hoops or kicking a football up and down the yard. I was about ten years old when I had an accident. On a Sunday afternoon I took a bad fall and fractured my skull. A year or two earlier I had broken a collar bone, also on a Sunday afternoon. On both occasions I experienced a degree of guilt because I was out doing what I should not have been doing on Sunday. I entertained the thought, "That's what happens when you don't remember to keep the Sabbath Day." I now realize that reference to a "Christian Sabbath" is a misnomer and that there can be no such thing as a partial observance of the Sabbath.

A CHALLENGE TO THE THESIS

And now, many years later, I find myself defending the central argument of this writing -- if something is not exhorted in the New Testament epistles, it probably should not be regarded as a matter of emphasis in the Christian life. The fourth commandment is not the subject of exhortation or admonition anywhere in the Letters to The Churches. We are not enjoined to keep the Sabbath in the writings of Paul or Peter or John or any of the New Testament writers. The content of the other nine commandments are carried forth into the Epistles, but that of the fourth is not. That poses a very interesting question; how is it that something so central to the Law of Moses and so controversial in the life of Jesus is not exhorted in the Epistles?

There may be readers who, at this point, are tempted to reject the thesis of this writing. After all, we have in view one of the Ten Commandments. How can we say that it is not to be kept in our day? I certainly recognize the importance of addressing this question and therefore view this present chapter as being very necessary with respect to defending my argument. As to personal prejudices (I surely do not assume this of the reader.), Lewis Sperry Chafer speaks to the importance of making a distinction between the two commemorative days, the Lord's Day and the Sabbath:

> The distinction between the reign of law and the reign
> of grace is at no point more sharply drawn than in the
> question of the observance of the seventh day of the
> week or the first day of the week; for these two days are
> symbolical of the dispensations to which they are related.
> Likewise, at no point is personal religious prejudice, which
> is born of early training and sentiment, more assertive than
> on the Sabbath question. It was the liberal teaching on the
> observance of the Sabbath which, more than aught else,
> provoked the wrath of the Jewish leaders against Christ;

and, it may be observed, there is no religious subject today which so draws out personal convictions and opinions. The reason is evident. Few have really compre-hended the exact character and principle of grace. To many, Christianity is a system of human works and character building from which merit accrues. And the observance of a Sabbath day presents extraordinary opportunities for the observance of meritorious works.[57]

The subject is not an easy one, but I have come to a place of resolution in my own mind concerning the theology of it and the application of that theology to our day. Also, as I will say later in this writing, I believe the Sabbath has taken a different form and that is stated as such in the book of Hebrews.

USE YOUR IMAGINATION

Let us begin our consideration by examining a passage from the book of Romans, chapter two. In that chapter the Apostle Paul is bringing God's indictment down upon the human race, arguing that all are guilty, both Jews and Gentiles. Beginning in verse twelve of that chapter we have these words:

> For all who have sinned without the Law will also perish without the Law, and all who have sinned under the Law will be judged by the Law; for it is not the hearers of the Law who are just before God, but the doers of the Law will be justified. For when Gentiles who do not have the Law do instinctively the things of the Law, these, not having the Law, are a law to themselves, in that they show the work of the Law written on their hearts, their conscience bearing witness and their thoughts alternately accusing or else defending them, on the day when, according to my gospel, God will judge the secrets of men through Christ Jesus (Romans 2:12-16).

---

[57] Lewis Sperry Chafer, *Systematic Theology,* vol. four, (Grand Rapids, MI: Kregel Publications,1948), p. 101.

The point of interest here is found in the words, "written on the heart" (Romans 2:15). According to Paul, the work of the Law is written on the hearts of Gentiles who have never been given the Law through Moses. Paul seems to be saying that men instinctively know that murder is wrong, stealing is wrong, and adultery is wrong. He says in verse Romans 2:15 that their "conscience bears witness against them." Paul speaks elsewhere of the fact that the conscience can be "seared" (I Timothy 4:2) "as with a branding iron." But generally speaking, the requirements of the moral law of God are written on the heart. Men instinctively know right from wrong when it comes to the great commandments of His Word.

But now the reader is invited to use his or her imagination. Imagine a man who, because he is living in some remote part of the world completely untouched by any form of civilization, has never heard of the commandments of God that are found in the Bible. He is among primitive people in some remote area in the deepest part of the jungle of the Amazon, or in Papua New Guinea, or in some other remote area, who have never had one speck of exposure to Judeo-Christianity. It would be difficult to prove that somewhere along the line some form of contact had never happened. But for the sake of argument we assume his complete isolation from civilization to be true. The question now is this: Does he have any sense at all of the fourth commandment, that he is to "remember the Sabbath Day, to keep it holy" (Exodus 20:8)? If, as Paul implies, he knows that committing murder, adultery, coveting, and bearing false witness are wrong and that he should honor his parents, etcetera...., does his conscience bother him at all about the matter of keeping the seventh day as a day of rest? When he kindles a fire on that day, does he inwardly believe it is wrong to do so (Exodus 35:3)? Does he know that no food is to be prepared, no journey undertaken, no burden borne and that no buying or selling is to take place (Exodus 16:22-26; Neh. 10:31, 13:15-21; Lev. 25:4, I Chron. 36:21)? And does he know that the penalty for profaning the day is death (Exodus 31:14)?

As you have imagined such a case, what answer has come to mind? Is the fourth commandment written on the heart of pagan man? Perhaps you reason that such a man knows in part. He may not know all the details, but he knows that part of his time each week belongs to God. Let us table the matter for now and move on to consider the importance of the Sabbath as revealed to man in the Scripture.

WHERE DID IT ALL BEGIN?

There is one definitive passage of Scripture that tells us precisely where and when God revealed the Sabbath to his people. No, it is not Genesis 2:3 which reads, "Then God blessed the seventh day and sanctified it, because in it He rested from all His work which God has created and made." Because God blessed the day at the time of a finished creation does not mean that it was instituted for mankind at that time. Rather, the defining passage is Nehemiah 9:9-14. After praising God because He had performed signs and wonders for them in Egypt and brought them through that Red Sea experience, Nehemiah says:

> Then You came down on Mount Sinai, and spoke with them from heaven; You gave them just ordinances and true laws, good statutes and commandments. So You made known to them Your Holy Sabbath, and laid down for them commandments, statutes and law, through your servant Moses (Nehemiah 9:13-14).

According to this passage, it began at Sinai, when God revealed it all through Moses. It is said that when God came down on Mount Sinai, He made known to them His Holy Sabbath. Actually, the first hint of it took place in the wilderness a short time before, when God provided the manna for His people, commanding them not to gather it on the seventh day (Exodus 16:13-31). We read in verse 31, "The house of Israel named it manna, and it was like coriander seed, white, and its taste was like wafers with honey" Exodus 16:31) Chafer points out that according to the historical record, seven days previous to the Sabbath observance that we read of in Exodus 16, the people of Israel had traveled from Elim to the wilderness of Sin, a distance of some twenty miles.[58] That would suggest that they were not in the habit of keeping the Sabbath before this, because such a journey would

---

[58] Ibid., p.104

not have been allowed. This was their first experience with the practice of Sabbath observance. We might say that the Sabbath commanded in Exodus sixteen was something of a preview of that which was to be instituted in chapter twenty (the giving of the ten commandments). It took place within the same general time frame.

There is another passage of scripture that fixes the exact time when the Sabbath was given to the people of Israel:

> So, I took them out of Egypt and brought them into the wilderness. I gave them my statutes and informed them of My ordinances, by which, if a man observes them, he will live. Also, I gave them My sabbaths to be a sign between Me and them, that they might know that I am the LORD who sanctifies them (Ezekiel 20:10-12).

Not only do these verses parallel the passage that is cited in Nehemiah (9:10-14). but they also connect with the words of Exodus 31:12-18 where the Sabbath is said to be the sign of the Mosaic Covenant:

> The Lord spoke to Moses saying, "But as for you, speak to the sons of Israel, saying 'You shall surely observe My sabbaths; for *this* is a sign between Me and you throughout your generations, that you may know that I am the LORD who sanctifies you. Therefore, you are to observe the sabbath, for it is holy to you. Everyone who profanes it shall surely be put to death; for whoever does any work on it, that person shall be cut off from among his people. For six days work may be done, but on the seventh day there is a sabbath of complete rest, holy to the LORD; whoever does any work on the sabbath day shall surely be put to death. So the sons of Israel shall observe the sabbath, to celebrate the sabbath throughout their generations as a perpetual covenant.' It is a sign between Me and the sons of Israel forever; for in six days the LORD made heaven and earth, but on the seventh day He ceased *from labor*, and was refreshed." When He had finished speaking with

him upon Mount Sinai, He gave Moses the two tablets of the testimony, tablets of stone, written by the finger of God. (Exodus 31:12-18)

THE SIGN OF THE COVENANT

Twice in the above passage it is stated that Sabbath observance was to be a sign between the LORD and the people of Israel. My professor of Hebrew in seminary stressed on a number of occasions that repetition in the Hebrew language was for the sake of emphasis. Indeed, this passage of scripture is emphatic in many respects. We must acknowledge that the Fourth Commandment as presented in these Old Testament scriptures is central; it is all important to the very fabric of the Mosaic Law.

TWO REASONS—CREATION AND REDEMPTION

Actually, in the context of the institution of the Fourth Commandment there are two reasons given for its observance. First of all, it was mandatory for the people of Israel so that they might honor the God of creation; "For in six days, the LORD made the heavens and the earth, the sea and all that is in them, and rested on the seventh day; therefore the LORD blessed the Sabbath day and made it holy" (Exodus 20:11).

But in Deuteronomy, where we have a second giving of the Law, the Ten Commandments are given again in chapter five. In connection with the giving of the Fourth Commandment we have these words, "You shall remember that you were a slave in the land of Egypt, and the LORD your God brought you out of there by a mighty hand and by an outstretched arm; therefore the LORD your God commanded you to observe the sabbath day" (Deuteronomy 5:15). In this verse we see that they were to remember that they worshipped their God who had redeemed them from the slavery of Egypt. Not only were they to honor the God of *creation*, they were also to honor the God of *redemption*.

This reminds me of two wonderful chapters in the book of Revelation, chapters four and five. In chapter four we find gathered around God's throne in heaven "the four living creatures" (angels, I believe) and also "the twenty four elders" (God's people, I believe) and in Rev 4:11 we read, "Worthy are You, our Lord and our God, to receive glory and honor and power; for You created all things, and because of Your will they existed, and were create" Revelation 4:11). In chapter four God is worshipped as the Creator.

In chapter five we have another great worship scene. Now, with regard to the worship of the Lamb of God, we read, "And they sang a new song, saying 'Worthy are You to take the book and to break its seals; for You were slain, and purchased for God with Your blood *men* from every tribe and tongue and people and nation. You have made them *to be* a kingdom of priests to our God; and they will reign upon the earth" (Revelation 5:9).

First there is worship of the God of Creation. And then there is worship of the God of Redemption. All of this was foreshadowed in the manner in which the people of Israel were to observe their Sabbath day. Indeed, Paul tells us in his letter to the Colossians that much of the Mosaic Law typified, or foreshadowed that which was to come. "Therefore no one is to act as your judge in regard to food or drink or in respect to a festival or a new moon or a Sabbath day—things which are a *mere* shadow of what is to come; but the substance belongs to Christ" (Colossians 2:16-17).

SABBATH OBSERVANCE BEFORE MOSES

There was none, as far as we can tell from the sacred record. There is no mention of it in the lives of Abraham, Isaac, Jacob, Job or any other patriarch of that time period. There are prayers, altars, sacrifices, and even tithing (Genesis 14:20), but no mention of Sabbath observance from creation to Moses. Concerning that fact, Chafer states, "It is incredible that this great institution of the Sabbath could have existed during all these centuries and there be no mention of it in the Scriptures dealing with that time."[59] He goes on to say:

> The words of Job, who lived five hundred years and more before Moses, offer an illustration. His experience discloses the spiritual life of the pre-Mosaic saint, having

---

[59] Ibid., p. 103

no written Scriptures, and striving to know his whole duty to God. Job and his friends refer to creation, the flood, and many details of human obligation to God; but not once do they mention the Sabbath. Again, it is impossible that this great institution, with all that it contemplated of relationship between God and man, could have existed at that time and not have been mentioned in any portion of the argument of the book of Job.[60]

We can add to that comment the fact that there are forty- two long chapters in the book of Job. Job and his friends dialogue concerning a multitude of issues, but we find no reference at all to Sabbath day observance or the Sabbath day. The life of Abraham, the father of the Jewish people, is recorded in fourteen wonderful chapters of the book of Genesis. He is presented as a spiritual giant, a great man of faith, even the "friend of God" (James 2:23). But there is no record that he ever observed the Sabbath day. Lewis Sperry Chafer comments on the theological significance of the Biblical testimony:

> Two theories obtain concerning the question of Sabbath observance during this period. There are those who contend that the Sabbath was committed to man In Eden, and there are those who contend that the Sabbath was given to Israel only, at the hand of Moses. The first theory is usually advanced with a view to applying the institution of the Sabbath to *all men* before the law even was given, in order that the Sabbath law may be treated as now applicable to *all men*, even after the termination of the Mosaic Law in the cross. This form of argument is not restricted to the Seventh Day legalists; it is employed by many writers and religious leaders who are attempting to transfer the Biblical authority concerning the Jewish Sabbath to the observance of the Lord's day.[61]

---

[60] Ibid., p. 103
[61] Ibid., p. 102

Yes, we do read in Genesis 2:1-3 that God "...rested on the seventh day from all His work which He had done," and as noted earlier "God blessed the seventh day and sanctified it...." There are many who assume that the Sabbath was imposed on man at Eden and that these verses so teach that supposition, but as Chafer points out, it is not necessarily implied in the passage. He reminds us, also, that Genesis was not written until the time of Moses.[62] As Moses is inspired by the Holy Spirit to write the book of Genesis, he is directed to include in it the blessing of the seventh day with a view to the fact that the Sabbath day is to be the sign of the Mosaic Covenant and the central observance of the Law given to the people of Israel at Sinai.

It is to be noted that there is no evidence at all that the Sabbath was given to anyone except the people of Israel. It was the *sign* of their unique relationship to Jehovah.

THE SABBATH AND JESUS

The question of the Sabbath seems to have been the longest continuing area of controversy in the life and ministry of Christ. It should be remembered that the Law of Moses was still in effect during his lifetime. He lived under that law and, unlike any other man, never broke it. He was, however, viewed by the Pharisees as being a liberal on the subject because he insisted on delineating between the Law as given by His Father and the man-made and sometimes ridiculous additions (e.g.-prohibition against false teeth as bearing a burden on the Sabbath) that the religious leaders had superimposed on that Law. He claimed to be the "Lord of the Sabbath" (Matthew 12:8) and thus, was claiming an authority on the subject that implied His deity. Such claims and His insistence on ministering to the sick even on the Sabbath day (e.g., John 9:13-14) infuriated the Pharisees and fanned the flames of the anger that eventually put Him on the cross.

THE SABBATH WAS MADE FOR MAN

There are many who insist that Christ extended the matter of observing the Sabbath to all men when He said, "The Sabbath was made for man, and

---

[62] Ibid., p. 1-3

not man for the Sabbath" (Mark 2:27). On the surface this might suggest that at the time of creation the Sabbath was given to all men as a time of rest for body and soul. The question is: What is the intended meaning of the word "man?" Chafer points out that:

> ...the word man is used in the Old Testament no less than 336 times when referring to Israel alone, and many times in the New Testament when referring only to Christians. It is said, "The head of every man is Christ"; the manifestation of the Spirit "is given to every man"; "if any man build upon this foundation"; "Every man shall have praise"; "that we may present every man perfect in Christ Jesus." In all these Scriptures the word *man* has only the limited meaning. It is therefore evident that Christ said, in harmony with all Scripture, that the Sabbath was made for Israel; for there is no Biblical evidence that Christ ever imposed the Jewish Sabbath on either Gentiles or Christians, but, true to the law, He did recognize its important place and obligation in relation to Israel until the reign of the law should be terminated through His death.[63]

The above examples as to how the word *man* is sometimes used in Scripture should call into question the insistence on the part of many that the word *man* refers to all humankind.

CONSPICUOUS BY ITS ABSENCE

It is worth noting that mention of the Sabbath does not occur in several places where we might expect to find it. For example, in the Gospel of John, chapters 13-17 we find that which is referred to as *The Upper Room Discourse*. On that occasion Jesus, on the night of His betrayal, imparts to His twelve disciples at length some final instructions before He goes to the Cross. In that discourse He prepares them and us, by the way, for

---

[63] Ibid., p. 107

the days to come. Contained in five wonderful and profound chapters of John, six if you include His High Priestly Prayer for us as found in John 17, we have teaching that is not only vital but precious for the believer who desires to enjoy a close walk with his or her Lord. However, we notice that there is no reference to the Sabbath Day. An observance that had been so central to the Mosaic economy and so controversial in the earthly life of Jesus is not mentioned.

Furthermore, in that all- important Council at Jerusalem, which is recorded for us in Acts fifteen, instruction with regard to the Sabbath is again conspicuous by its absence. Concerning Gentiles who were being added to the church of Christ we read that "…some of the Pharisees who had believed stood up, saying, 'It is necessary to circumcise them and to direct them to observe the Law of Moses'" (Acts 15:5). And so, "The apostles and the elders came together to look into this matter" (Acts 15:6). After much debate, James, who was the leader of the church in Jerusalem, issued this statement as found in verses 19-21:

> …Therefore, it is my judgment that we do not trouble those who are turning to God from among the Gentiles, but that we write to them that they abstain from things contaminated by idols and from forni-cation and from what is strangled and from blood. For Moses from ancient generations has in every city those who preach him, since he is read in the synagogues every Sabbath. (Acts 15:19-21)

It is important here to recall the reason for this council and the subject of the debate. The Pharisees were insisting that Gentile believers should be circumcised and directed to observe the *Law of Moses*. Keeping the Sabbath, as we have stated, was central to the keeping of the Law of Moses, yet there is no mention of the Sabbath in the words of the decision that is passed down. There is only reference made to that which would be blatantly offensive to Jews, who were found in just about every city of the known world at that time (Acts 15:21). Verse 20 reads, "but that we write to them that they abstain from things contaminated by idols and from fornication and from what is strangled and from blood"(Acts 15:20).

The latter reference leads to another observation, the absence of any mention in the book of Acts that believers were observing the Sabbath day. The word Sabbath is found nine times in the book of Acts, but in each case the observance has to do with unbelieving Jews, who, as would be expected continued to keep their most Holy day. Yes, we read that Paul often went on the Sabbath into the Jewish synagogues and reasoned with his countrymen on the Sabbath and we can understand that it was expedient for him to do so. Paul had a heart for his people and in the synagogue on the Sabbath Day, that is where he could find them gathered. But not once do we read, or is it implied, that Christians observed the Sabbath.

Of course, as stated by Merrill Unger in his Bible Dictionary, Jewish believers did continue to observe the seventh day. He writes:

> Jewish Christians at first continued to frequent the temple and synagogue services, but at a very early date "the first day of the week" took the place of the Jewish Sabbath as the chief time of public worship (Acts 20:7; I Cor. 16:2) in many of the churches of Jewish Christians. …The Jewish Christians at first observed both the seventh and the first day of the week, but the Gentile Christians kept the "Lord's Day" from the beginning. The relation of the seventh to the first, as understood by the Jewish Christians may not be easy to determine, yet there seem to be indications that the seventh was regarded as a day of preparation for the first. The idea of Christian worship would attach mainly to the one; the obligation of rest would continue attached to the other; although a certain interchange of characteristics would grow up, as worship necessitated rest, and the rest naturally suggested worship.[64]

The above is very interesting and stimulates our imagination as to the practice of the early church. Does it not seem likely that, in accordance with the structure of their culture at that time, many Jewish believers would have to go about their means of livelihood on the first day of the week? Wouldn't it have been a normal working day? Our point here,

---

[64] Merrill Unger, *Unger's Bible Dictionary*, (Chicago: Moody Bible Institute, 1957), p. 1050.

however, is that Sabbath observance by Christians is excluded from the book of Acts and that, we believe, is by reason of the divine inspiration of the writing.

Finally, as noted earlier, there is no commandment, no exhortation, or admonition to keep the Jewish Sabbath in the Epistles. And that, as may be recalled, is the reason for the writing of this chapter.

THE DAWNING OF A NEW DAY

"This is the day which the LORD has made; Let us rejoice and be glad in it" (Psalm 118:24). This prophetic passage from a psalm of thanksgiving speaks of the appointment of a new day under God's grace. Verses 22-24 read as follows:

> The stone which the builders rejected has become the chief corner stone. This is the LORD'S doing; It is marvelous in our eyes. This is the day which the LORD has made; Let us rejoice and be glad in it. (Psalm 118;22-24)

The importance of this verse can be seen in the fact that the first part of it is repeated in a number of New Testament passages. It is found in Matthew 21:41, Mark 12:10-11 and Luke 20:17 in connection with the parable of the landowner who planted a vineyard and sent his servants in to check on the produce of it. We read that the vine-growers beat and killed all the servants who were sent in. Finally, the landowner sent in his son thinking that they would respect him. But the son was killed as well. That of course speaks of the rejection of God's Son who was sent into the vineyard of this world.

Paul in Ephesians 2:20 and Peter in I Peter 2:7 quote the words, "The stone which the builders rejected has become the chief corner stone" in connection with the spiritual temple, the church of Christ, which is under construction, even to this day." In all of these passages it is obvious that both the death and resurrection of Christ are in view. This is especially so in the quotation that is found in the fourth chapter of the book of Acts where Peter says in verses 10-12:

...let it be known to all of you and to all the people of Israel, that by the name of Jesus Christ the Nazarene, whom you crucified, whom God raised from the dead— by this *name* this man stands here before you in good health. He is the STONE WHICH WAS REJECTED by you, THE BUILDERS, *but* WHICH BECAME THE CHIEF CORNER *stone.* And there is salvation in no one else; for there is no other name under heaven that has been given among men by which we must be saved. (Acts 4:10-12)

The words of Peter on the day of Pentecost and soon after are powerful and convicting. Peter says, "You nailed Him to a cross, but God raised Him up" (Acts 2:23-24). But ye denied the Holy One and the Just, and desired a murderer to be granted unto you; and killed the Prince of Life, whom God hath raised from the dead; whereof we are witnesses (Acts 3:14-15 / KJV). "You crucified Him, but God made Him both Lord and Christ" (Acts 2:36). And again, in Acts 4, "Be it known unto you all, and to all the people of Israel, that by the name of Jesus Christ of Nazareth, whom ye crucified, whom God raised from the dead, even by him doth this man stand here before you whole. This is the stone which was set at nought of you builders, which is become the head of the corner" (Acts 4:10-11 /KJV).

We are here speaking to the fact that the very great emphasis of these early chapter of the book of Acts is the Resurrection of Christ. We read, "And with great power the apostles were giving testimony to the resurrection of the Lord Jesus, and abundant grace was upon them all" (Acts 4:33).

Coming back to Psalm 118 we read, "This is the day the Lord has made" (Psalm118:24). The day was appointed and ordained by God to be a day of gladness and a celebration of victory.

On that appointed day, the first day of the week following His crucifixion, Jesus Christ rose from the dead. The phrase, "the first day of the week" is prominent in John's account. "Now on the first day of the week Mary Magdalene came early to the tomb" (John 20:1). "So, when it was evening on that day, the first day of the week, and when the doors were shut where the disciples were, for fear of the Jews, Jesus came and stood in their midst and said to them, 'Peace be with you'" (John 20:19). "After eight days (NIV-a week later) His disciples were again inside, and Thomas with them" (John 20:26).

Coming to Acts chapter one we note that, as calculated, the Holy Spirit came at Pentecost on the first day of the week. In Acts chapter 20 we find Paul meeting with believers to "break bread" on "the first day of the week" (Acts 20:7). It would seem that Paul had a choice. Because of the fact that he spent seven day in Troas, he could have met with them on the seventh day or the first day. The fact that they met on the first day suggests that they were in the habit of meeting on the first day of the week, commemorating the blessed truth that Jesus rose on the first day of the week.[65]

In support of the view that they were in the habit of meeting on the first day of the week we have the words of Paul in I Corinthians 16:2, "On the first day of every week each one of you is to put aside and save, as he may prosper, so that no collections be made when I come."

In his Bible dictionary Unger writes the following:

> Sunday is the first day of the week, adopted by the first Christians from the Roman calendar (Lat. *Dies Solis, Day of the Sun*), because it was dedicated to the worship of the sun. The Christians reinterpreted the heathen name as implying the Sun of Righteousness, with reference to this "rising" (Mal. 4:2). It was also called *Dies Panis* (*Day of Bread*), because it was an early custom to break bread on that day. In *the Teaching Of the Twelve* it is called the "Lord's Day of the Lord" (*Kuriaken de Kurious*). ...It was the day of the resurrection of Christ, of most of His appearances to the disciples after the resurrection, and on this day the Holy Spirit was poured out at Pentecost. For these reasons, and especially after the destruction of the sacred city had rendered the sacrificial service of the temple impossible, Sunday became the recognized day of assembly for fellowship and for the celebration of the Lord's supper.[66]

---

[65] Chafer, p. 119.
[66] Unger, p. 1050.

BEFORE CONSTANTINE

It is maintained by some that the emperor Constantine, by proclamation in A.D. 321 is responsible for the big change, the substitution of Sunday for the Sabbath. Others suggest that the change took place even later, by action of the Pope of Rome.[67] Indeed, Constantine did have a role to play as described by Merrill Unger:

> The reign of Constantine marks a change in the relations of the people to the Lord's Day. The rescript of the emperor, commanding the observance of Sunday, seems to have had little regard for its sanctity as a Christian institution; but the day of the sun is to be generally regarded with veneration…Later enactments made plain the duties of civil and ecclesiastical officers respecting the observance of Sunday, until it takes its place as an institution to be guarded and regulated by the government.[68]

However, the testimony of a number of the early church Fathers supplies ample proof that Christians were observing the Lord's Day as their day of worship long before 321 A.D. Chafer, in his systematic theology, quotes a number of the Fathers, ordering the writings from the most recent to the earliest:

> Eusebius, 315 A.D. says: "The churches throughout the rest of the world observe the practice that has prevailed from Apostolic tradition until the present time so that it would not be proper to terminate our fast on any other day but the resurrection day of our Savior. Hence there were synods and convocations of our Bishops on this question and all drew up an ecclesiastical decree which they communicated to churches in all places – that the mystery of the Lord's resurrection should be celebrated on no other day than the Lord's Day." Peter, Bishop of

---

[67] Chafer, p. 120.
[68] Unger, p. 1050.

Alexandria, 300 A.D., says: "We keep the Lord's Day as a day of joy because of him who rose thereon." Cyprian, Bishop of Carthage, 253 A.D., says: "The Lord's Day is both the 1ˢᵗ, and the 8ᵗʰ day." Tertullian, of Carthage, 200 A.D., says, speaking of the "Sun Worshippers": "Though we share with them Sunday, we are not apprehensive lest we seem to be heathen." Clement of Alexandra, 194 A.D., says: "The old sabbath day has become nothing more than a working day [to Christians]." Irenaeus, Bishop of Lyons, 178 A.D., says: "The mystery of the Lord's resurrection may not be celebrated on any other day than the Lord's Day." Bardesanes, 180 A.D., says: "Wherever we be, all of us are called by the one name of the Messiah, namely Christians, and upon one day, which is the first day of the week, we assemble ourselves together and on the appointed days we abstain from food." Justin Martyr, 135 A.D., says: "Sunday is the day on which we all hold our common assembly, because it is the first day on which God having wrought a change in the darkness and matter made the world and Jesus Christ, our Savior on the same day rose from the dead. . .On the Lord's Day all Christians in the city or country meet together because that is the day of our Lord's resurrection; and then we read the apostles and prophets. This being done, the president [presiding minister] makes an oration [verbal admonition] to the assembly exhorting them to imitate and to practice the things which they have heard, and then we all join in prayer, and after that we celebrate the Lord's Supper." Ignatius, Bishop of Antioch, 110 A.D., says: "Those who walked in the ancient practices attain unto newness of hope no longer observing sabbaths, but fashioning their lives after the Lord's Day, on which our life also rose through him, that we may be found disciples of Jesus Christ our only teacher." Barnabas, one of the Apostolic Fathers, 70 A.D. says: "Finally He saith, 'Your present Sabbaths are not acceptable to me. I shall make

a new beginning of the eighth day, that is the beginning
of another order of the world,' wherefore also we keep the
Lord's Day with joyfulness, the day also on which Jesus
rose from the dead."[69]

Combining the above testimony with that of the New Testament and
considering the fact that we are not exhorted to keep the Sabbath in any
of the Epistles, it seems clear to this writer, that God, by means of the
Resurrection of His Son and His sovereign control over the affairs of men,
has brought in the new day of worship and celebration.

WHY DO YOU JUDGE YOUR BROTHER?

These are the words of Paul as found in verse 10 of Romans 14 with
regard to the subject of the liberty that we now have in Christ. The
particulars of his discussion are that of eating certain kinds of food and
observing certain days. The subject is presented in chapter 14 and occupies
much of chapter 15. Reference is made to the one who "is weak in the
faith" (Romans14:1) and those who are "strong" (Romans 15:1). The one
who is strong is he or she who understands the liberty that can be realized
in Christ. Those who are weak are those whose conscience dictates a
concern with regard to, as we said above, eating certain food and observing
certain days. Of course, when we speak of the freedom that we have in
Christ, we are not speaking about moral absolutes, those matters that are
clearly laid out in Scripture as being right or wrong. For example, killing,
stealing, adultery and other behavior that violates love for God or neighbor
is clearly not up for debate. The subject here in this section of Romans, as
well as in chapters 8 and 9 of I Corinthians, is the matter of *questionable
things*, involving areas of disagreement among Christian brothers or sisters.

It is very likely that the issues mentioned in the first ten verses of
Romans 14 relate to the opinions of Jewish believers as opposed to Gentile
believers. The verses read as follows:

---

[69] Chafer, pp. 120-121.

Now accept the one who is weak in faith, but not for *the purpose of* passing judgment on his opinions. One person has faith that he may eat all things, but he who is weak eats vegetables only. The one who eats is not to regard with contempt the one who does not eat, and the one who does not eat is not to judge the one who eats, for God has accepted him. Who are you to judge the servant of another? To his own master he stands or falls; and he will stand, for the Lord is able to make him stand. One person regards one day above another, another regards every day *alike*. Each person must be fully convinced in his own mind. He who observes the day, does so for the Lord, and he who eats, does so for the Lord, for he gives thanks to God; and he who eats not, for the Lord he does not eat, and gives thanks to God. For not one of us lives for himself, and not one dies for himself; for if we live, we live for the Lord, or if we die, we die for the Lord; therefore whether we live or die, we are the Lord's. For to this end Christ died and lived again, that He might be Lord both of the dead and of the living. But you, why do you judge your brother? Or you again, why do you regard your brother with contempt? For we will all stand before the judgment seat of God. (Romans 14:1-10)

The notes of the NIV Study Bible read at verse 1: "Probably Jewish Christians at Rome who were unwilling to give up the observance of certain requirements of the law, such as dietary restrictions and the keeping of the Sabbath and other special days."[70]

"THE DAY"

Of particular interest in the above passage and relevant to our discussion are verses 5 and 6 of Romans 14. After observing that one person may regard "one day above another" while another "regards every

---

[70] NIV Study Bible, (Grand rapids, MI: Zondervan Bible Publishers, 1985), p. 1727.

day alike," Paul says, "He who observes the day, observes it for the Lord" (Romans 14:5-6). There is one factor here that leads me to believe that the apostle is referring to a disagreement concerning the Sabbath day. Paul refers to *the day*. The definite article is used here in the English and in the Greek text. *The day*, the Sabbath day, had been the area of on-going area of controversy in the earthly ministry of Christ. *The day* was the sign of the Mosaic economy and central to that whole theocratic system. If this is not what the apostle meant to say, he could certainly have put another way when writing the Greek text.

I find it interesting that so many Bible commentators cannot accept that Paul is referring to the Sabbath day. They notice that verse 5 suggests that while one person regards one day above another, another person regards "every day alike" (Romans 14:5). They perhaps ask, "How can that possibly have reference to the Sabbath? Certainly, God has sanctified it and made it to be more important than any other day." For example, when dealing with Romans 14:4- 6 Albert Barnes does not mention the Sabbath, rather he suggests that they refer to "the distinctions of the days of Jewish fastings, etcetera…"[71] I suggest that he is pulling that reference *out of the blue*. The Mosaic days of fasting are not in view, but *the day*, the Sabbath day, is the more likely reference. Christendom is so steeped with respect to a lack of distinction between Law and Grace, between the Sabbath and the Lord's Day that men of God cannot accept the fact that the Sabbath day might be referred to in these verses.

To be fair, we should call attention to the fact that the word "alike" (Romans 14:5) is in italics in our English Bibles, indicating that the word is not found in the Greek text. The Greek may be saying that while one man may regard one day as above or beyond another, another man judges or esteems every day. He regards every day as consecrated to the Lord. That is a possible rendering of the text, nevertheless, all of the major English versions do use the word "alike", although rendered in italics.

It is, therefore, interesting to note that while there is not one passage in the Epistles that exhorts us to keep the Seventh day, there does seem to be one passage that exhorts us not to judge one another on the matter.

---

[71] Albert Barnes, *Albert Barnes' Notes on the Bible,* (computer program, e-Sword, version 7.9.5. Rich Meyers, 2001).

CHAPTER ELEVEN

A SEARCH FOR THE
TRUE SABBATH

Digging deeper

Have you ever wondered why the requirements for the observance of the Jewish Sabbath were so strict? No journey was to be undertaken; no wood gathered; no fire kindled; no food prepared; no buying or selling permitted and no burden was to be borne. A day of absolute rest was binding upon the whole nation of Israel and the penalty for violating the day was death. While it is easy to agree with the thought that a day of rest each week is good for body and soul and that it just might be a God-given principle to which we would do well to heed, the requirements of the Jewish Sabbath in the Mosaic economy seem harsh and unnecessary. Why was it such a serious matter in the eyes of our God in the days of Moses and in the centuries that followed up through the time of Christ on earth?

As a pastor of two churches over the course of forty-six years my day of rest was Monday, not the first, but the second day of the week. Needless to say, Sunday was my busiest day and at the same time my most enjoyable day. With a Sunday school class, a morning sermon, an evening sermon for many of those years, occasional ministries to nursing homes, hospital visits when important, classes for baptism when called for, and at times meetings to interview people for church membership, etc., etc., it was not only a fulfilling day but an exhausting one. Needless to say, on Mondays I was not very productive, at least mentally. I have learned that not all pastors feel that drained on Mondays, but many do. To be noted is the fact that there was a good deal of work and stress leading up to those Sunday presentations.

But Mondays were, nevertheless, a needed blessing. It was the one day during which I felt free. Because of the fact that a pastor's life is not one of ridged structure, I could take time to pursue interests other than that of the ministry; but there would usually be, at least, a little bit of tension or guilt, if you please, about not being in the office or visiting a parishioner or taking care of correspondence during the week. But on Mondays, I was completely free from such stress. I could resist the occasional suggestion that we ought to have a board meeting on a Monday evening; I could say no to such a request because I felt entitled to that one day of rest.

But the point of what I am saying is this: I somehow believed that by reason of a divine principle I could, and even should, take a Sabbath day. With very little thought as to all that we have been considering in these chapters, I acknowledged the rule of one day in seven as a day of rest. I thought of it, though, as a matter of good principle, not Law. My Sabbath was Monday.

However, I am now questioning the Biblical basis for the assumption to which I adhered through the years. I had been assuming some sort of a Christian Sabbath—the thought that I could accept a part of the Sabbath, but leave the Jewish observance out of it. What Biblical basis is there for that kind of thinking? In the last chapter we traced somewhat the change over from the Sabbath to the Lord's Day. The Lord's Day is now a day of worship and celebration of our Lord's victory over the grave, but for many evangelicals today, especially those who are viewed as being dedicated Christians, it is a day of great activity.

We come back now to the question of the Jewish Sabbath. Why was the Lord God so serious about it being a day of absolute rest, so serious that to violate it made one worthy of death?

IT'S ABOUT TYPOLOGY

As the reader may know, typology is a phenomenon of Scripture whereby an event, or person or thing that is spoken of in the Old Testament looks ahead or foreshadows a corresponding event, person or thing that is found in the New Testament. For example, when it is recorded that

Abraham, in obedience to God's command proceeded to offer up his only son, Isaac, on Mount Moriah as a sacrifice (The Lord prevented him from going through with it), we have a case of typology. Isaac is the *type*, while Jesus dying on the cross is the *antitype*. Abraham is the *type* or adumbration of the Heavenly Father offering up His only begotten Son. This typology is implied in Hebrews 11:17- 19 where we read that "Abraham, when he was tested, offered up Isaac, and he who had received the promises was offering up his only begotten son" (Hebrews 11:17): We also read there that, "He considered that God is able to raise *people* even from the dead, from which he also received him back as a type" (Hebrews 11:19). It is important to bear in mind that an Old Testament *type* is to be taken literally. That is, the person or event or thing referred to is literal and historical. The story of Abraham and Isaac is a story about real people who lived, perhaps, two thousand years before Christ. God so ordered their lives as to make their story a foreshadowing of Himself offering up His Son on the cross.

Merrill Unger believes that we have typology in the institution of the Jewish Sabbath Day. He writes:

> The Sabbath commemorates God's creation rest. It marks a finished creation. After Sinai it was a day of legal obligation. The Sabbath is mentioned often in the Book of Acts in connection with the Jews. In the rest of the N.T. it occurs but twice (Col. 2:16,17; Heb. 4:4). In these passages the Sabbath is set forth not as a day to be observed, but as typical of the present rest into which the believer enters when "he also ceases from his own rest" and trusts Christ.[72]

We move now to a consideration of one of the passages mentioned in the above quotation from Unger. Of interest in these verses (Colossians 2:16-17) is the use of the word "shadow." Paul writes:

> Therefore no one is to act as your judge in regard to food or drink or in respect to a festival or a new moon or a Sabbath day – things which are a *mere* shadow of what is

---

[72] Merrill Unger, *Unger's Bible Dictionary*, (Chicago: Moody Bible Institute), p. 941.

to come; but the substance belongs to Christ. (Colossians 2:16-17)

Verse 16 begins with "therefore," which refers us to the preceding context. Here the apostle exhorts us not to let anyone act as our judge (vs. 16) because of that which has been nailed to the cross (vs. 14). Paul declares that the "certificate of debt consisting of decrees against us, which was hostile to us; …He has taken it out of the way, having nailed it to the cross" (Colossians 2:14,15. Concerning verse 14 the NIV Study Bible has the following footnote:

> "*written code*." A business term, meaning a certificate of indebtedness in the debtor's handwriting. Paul uses it as a designation for the Mosaic Law, with all its regulations, under which everyone is a debtor to God.[73]

Because of the fact that the written code has been "taken out of the way" and "nailed to the cross," "therefore" (Colossians 2: 16), no one is to act as your judge in regard to food or drink or in respect to a festival or a new moon or a sabbath day-- …" The apostle then goes on to say that these things are but a *shadow* of that which is to come (Colossians 2: 17), but the substance or the reality belongs to Christ. There are some who submit that the sabbaths referred to here are special days other than the seventh day of the week, such as the first and last days of the Feast of Tabernacles (Leviticus 23:34-42). It is inconceivable to them that the weekly Sabbath could be but a shadow of things to come. Others, like Normal Geisler[74] and Lewis Sperry Chafer,[75] insist that we have here a reference to the weekly Sabbath day.

It is not my purpose at this point to endeavor to settle this difference of interpretation. Whether the reference is to a sabbath day or the Sabbath

---

[73] NIV. Study Bible, (Grand rapids, Michigan: Zondervan Bible Publishers, 1985), p. 1815.

[74] Norman Geisler, "Colossians," *The Bible Knowledge Commentary*, editors John F. Walvoord and Roy B. Zuck, (Wheaton, Illinois: Victor Books, 1983), p. 678.

[75] Lewis Sperry Chafer, *Systematic Theology*, vol. 4, (Grand Rapids, MI: Kregel Publiations, 1948), p. 110.

day, there is still the question as to typology that may be involved with regard to sabbath rest.

MORE SHADOWS

In Hebrews chapter 8 the writer refers to the work of the priests who offered up "gifts and sacrifices" (Hebrews 8:3) and then goes on to say, "...who serve a copy and shadow of the heavenly things (Hebrews 8:5)." The word *shadow* is found again at chapter ten, verse one of Hebrews, "For the Law, since it has *only* a shadow of the good things to come *and* not the very form of things, can never, by the same sacrifices which they offer continually year by year, make perfect those who draw near." (Hebrews 10:1) The question that intrigues me is, "What about the Sabbath with respect to typology? If the animal sacrifices offered by the Old Testament priests looked forward to the one all-sufficient sacrifice for sins that took place at Calvary, what might be foreshadowed in this that was the sign of the Mosaic Covenant? Could the reason for the strict observance of that day demanded by Jehovah be found in God-inspired typology? Is there deeper theological truth to be considered?

CLASSIC TYPOLOGY

Unmistakable and significant typology is found in a passage that presents to us the first recorded instruction concerning Sabbath observance. In Genesis we read that God rested on the seventh day of the creation week and blessed the day "because in it He rested from all His work ..." (Genesis 2:2-3). Nothing is said about Sabbath observance, however, until we come to Exodus 16.

The people of Israel, having been delivered from the slavery of Egypt, are journeying toward Sinai where they will receive the Ten Commandments. We read in the text that they came to the "wilderness of Sin." That name is strangely appropriate because we read in the next verse that the "whole congregation of the sons of Israel grumbled against Moses and Aaron in the wilderness" (Exodus 16:2).

In response to the grumbling of His people the Lord responded with grace. He said to Moses, "I will rain down bread from heaven" (Exodus16: 4). Those exact words, "bread from heaven," should be noted. With respect to the heavenly food, the Manna, that God provides, the procedure for a Sabbath day observance is commanded. They were to gather each morning a supply for the day, depending upon the number of people in each household. They could not keep any of it over until the next day because, as some found out (Exodus 16: 20), it would breed worms and turn foul. In spite of that phenomenon, on the sixth day they were to gather twice as much so that the work of gathering would not take place on the seventh day. It was to be a day of complete rest. Miraculously, the supply gathered on the sixth day did not turn foul or breed worms.

With respect to this first body of teaching concerning Sabbath day observance two important points can be made. First to be noted is God's miraculous provision for His people. This can be seen in two aspects: Firstly, He gave them food from heaven. It somehow came down with the dew. "When the layer of dew evaporated, behold, on the surface of the wilderness there was a fine flake-like thing, fine as the frost on the ground" (Exodus 16:14). It may have looked like frost, but it wasn't frost; it was life-nurturing food.

Just as significant as that miraculous provision of food, and perhaps more so, was the fact that on the morning of the 7th day the manna had not turned foul. And that aspect of the miraculous presents us with, I believe, a clue as to the meaning of the fourth commandment, which will be delivered to them at Sinai a short time later.

This leads us to a second major point of observation: The Manna is a type of Christ. This is made very plain in the 6th chapter of John where Jesus says, "I am the bread of life" (John 6:35).

In verse 30 of chapter 6 of John the Jewish leaders ask for a miraculous sign. "What then do You do for a sign, so that we may see, and believe You? What work do you perform? Our fathers ate the manna in the wilderness; as it is written, 'HE GAVE THEM BREAD OUT OF HEAVEN TO EAT'" (John 6:30).

Jesus responds, "Truly, truly, I say to you, it is not Moses who has given you the bread out of heaven, but it is My Father who gives you the true bread out of heaven. For the bread of God is that which comes down out of heaven, and gives life to the world. ...I am the bread of life; he who comes to Me will not hunger, and he who believes in Me will never thirst" (John 6:32-35).

The typology is unmistakable and very significant. The Manna is introduced to the people of Israel in the connection with the institution of Sabbath day observance. In John 6 Jesus refers to the "true bread out of heaven" (John 6:55,58) The question for us is: If there is the *true bread* out of heaven, is there a *true Sabbath*?

THE BELIEVER'S REST

A very remarkable statement is found in the fourth chapter of the book of Hebrews. In verse 9 we read, "So there remains a Sabbath rest for the people of God" (Hebrews 4:9). The chapter begins, "Therefore, let us fear if, while a promise remains of entering His rest, any one of you may seem to have come short of it" (Hebrews 4:1). The subject of God's people finding rest is an important theme in the Old Testament record.

Let's begin with Deuteronomy 3:18 where Moses says, "Then I commanded you at that time saying, 'The LORD your God has given you this land to possess it; all your valiant men shall cross over armed before your brothers, the sons of Israel'" (Deut. 3:18). He continues, "until the LORD gives rest to your fellow countrymen as to you, and they also shall possess the land which the LORD your God will give them beyond the Jordan" (Deuteronomy 3:20).

As Joshua assumes command of Israel, he admonishes the people to remember the promise, "Remember the word which Moses the servant of the LORD commanded you, saying, 'The LORD your God gives you rest and will give you this land'" (Joshua 1:13).

In Psalm 95:8-11, however, we read about God's anger against an entire generation of people who wandered in the wilderness for forty years because they could not believe in what He had promised:

> Do not harden your hearts, as at Meribah, as in the days of Massah, in the wilderness, when your fathers tested Me, they tried Me, though they had seen My work. For forty years I loathed that generation, And said they are a people who err in their heart, and they do not know My

ways. Therefore, I swore in My anger, truly they shall not enter my rest. Psalm 95:8-11)

The writer of Hebrews refers to this Psalm of David and implies that the people of Israel never did truly realize the kind of rest that God wanted them to enjoy beyond the Jordan. "He again fixes a certain day, 'Today,' saying through David after so long a time just as has been said before, 'TODAY IF YOU HEAR HIS VOICE, DO NOT HARDEN YOUR HEARTS.' For if Joshua had given them rest, He would not have spoken of another day after that. So there remains a Sabbath rest for the people of God" (Hebrews 4:7-9).

CROSSING THE JORDAN

What is meant by the expression, "crossing the Jordan?" I wonder how many gospel songs have carried along that theme suggesting that to "cross the Jordan" means to enter into eternal bliss, to pass over from the weariness of this life into the land of eternal rest. I submit that the writer of Hebrews chapter four is addressing an entirely different matter, one that is of vital importance for us to understand.

Please notice first of all, that reference is made to God resting on the seventh day at the time of creation, "For we who have believed enter that rest, just as He has said, 'AS I SWORE IN MY WRATH, THEY SHALL NOT ENTER MY REST,' although His works were finished from the foundation of the world. For He has said somewhere concerning the seventh day: 'AND GOD RESTED ON THE SEVENTH DAY FROM ALL HIS WORKS.' (Hebrews 4:3-4). The writer seems to be saying that God wants us to enter into the kind of rest that He has enjoyed since the beginning.

Secondly, we notice references that speak of a cessation from work, "...AND GOD RESTED ON THE SEVENTH DAY FROM ALL HIS WORKS" (Hebrews 4:4) And then after declaring that there is "a Sabbath rest for the people of God" (Hebrews 4:9) the writer states, "For the one who has entered His rest has himself also rested from his works, as God did from His" (Hebrews 4:10). Note: The one entering rest has "rested from his works."

I suggest that verse 10 of Hebrews 4 is the key to understanding what this passage is all about. It has to do with one of the more important theological points of the New Testament – salvation is not about works, but about the finished work of Christ on the cross. There are two great errors which characterize the theology of the modern-day cult. Those who adhere to cult theology are wrong about two things; they are wrong about the person of Christ and they are wrong about the terms of our eternal salvation. On the one hand they present Jesus Christ, as being something less than He is, an angel, perhaps, or a lesser god. On the other hand, they add works to faith as being necessary for salvation. On this latter error the Apostle Paul reveals his passion on the matter in the first chapter of the book of Galatians, verses 6-9:

> I am amazed that you are so quickly deserting Him who called you by the grace of Christ, for a different gospel; which is really not another; only there are some who are disturbing you and want to distort the gospel of Christ. But even if we, or an angel from heaven, should preach to you a gospel contrary to what we have preached to you, he is to be accursed! As we have said before, so I say again now, if any man is preaching to you a gospel contrary to what you received, he is to be accursed! (Galatians 1:6-9)

Paul, in the book of Galatians, speaks to the problem of those in the church who insisted on adding the tenets of Judaism to the Gospel as being necessary for salvation; but his words apply to any such additions to the finished work of Christ. The words of Ephesians 2:8-9 are familiar to many, "For by grace you have been saved through faith; and that not of yourselves, *it is* the gift of God; not as a result of works, so that no one may boast." Paul writes at length on the subject of faith without works in the book of Romans (3:21-4:25).

My question at this point is: Does the passion of Paul on the subject, saying that those who preach another gospel, a gospel that includes works, are worthy of being accursed, connect with a deeper meaning of the Old Testament Sabbath, during which <u>day no works were to be tolerated?</u> The penalty for violation was death. Does the fact that our God presented the observance of the Sabbath in such a serious way speak to the importance of resting in the finished work of His Son on our behalf?

BLESSED ASSURANCE

According to the writer of the book of Hebrews, God seriously desires that we enter into His rest. It is a rest that involves a complete turning away from our works. I believe that it is a rest of heart and mind with regard to our eternal salvation. It is a rest whereby we trust fully in the value of the finished work of Christ on the cross. I suggest that there is hardly anything more important to the eyes of our Heavenly Father than the death of His Son on that cross. That transaction whereby our sins were placed under that precious blood cost Father and Son more than we can possibly imagine. How it must displease Him when we try to add our good works to the finished work of Christ! Rather, He desires that we have a *blessed assurance* concerning our relationship with Him, a manna of peace and joy far more satisfying than that which God provided His people during their wilderness wanderings. It is spiritual rest, however, that the people, to whom the book of Hebrews is written, were finding difficult to realize.

CONSIDERING THE CONTEXT

It seems to me, from a study of these chapters in the book of Hebrews, that the people, to whom this epistle was written, were struggling with the terms of salvation and the achievement of assurance concerning their relationship with God. They found themselves enduring a good deal of persecution and at the same time witnessing a number of people in their midst, whom they thought to be their brothers and sisters in Christ, turning away from the things of God. It must have been extremely disconcerting to see some folks leaving their midst, apparently turning away from things of Christ.

At the end of chapter four, we find the writer endeavoring to inspire their confidence in the work of our great High Priest:

Therefore, since we have a great high priest who has passed through the heavens, Jesus the Son of God, let us hold fast our confession. For we do not have a high priest who cannot sympathize with our weaknesses, but One who has been tempted in all things *as we are, yet* without sin. There-fore let us draw near with confidence to the throne of grace, so that we may receive mercy and find grace to help in time of need (Hebrews 4:14-16).

At the end of chapter 5 he admonishes them concerning a lack of growth with respect to their spiritual understanding of God and His Word:

Concerning him we have much to say, and *it is* hard to explain, since you have become dull of hearing. For though by this time you ought to be teachers, you have need again for someone to teach you the elementary principles of the oracles of God, and you have come to need milk and not solid food. For everyone who partakes *only* of milk is not accustomed to the word of righteousness, for he is an infant. But solid food is for the mature, who because of practice have their senses trained to discern good and evil (Hebrews 5:11-14).

We notice in particular the emphasis in Hebrews 5:11,12 and the words "again" and "elementary" principles. I believe that these people had come to those elementary principles before and had become true believers in Christ for their salvation. But something now is causing them to go back and review the matter. On the one hand they had not been growing in the things of Christ and the Word as they should and now, in the face of some persecution, they were seeing some people apparently leaving the faith.

The writers concern for these people of God is carried forward into chapter six, a chapter that has been the cause of much controversy and diversity of interpretation. My belief that the people to whom the writer is speaking are genuine believers is confirmed by the words of verse 9 of Hebrews 6, "But beloved, we are convinced of better things concerning you, and things that accompany salvation, though we are speaking in this way" (Hebrews 6:9). Earlier in this chapter, however, the writer had found it necessary to explain the situation with regard to people who were turning away from Christ (Hebrews 6: 4-8).

Bringing his argument from chapter five into chapter six (there were no chapter divisions in the original manuscripts), he admonishes the believers to "leave the elementary teaching about the Christ, and press on to maturity" (Hebrews 6:1).

AN IMPEDIMENT TO GROWTH

The writer wants them to press on to maturity; but there seems to have been an impediment to their growing in the grace and knowledge of Christ. We can also say, in connection with the apostle's words in chapters three and four, that there is an impediment to an enjoyment of the kind of Sabbath rest that God wanted them to have.

I am suggesting the above with a view to the words found in verses 4-8 of chapter six. Beginning in Hebrews 6:4 the writer of Hebrews addresses the problem by referring to some people who were apparently turning away from the faith. He writes:

> For in the case of those who have once been enlightened and have tasted of the heavenly gift and have been made partakers of the Holy Spirit, and have tasted the good word of God and the powers of the age to come, and *then* have fallen away, it is impossible to renew them again to repentance, since they again crucify to them selves the Son of God and put Him to open shame (Hebrews 6:4-6).

It seems to me that the true believers in Christ, for whom this letter is written, found themselves in some degree of confusion and consternation concerning a number of people who had left their midst and had apparently turned away from Christ. Add to this consternation the probability that they were enduring some persecution, as many Bible commentators believe to have been the case, and we can perceive a possible cause for stalling with regard to growing in Christ as well as a temptation to withdraw to some form of Judaism. The writer of this epistle endeavors then to explain the case of some who were apostatizing or falling away from the Faith.

It has been my personal observation as a pastor that people are troubled when people leave a church, for whatever reason. If a family leaves, not because they are moving away from the area, but to attend another church, people are somewhat upset and share with one another their concern. "Whose fault is this? What are we doing wrong? Has anyone found out the reason for their departure?" People are especially concerned when two or three families leave. We bear in mind that this is the case when those who leave are believers in Christ. But the words of Hebrews six suggest that people are not only leaving the fellowship of believers, but are turning away from their faith in Christ. The writer therefore endeavors to explain the phenomenon that was troubling them and hindering their own growth in Christ.

THE PROBLEMATIC CLAUSE OF HEBREWS SIX

The troubling words of Hebrews 6:6 are: "…it is impossible to renew them again to repentance…." That clause has been the source of many and diverse interpretations. Some say that the words of Hebrews 6:4-6 serve as a severe warning to true believers in Christ who are in danger of losing their salvation. The alarming part of the whole passage is the statement that if they lose their salvation, they cannot be restored to true faith in Christ. Others suggest that the people in question are not true believers at all.

They say that the warning concerns those who have professed Christ, but never really possessed Christ. They have "tasted the heavenly gift" and "tasted the good word of God" (Hebrews 6:5). They have been enlightened with regard to the convicting influence of the Holy Spirit as to who Jesus is and what He did on the cross.

I lean to this view and look at it this way: Under the eye-opening influence of the Holy Spirit they have been brought to the foot of the cross to behold the Savior who was crucified for them. They tarry there for a while and in the process seemingly fellowship with true believers in the church. But in due time, they turn away, making the decision to reject Him, and as the writer puts it, "…crucify to themselves the Son of God…."

We notice that the word "taste" is used twice in the passage. This would seem to comprise an emphasis on the *tasting* as opposed to full acceptance. Some, objecting to this point, refer us to Hebrews 2:9 where we read that Jesus *tasted death* for us all. "Doesn't that mean that He really died?" Yes, but He didn't stay dead. He rose from the grave. He did, however, experience death for us all. Perhaps we are quibbling about the use of words, but generally speaking, when we taste something, we may go ahead and eat it or throw it away. I interpret the words here to mean that they tasted the things of God, but decided to throw it all way.

NOT SO MUCH A WARNING, AS AN EXPLANATION

But what about that problematic clause: "it is impossible to renew them again to repentance since they again crucify to themselves the Son of God and put Him to open shame" (Hebrews 6:6)? I have read a number of interpretations of these words, but I find none of them to be very satisfying.

With regard to the last part of the above statement, it should be noted that the Greek New Testament has only these words: "crucifying to themselves the Son of God" (Hebrews 6:6).

The English translators have, by necessity, added some words so as to make it complete. Grammatically the word "crucifying" is a present participle in the Greek clause, speaking of a continuous action. The word "since," which is added to the clause by the translators, makes it a causal participle. It seems to say that these people cannot be renewed repentance because or since or because they are crucifying to themselves the Son of God.

I submit the possibility that the writer may have intended the meaning to be that of a *temporal participle*. If that is the case it would then be rendered this way: "It is impossible to renew them to repentance *as long as*, or *while* they are crucifying for themselves the Son of God. The writer is not saying that such people can never be renewed to repentance, but that they cannot be renewed to repentance as long as they continue in a state of mind whereby. they are rejecting Christ. There is nothing in the clause itself that would tell us whether the writer intends it to be a causal participle or a temporal participle. The Greek simply reads, "crucifying to themselves the Son of God…"(Hebrews 6:6).

Perhaps the writer of Hebrews is saying to his disconcerted readers,

"These Christ deniers have come to a decision to turn away from Jesus and there is not much we can do about it but pray for them." They seem to have their minds made up. We note also the use of the very strong word, "crucifying." He says, "This is not you, is it? You love Him. You don't want to reject Him as they did at Calvary, do you?"

Then he goes on to say in verse 9, "But, beloved, we are convinced of better things concerning you, and things that accompany salvation, though we are speaking in this way" (Hebrews 6:9). At this point we note the parallel passage of I John 2:18-20:

> Children, it is the last hour; and just as you heard that antichrist is coming, even now many antichrists have appeared; from this we know that it is the last hour. They went out from us, but they were not of us; for if they had been of us, they would have remained with us; but they went out, so that it would be shown that they all are not of us. But you have an anointing from the Holy One, and you all know. I have not written to you because you do not know the truth, but because you do know it, and because no lie is of the truth. (I John 2:18-20)

We observe that the argument given by the Apostle John is very much the same as that which we find in Hebrews six. First, he declares that the fact that they left us demonstrates that they were not really of us. And then, addressing the readers, he says, "But you are not like them. You have an "anointing from the Holy One" and you know the truth." [my paraphrase of I John 2:20-21). We also note that he calls the apostates, "antichrists") I John 2:18). This parallels the word "crucifying" found in Hebrews 6:6 with respect to a severe attitude. We are also reminded of Judas Iscariot who is a case in point. He spent three years with Jesus and the other disciples, but in my opinion was never a true child of God. In His high-priestly prayer of John chapter 17, Jesus called him, "the son of perdition" (John 17:12), which means "son of destruction." Judas is in bad company because the same terminology is used of the great Man of Sin, the Anti-Christ, in II Thessalonians 2:3.

THE GREAT NEGLECTED PART OF HEBREWS SIX

As stated, great has been the diversity of interpretation and the controversy surrounding the first several verses of Hebrews six. Are the people spoken of in verses 4-8 true believers who have lost their salvation or are they those who have professed Christ but never truly possessed Christ? Or, is there some other way of looking at this problematic passage? However, in the latter half of the chapter we have presented to us a very powerful analogy with respect to Abraham and the promises God gave him. The promises that God gave to Abraham are analogous to the promises that God has given to the believer and that analogy should give the believer "an anchor of the soul, a *hope* both sure and steadfast..." (Hebrews 6:19). It seems to me that verses 13-20 of Hebrews 6 have been somewhat neglected by many who have focused on the first part of the chapter.

At this point we want to bear in mind that we are tracing an argument in the book of Hebrews relevant to the question presented to us in chapters three and four. What is the nature of the "Sabbath rest" that God wants us to enjoy? We have previously suggested that it is a matter of salvation without works and a continued resting in the promises of God for our present and eternal well- being. We have also suggested that this Sabbath rest, which is of a spiritual nature, was foreshadowed or typified by the Old Testament observance of rest on the seventh day. The last several verses of chapter six go a long way towards solidifying the argument. Here is the passage:

> For when God made the promise to Abraham, since He would swear by no one greater, He swore by Himself, saying, "I WILL SURELY BLESS YOU AND I WILL SURELY MULTIPLY YOU." And so, having patiently waited, he obtained the promise. For men swear by one greater *than themselves*, and with them an oath given as confirmation is an end of every dispute. In the same way God, desiring even more to show to the heirs of the promise the unchangeableness of His purpose, interposed with an oath, so that by two unchangeable things in which it is impossible for God to lie, we who have taken refuge

would have strong encouragement to take hold of the hope set before us. This hope we have as an anchor of the soul, a *hope* both sure and steadfast and one which enters within the veil, where Jesus has entered as a forerunner for us, having become a high priest forever according to the order of Melchizedek (Hebrews 6:13-20).

THE ABRAHAM ANALOGY

The quotation in the above passage is taken from Genesis 22:16-17 and connects with the great and classic story whereby Abraham's faith is put to the ultumate test. He has been told: "take now your son, your only son, whom you love, Isaac, and go the land of Moriah, and offer him there as a burnt offering on one of the mountains of which I will tell you" (Genesis 22:2). In an incredible act of obedience Abraham's faith is confirmed and God reiterates His promise of blessing for him; the Angel of the LORD says, "By Myself I have sworn, declares the LORD, because you have done this thing and have not withheld your son, your only son, indeed I will greatly bless you, and I will greatly multiply your seed as the stars of the heavens and as the sand which is on the seashore; and your seed shall possess the gate of their enemies. In your seed all the nations of the earth shall be blessed because you have obeyed My voice" (Genesis 22:16-18).

THE ALL-IMPORANT ABRAHAMIC COVENANT

At this point it seems quite important to consider Genesis 22 in the context of all that God promised to this great man of faith as recorded in chapters 12-22 of Genesis, so as to understand what the writer of Hebrews calls "the unchangeableness (or immutability-KJV) of His purpose" (Hebrews 6:17). Theologians have labeled it the Abrahamic Covenant and the promises connected with it are found in Genesis 12:1-3; 13:14-17; 15:4-21; 17:1-22; and 22:1-18. The story begins in chapter 12:1-3 with these words:

Now the LORD said to Abram,
"Go forth from your country,
And from your relatives,
And from your fathers' house,
To a land which I will show you;   THE LAND
And I will make you a great nation,
And I will bless you,
And make your name great;   THE SEED
And so, you shall be a blessing;
And I will bless those who bless you,
And the one who curses you I will
curse.   THE BLESSING
And in you all the families of the earth
will be blessed (Genesis 12:!-3).

Thus, begins the promises of God to Abraham. There are three basic elements of the Abrahamic covenant and they are: the land, the seed (or descendants) and the blessing. Throughout the chapters which follow in Genesis there is reiteration and enlargement of the promise that Abraham would be the father of a great nation, that the land would be for them an everlasting possession and that he and his descendants would be greatly blessed and would provide a blessing for the world. A careful reading of chapters 13, 15, 17 and 22 reveals that these three elements are interwoven throughout the narrative. The three are all part of the covenant that God made with Abraham. The word *covenant* is found in Genesis 15:18; 17:2, 4, 7, 9,10,13,14,19, and 21.

UNILATERAL AND UNCONDITIONAL

Of vital important and central to the nature of the covenant that God made with Abraham is the solemn ceremony that is recorded for us in chapter 15:7-21:

And He said to him, "I am the LORD who brought you out of Ur of the Chaldeans, to give you this land to possess it." He said, "O LORD GOD, how may I know that I will possess it?" So, He said to him, "Bring Me a three- year old heifer, and a three year old female goat, and a three- year old ram, and a turtledove, and a young pigeon. Then he brought all these to Him and cut them in two, and laid each half opposite the other; but he did not cut the birds. The birds of prey came down upon the carcasses, and Abram drove them away. Now when the sun was going down, a deep sleep fell upon Abram; and behold, terror and great darkness fell upon him. *God* said to Abram, "Know for certain that your descendants will be strangers in a land that is not theirs, where they will be enslaved and oppressed four hundred years. ...Then in the fourth generation They will return here, for the iniquity of the Amorite is not yet complete." It came about when the sun had set, that it was very dark, and behold, *there appeared* a smoking oven and a flaming torch which passed between these pieces. On that day the LORD made a covenant with Abram saying, "To your descendants I have given this land, from the river of Egypt as far as the great river, the river Euphrates: the Kenite and the Kenizzite and the Kadmonite and the Hittite and the Perizzite and the Rephaim and the Amorite and ..." (Genesis 15:7-21)

It was sometimes the practice of two men who were entering into a contract to solemnize the agreement with a ceremony such as that which we read of here in Genesis fifteen. Animals would be killed and cut in pieces. The pieces would then be divided so as to form a corridor that stretched out between the two rows of slain animals. The two parties would then walk together between the rows to seal the agreement. The notes from the NIV Study Bible describe the situation as follows:

In ancient times the parties solemnized a covenant by walking down an aisle flanked by the pieces of slaughtered animals (see Jer. 34:18-19). The practice signified a self-maledictory oath: "May it be so done to me if I do not keep my oath and pledge." Having credited Abram's faith as righteousness, God now graciously ministered to his need for assurance concerning the land.[76]

The writer of the above commentary note goes on to make an interesting observation regarding the words "made a covenant" in verse 18 of Genesis 15. The literal meaning of the Hebrew is "cut a covenant" referring to the slaughtering of the animals."[77] We note also that the animals which are slain, with the exception of the birds, are said to be three years old. This age was typical with regard to animals sacrificed under the Mosaic law.

The most important point to be made, however, is that the covenant that was made in this case was unilateral and unconditional in nature. Abraham did not walk between the row of animal parts. He was put to one side and slept through the ceremony. We read, "As the sun was setting, Abram fell into a deep sleep, and a thick and dreadful darkness came over him" (Gen.15:12). The LORD GOD Himself, in the form of "a smoking firepot with a blazing torch appeared and passed between the pieces" (Gen.15:.17). Abraham was not allowed to promise anything. It was unilateral, with only one party involved in the covenant. It was unconditional as far as Abraham was concerned. He promised nothing. It all depended on the person of God Himself.

HUMAN WORKS NOT ALLOWED

As stated previously, most Evangelical commentators who write on the book of Hebrews, suggest that it was written to Jewish converts to Christ. Abraham was highly regarded in the Jewish community of the first century. It would seem that a great many of them would be familiar with this incident in the life of Abraham. Therefore, when the writer of Hebrews refers to the story of Genesis 22 where God says, "by Myself I have sworn, declares the LORD." (Gen. 22:16), the readers might also remember the solemn covenant that God *cut* as recorded in Genesis 15. By that act God was giving to Abraham a blessed assurance as to the *unchangeableness of*

---

[76] NIV Study Bible, p. 28
[77] Ibid., p. 28.

His purpose. The promises that He had made to Abraham would surely be fulfilled.

The fact that Abraham was not allowed to contribute human works to what God had promised is presented in Hebrews six as analogous to our salvation in Christ. Not only has God promised us eternal life by reason of our faith alone in Him, but He has guaranteed our salvation based upon the sacrifice of His Son on the Cross. We can't earn it to begin with. Neither can we maintain it by adding our works to what Christ has done for us. It is unilateral and unconditional. We enter the land of Sabbath rest by our faith alone and we enjoy that land of rest as we learn to trust Him more and more for our every need.

We began this section by asking about the reason for the strict seventh day rest that God demanded of His people in the days of Moses. We said that the answer was to be found in the area of typology. Adding our works to His provision for us is a very serious offense to Him because nothing is more important to Him than the worth of His Son's sacrifice at Calvary. Above all else our Heavenly Father desires that we rest in Him, not only for our salvation, but for all our needs. We read in Hebrews 4:15-16, "For we do not have a high priest who cannot sympathize with our weaknesses, but One who was tempted in all things as we are, yet without sin. Therefore, let us draw near with confidence to the throne of grace, so that we may receive mercy and find grace to help in time of need."

BACK TO AN EARLIER QUESTION

If the works of the law are written on the hearts of men, as stated in Romans 2:15, does that mean that the fourth commandment is written there also? I do not believe so. The Scripture indicates that it was given to the nation Israel, beginning in the days of Moses. Furthermore, we do not find any admonition or exhortation or commandment in the New Testament epistles that we observe the Old Testament demands of Seventh day observance.

A FINAL EXHORTATION FROM HEBREWS

We still have Sunday here in our land, whereby most people are not required to pursue their means of livelihood. Since the Lord in His providential work on our behalf has arranged that we have now freedom to worship on the first day of the week, let us take note of what is exhorted later in the book of Hebrews, chapter 10:22-25:

> Let us draw near with a sincere heart in full assurance of faith, having our hearts sprinkled *clean* from an evil conscience and our bodies washed with pure water. Let us hold fast the confession of our faith without wavering, for He who promised is faithful; and let us consider how to stimulate one another to love and good deeds, nor forsaking our own assembling together, as is the habit of some, but encouraging *one another*; and all the more as you see the day drawing near. (Hebrews 10:22-25)

It is important that we take advantage of the Lord's Day as an opportunity to assemble together, so that we might not only worship our God, but nurture one another with regard to the faith-rest that He wants us to enjoy.[78]

---

[78] See Appendix for "More thoughts on Hebrews 6 and 10."

CHAPTER TWELVE

LOOKING FOR SIGNS
AND WONDERS

AN AID TO EVANGELISM?

Next door to the Citgo station was a delicatessen which specialized in good German food. Occasionally, during a visit with my friend who managed the station, he would take a break from pumping gas so that we might go next door to the deli. Located in the back room of that establishment was a ping pong table, which the owner allowed us to use. One day, in the spring of 1969, after our round of Table Tennis, my friend did something which he had done on a number of occasions; he invited the owner of the deli to come to church. That invitation had never met with success, so on this day he presented it in a different way.

He said to the man, "If the Mets win the World Series this year, will you come to church with me some Sunday morning soon after?"

Much to our surprise, the owner of the deli said, "Yes, okay, if the Mets win the Series this year I will come to church."

It should be noted at this point that the New York Mets baseball team had not done well the previous year. In fact, they finished in last place in their division. Therefore, the prospect of their winning the World Series in 1969 was not good. It was not very likely that they would win the trophy, but they did. The amazing Mets pulled off a miracle, it seems. They were the Miracle Mets.

With tongue in cheek we might say that the Lord performed a miracle for the benefit of the owner of that deli. who had promised to come to church if such an event took place. But he never did. He went back on his promise.

Even at that time, many years ago, a Biblical truth came to my mind concerning the *signs and wonders* that Jesus performed during the course of His ministry on earth. For the most part, people did not respond in a positive way to the miracles that took place by His hand. Those wonderful displays of God's power working through Him did not, as a rule, command the faith of the multitudes. Of course, the Mets winning the World Series should not be classified as a true miracle -- a providential working perhaps, but not truly analogous with the miracles that Jesus did. Nevertheless, the lesson pertaining to the man in the above story can be seen as analogous to the response of people in Jesus' day. People will not respond in a positive way to whatever God does, unless there is within a heart inclined to seek Him.

THEY SIMPLY WOULD NOT BELIEVE

It is not known just how many miracles Jesus did during His earthly ministry. There are a number of Scripture passages that imply that, indeed, there were a great many. Matthew gives us a good summary of His healing ministry in the fourth chapter of his gospel, Mathew 4:23-25:

> Jesus was going throughout all Galilee, teaching in their synagogues and proclaiming the gospel of the kingdom, and healing every kind of disease and every kind of sickness among the people. The news about Him spread throughout all Syria; and they brought to Him all who were ill, those suffering with various diseases and pains, demoniacs, epileptics, paralytics; and He healed them. Large crowds followed Him from Galilee and the Decapolis and Jerusalem and Judea and from beyond the Jordan. (Matthew 4:23-25)

The above passage serves to emphasize the great compassion of Jesus as well as the capability of the long- awaited Messiah to care for His people. There is also, of course, the matter of authenticating His person and ministry with miraculous signs. Peter speaks to this during his sermon on the Day of Pentecost; "Men of Israel, listen to these words: Jesus the Nazarene, a man attested to you by God with miracles and wonders and signs which God performed through Him in your midst, just as you yourselves know …" (Acts 2:22).

When John the Baptist sent a message to Jesus from prison, asking if He indeed was the "expected one," Jesus replied, "Go and report to John what you hear and see; *the* BLIND RECEIVE SIGHT and *the* lame walk, *the* lepers are cleansed and *the* deaf hear, *the* dead are raised up, and *the* POOR HAVE THE GOSPEL PREACHED TO THEM. And blessed is he who does not take offense at Me." (Matthew 11:3-6).

Especially noteworthy concerning the miraculous display of power that authenticated His person and ministry is the fact that the majority refused to believe. In Matthew chapter twelve Jesus calls them "an evil and adulterous generation" (Matt. 12:39) because they kept demanding more signs while evading the truth about Him. There are several passages that speak to this phenomenon. The passage in Matthew twelve reads:

> Then some of the scribes and Pharisees said to Him, "Teacher, we want to see a sign from You." But He answered and said to them, "An evil and adulterous generation craves for a sign; and yet no sign will be given to it but the sign of Jonah the prophet; for just as JONAH WAS THREE DAYS AND THREE NIGHTS IN THE BELLY OF THE SEA MONSTER, so will the Son of Man be three days and three nights in the heart of the earth. The men of Nineveh will stand up with this generation at the judgment, and will condemn it because they repented at the preaching of Jonah; and behold, something greater than Jonah is here" (Matthew 12:38-41).

Many Bible students consider this to be a defining moment in the life of Christ. At this point in time the rejection of Him by the nation Israel is obvious. The nation has made its decision; that decision needs only to be formalized at the cross. It is for this reason that Jesus declares that there will be no more signs except that of the prophet Jonah. There will be some miraculous healings, but no miracles designed to authenticate His person, except that of His resurrection from the grave.

It is also interesting to note that Jonah did no miracles during the time of his preaching in Nineveh, but they repented, while the people of Israel witnessed an abundance of miracles and refused to believe.

He said that there would be no more signs, but the religious leaders kept asking for them. Later on, as recorded in Matthew 16:1, "The Pharisees and Sadducees came up, and testing Jesus, they asked Him to show them a sign from heaven."

THE UNPARDONABLE SIN

The occasion for Jesus' statement that an unpardonable sin was being committed is recorded in Matthew 16:22-23. A demon-possessed man is brought to Jesus. After the man, who was both mute and blind, gave evidence of being completely healed, we read that the crowds were amazed and began to debate as to whether or not Jesus was the Messiah saying, "This man cannot be the Son of David, can he" (Matt. 12;23)? The Pharisees respond by declaring that the miracle had been done by the power of Beelzebul, the ruler of the demons (Matt. 12:24). Jesus replies with the following argument:

> And knowing their thoughts Jesus said to them, "Any kingdom divided against itself is laid waste; and any city or house divided against itself will not stand. If Satan casts out Satan, he is divided against himself; how then will his kingdom stand? But if I by Beelzebul cast out demons, by whom do your sons cast *them* out? For this reason they will be your judges. But if I cast out demons by the Spirit of God, then the kingdom of God has come upon you" (Matthew 12:25-28).

Jesus then proceeds to declare that what the religious leaders were doing constituted blasphemy against the Holy Spirit -- that is, attributing to Satan what God had done. Their response to this one miracle prompts Jesus to characterize that generation as evil and a people who were always demanding signs and to declare that there would be no more signs, except that of the prophet Jonah (the miracle of His resurrection). There are many who believe that the *unpardonable sin* was the sin of that generation of Israelites who rejected their Messiah, in spite of all the claims that He had made, authenticated by many signs and wonders. We note in particular Matt. 12:28, "But if I cast out demons by the Spirit of God, then the kingdom of God has come upon you." As a people, they rejected their king and His kingdom. All of the miracles that Jesus had done by the enabling power of the Holy Spirit, did not command their faith in Him. They simply refused to believe.

A CASE IN POINT

There is one miracle done by Jesus that is found in all four Gospels. The feeding of the five thousand is recorded for us in Matthew, Mark, Luke, and John, but the fullest treatment of it is found in John, due in part to his account of the subsequent reaction of the people to it.

Their first response to the great miracle is stated in John 6:14 "Therefore when the people saw the sign which He had performed, they said, 'This is truly the Prophet who is to come into the world.'" However, the nature of their appreciation of the sign is laid out for us in the verses that follow. We read in John 6:15 that "they were intending to come and take Him by force to make Him king." Jesus withdrew from them and, soon after, crossed the Sea of Galilee to Capernaum. The next day the crowds caught up with Him and said, "Rabbi, when did You get here" (John 6:25)?

Jesus responds to them by coming right to the point, "Truly, truly, I say to you, you seek Me, not because you saw signs, but because you ate of the loaves and were filled. Do not work for the food which perishes, but for the food which endures to eternal life, which the Son of Man will give to you, for on Him the Father, God, has set His seal" (John 6:26-27).

In other words, their interest in Jesus was confined to the realm of the physical. They appreciated the banquet of food that He had provided for them, but they showed no interest in relating to Him as the One who could satisfy their spiritual needs. Jesus admonishes them to seek out the spiritual food that endures to eternal life (Matthew 6:27).

HIS HOMETOWN MINISTRY

From a human point of view, His hometown ministry seemed to be a failure.

We read in Mark 6 that "He could do no miracles there except that He laid His hands on a few sick people and healed them" (Mark 6:5). And then Mark says, "And He wondered at their unbelief" (Mark 6:6).

According to Mark's account the people of Nazareth were amazed, not only by His teaching, but by His miracles. We read in verses 2-4 of Mark 6:

> When the Sabbath came, He began to teach in the synagogue; and the many listeners were astonished, saying, "Where did this man get these things, and what is this wisdom given to Him, and such miracles as these performed by His hands. Is not this the carpenter, the son of Mary, and brother of James and Joses and Judas and Simon? Are not His sisters here with us?" And they took offense at Him. (Mark 6:2-4)

For some reason, "they took offense at Him saying, "Is he not a common worker with his hands like the rest of us" (Mark 6:2)? "They saw no reason to believe that he was different from them, much less that he was specially anointed by God."[79]

Our point here is that the miracles of Jesus did not command their faith. Again, we note the statement of Mark 6:6., "And He wondered at their unbelief."

But what is meant by Mark's statement that "He could do no miracles there..." (Mark 6:5). John Wesley, in his *Explanatory Notes* writes:

> It being inconsistent with his wisdom to work them there, where it would not promote his great end; and with his goodness, seeing he well knew his countrymen would reject whatever evidence could be given them, and

---

[79] NIV Study Bible, (Grand rapids, Michigan: Zondervan, 1985), p. 1504.

therefore to have given them more evidence, would have only increased their damnation.[80]

While He could physically perform more miracles there, He could not do so in accordance with His wisdom. In that sense He could not give them any more authenticating signs, yet out of compassion He could lay "hands on a few sick people" (Mark 6:5) and heal them.

THE APOSTLE PAUL SUMS IT UP.

To sum up what has been thematic in our consideration of this subject so far, we quote the words of Paul as found in I Corinthians 1:22: "For indeed Jews ask for signs and Greeks search for wisdom, but we preach Christ crucified, to Jews a stumbling block and to Gentiles foolishness." The Greek verb translated "demand" can certainly be taken that way, and in accordance with what we have seen in the Gospel accounts, should be taken that way. No matter what evidence Jesus had already provided, they never stopped asking for signs. It seems that they could not or would not believe the signs that Jesus did.

BUT SOME DID BELIEVE.

After declaring that "…we preach Christ crucified, to Jews a stumbling block and to Gentiles foolishness" (I Cor. 1:23). he goes on to say, "but to those who are called, both Jews and Greeks, Christ the power of God and the wisdom of God" (I Corinthians 1:23-24). We take note now of the fact that there were some who did respond to the miracles of Christ in a positive way. The impression given by the passages we have considered is that those who responded in a positive way to the miracles of Christ were in the minority. There are several passages that speak of people believing in Christ in connection with the miracles that took place.

---

[80] John Wesley, *John Wesley's Explanatory Notes on The Whole Bible*, (e-Sword, Rick Meyers).

HE TURNED THE WATER INTO WINE.

The first miracle that took place, according to John's Gospel, took place in Cana of Galilee. After He turned the water into wine at a wedding feast, we have these words: "This beginning of His signs Jesus did in Cana of Galilee, and manifested His glory, and His disciples believed in Him" (John 2:11). Without question the faith of the disciples is connected with that first miracle. However, we should not lose sight of all that takes place as recorded in the first chapter of John. John the Baptist is preaching and testifying as to the person of Jesus. In John 1:29 we read, "The next day he saw Jesus coming to him and said, 'Behold, the Lamb of God who takes away the sin of the world!'" That message, which points to His forthcoming sacrifice on the Cross, is repeated in verse 36, of John chapter one, "Behold, the Lamb of God!" John the Baptist says in John 1:24, "I myself have seen, and have testified that this is the Son of God."

In the verses immediately following, we have the account of how several of the first disciples of Jesus responded to the message of John and began to follow Jesus. In response to the words, "Behold, the Lamb of God" (John 1:36), two disciples, who had heard Him speak, began to follow Jesus (John 1: 37). One of the two was Andrew, brother to Simon Peter. Andrew testified about Jesus to Peter (John 1:41). Then we read of Philip who took the message to Nathanael. Nathanael said, "Rabbi, You are the Son of God; You are the King of Israel" (John 1:49). "Jesus answered and said to him, 'Because I said to you that I saw you under the fig tree, do you believe? You will see greater things than these'" (John 1:50).

THE PREACHING OF THE CROSS

The order of events presented in this passage would seem to be of vital importance. First, there is the preaching of the Cross. We do not mean to say that these disciples had an understanding or perception of that which would take place at Calvary. But when John preaches, "Behold, the Lamb of God who takes away the sin of the world" (John1:29) the message of Christ crucified is inherent in that announcement. Whatever their comprehension of what John was preaching, they did respond to it. They began to follow Jesus and to recruit others to follow Him. In

John 1:49 we read of Nathanael's statement of faith, "Rabbi, You are the Son of God; You are the King of Israel" (John 1:49). First the message is preached. Secondly, the disciples respond to that message with, at least, some degree of faith. To what degree their faith had matured, we do not know, but they are certainly moving in the right direction. And finally, in this passage, there is the promise of a display of "greater things (John 1:50." The implied promise to Nathanael is that signs and supernatural wonders would be forthcoming.

Yes, we read in chapter two that the disciples believed in response to the first miracle that Jesus did, but can't we say that they had already displayed some faith in Him? Could we, perhaps, say the same of Nicodemus? In chapter three of John verse 2 we read, "...this man came to Jesus by night and said to Him, 'Rabbi, we know that You have come from God as a teacher; for no one can do these signs that You do unless God is with him.'" Certainly, Nicodemus is responding to the miracles of Jesus in a positive way. However, we do not know when he began to seek God, before or after he saw a miracle. His is an interesting case, because, as a religious leader ("ruler of the Jews" (John 3:1), he is seen in marked contrast to the Pharisees and Sadducees who attributed the miracles of Jesus to Beelzebul. Nevertheless, we have to say that Nicodemus was properly impressed by the miracles which Jesus had done. He looks upon them as evidence that God was with Him (John 3:2).

BELIEVERS AT JERUSALEM

Once again, the apostle John in his Gospel proves to be helpful with regard to the subject we are considering. He writes in chapter two:

> Now when He was in Jerusalem at the Passover, during the feast, many believed in His name, observing His signs which He was doing. But Jesus, on His part, was not entrusting Himself to them, for He knew all men. And because He did not need anyone to testify concerning man, for He Himself knew what was in man. (John 2:23-25)

John informs us that many people in Jerusalem believed in His name as they observed the signs that were taking place. But then, that statement is qualified by the next verse that tells us that Jesus did not necessarily believe in them (John 2:24). John implies that Jesus knew that, with regard to many of them, the faith was not genuine. This connects with a passage found toward the end of chapter six where we read, "'But there are some of you who do not believe,' For Jesus knew from the beginning who they were who did not believe, and who it was that would betray Him. And He was saying to them, 'For this reason I have said to you, that no one can come to Me unless it has been granted him from the Father.' As a result of this many of His disciples withdrew and were not walking with Him anymore" (John 6:64-66).

FAITH BEYOND THE JORDAN

There is a passage of great interest found at the end of John chapter ten. It is a very different story, one in which there is the development of faith apart from miracles. We read in verses 40-42 of John chapter ten.

> And He went away again beyond the Jordan to the place where John was first baptizing, and He was staying there. Many came to Him and were saying, "While John performed no sign, yet everything John said about this man was true." Many believed in Him there (John 10,40-42).

This testimony to faith seems to be quite different from much of that which we have been considering in the Gospel of John. The impression is given, I believe, that the faith of these people was genuine. They had not responded to miracles performed for them. They stated that John had performed no sign, but they had come to believe that what John said about Jesus was true.

We are led to believe, from what John tells us throughout his Gospel, that this is the better way – coming to faith in response to the Word preached.

MORE THAN A PROPHET

In a moving tribute to John the Baptist, Jesus declares that "among those born of women there has not arisen *anyone* greater than John the Baptist" (Matthew 11:11). He states that John was not only a prophet, but "more than a prophet" (Matthew 11:9). How are we to interpret these words?

D.A. Carson, in a writing entitled "The Purpose of Signs and Wonders in the New Testament," comments on this passage. In what sense was John more than a prophet? He writes, "The Baptist is more than prophet, Jesus insists, because John not only spoke the Word of God, but was someone of whom the Word of God spoke."[81] Quoting

Malachi 3:1, Jesus points out that Malachi, the Old Testament prophet, wrote about John saying, "I will send my messenger ahead of you, who will prepare your way before you" (Matthew 11:10). Therefore, John was more than a prophet – destined to have a place of higher privilege than all the other Old Testament prophets.

NONE GREATER

D. A. Carson goes on to deal with another intriguing declaration concerning John. In His tribute to the Baptist Jesus says, "Truly I say to you, among those born of women there has not arisen *anyone* greater than John the Baptist! Yet the one who is least in the kingdom of heaven is greater than he" (Matthew 11:11). Carson writes:

> The second part of the verse shows that Jesus means John is the greatest born of woman *up to that time*. From the time of the kingdom onward, John is outstripped in greatness by the least in the kingdom. Still, the first part of the verse must have raised a few eyebrows in the first century. It means that in the evaluation of Jesus John the Baptist is

---

[81] D.A. Carson, "The Purpose of Signs and Wonders in The New Testament," *Power Religion, The Selling Out of The Evangelical Church*, Ed. Michael Scott Horton (Chicago: Moody Press, 1992), p. 106.

greater than Moses, greater than King David, greater than
Isaiah or Jeremiah, greater than Solomon. Why?

It may be a minor point to bring out, but we ask, is Jesus saying that
John was the greatest up to that time, or that there had been none greater?
Carson concurs with those scholars of the Greek who suggest the meaning
of the idiom is "greater."[82] Either way, the statement is remarkable when we
think of those who had gone before, men venerated by the people of Israel,
people of faith such as Abraham, Moses, David, and Elijah.

In what sense was the tribute of Jesus true of John? D.A. Carson
interprets the passage in a good and logical way, I believe. He argues that
the greatness of John had to do with position and privilege. To him was
given the privilege of pointing Jesus out more clearly than any who had
gone before. Many had pointed to Jesus in one way or another in the past,
but John was pointing to Jesus "in time, on the plane of history, before
his peers."[83] The privilege of giving testimony to the person of Christ more
clearly than all who had gone before, lifted him into the realm of true
greatness. Carson observes the peculiar nature of this tribute to John in
that "He is in fact using John to point afresh to Himself."[84]

Concerning the next statement of the passage, that "...the one who
is least in the kingdom of heaven is greater than he" (Matthew 11:11), it
should be understood that the standard of greatness remains the same.
It seems logical to assume that. If John's greatness had to do with his
position of being able to witness clearly to the person of Christ, even so the
greatness of those in the new age has to do with the privilege of pointing
to the person and work of Christ with clarity. After the "Lamb of God"
has been sacrificed on the Cross, after His resurrection from the grave,
after the coming of the Holy Spirit on the Day of Pentecost, and after the
completion of the New Testament Scripture, we are able to give testimony
to Jesus Christ with far more clarity than did John.

Most modern versions translate: "he that is least." Even if that is
technically correct, it may be that the sense is, "but little." Generally
speaking, even the least of us in our day can exceed in privilege that of

---

[82] A.T. Robertson, *Word Pictures in the New Testament*, (e-Sword, Rich Meyers).

[83] Carson, p. 107.

[84] Ibid., p. 107.

John. We know so much more and can, therefore, testify more clearly as to His person and work.

D.A. Carson sums up his argument:

> All of us live this side of the cross and resurrection; none of us is slow to affirm that Jesus is simultaneously the conquering king and the suffering servant, the Davidic king and the priest in the order of Melchizedek, the sovereign Lord and the bleeding sacrifice, the crucified Messiah and the resurrected Savior. That which establishes the Christian's greatness: to us has been given the indescribably great privilege of bearing witness to Jesus' person and work. It does not depend on performing miracles, as John the Baptist's greatness did not depend on performing miracles (John 10:40-42): it depends on the privilege of knowing God in Christ Jesus, this side of the cross and resurrection, this side of the dawning of the promised kingdom.[85]

SIGNS AND WONDERS IN THE EARLY CHURCH

Without question, the manifestation of signs and wonders was a prominent phenomenon in the life of the early church. We read of it time and time again. "Everyone kept feeling a sense of awe; and many wonders and signs were taking place through the apostles" (Acts 2:43). "At the hands of the apostles many signs and wonders were taking place among the people; and they were all in one accord in Solomon's portico" (Acts 5:12). Being threatened by persecution from the authorities they prayed, "And now, Lord, take note of their threats and grant that Your bond-servants may speak Your word with all confidence, while You extend your hand to heal, and signs and wonders take place through the name of Your holy servant Jesus" (Acts 4:29-30).

Further on in the books of Acts we read concerning Paul and Barnabas, "Therefore they spent a long time *there* speaking boldly *with reliance* upon

---

[85] Carson, pp. 107-108.

the Lord, who was testifying to the word of His grace, granting that signs and wonders be done by their hands" (Acts14:3). Writing to the Corinthian church, Paul, referring to himself declares, "The signs of a true apostle were performed among you with all perseverance, by signs and wonders and miracles" (II Cor. 12:12). Compare also: Acts 6:8; 8:3; 15:12; and Romans 15:19.

There is some indication that, while most of the references to signs and wonders are tied to the ministry of the apostles, others were involved as well. Galatians 3:5 may be indicative of that. "So then, does He who provides you with the Spirit and works miracles among you, do it by the works of the Law, or by hearing with faith?"

A MATTER OF CONFIRMATION

In the second chapter of the book of Hebrews we have a passage that is explanatory, I believe, of the scriptures just quoted. Verses 3 and 4 of Hebrews 2 would seem to be central with regard to our understanding of that which took place in the early church. We read:

> …how will we escape if we neglect so great a salvation? After it was at the first spoken through the Lord, it was confirmed to us by signs and wonders and by various miracles and by gifts of the Holy Spirit according to His own will. (Hebrews 2: 3-4)

The author of Hebrews writes from the perspective of being one generation removed from the ministry of Jesus. Those who heard the teaching of Jesus, passed on the message of salvation to the next generation of believers as they were enabled by God to perform signs, wonders, various miracles, and gifts of the Holy Spirit. He says that God was testifying with them through the means of the miraculous display of His power.

Now the question is: Are we to seek to do the same? Can we expect God to testify to the world through us by means of signs and wonders? With regard to the grouping of spiritual gifts found in I Corinthians 12, we have said that they might be regarded as foundational gifts. We do find listed there "the effecting of miracles," along with the gift of tongues, the interpretation of tongues, gifts of healings, etc., These gifts, we suggested, are foundational, in that they were given with respect to the authority and ministry of the apostles as the early church is being established. In a previous chapter we traced the argument of the book of Acts with respect to the gift of tongues, noting how important it was for Jewish believers to accept Gentiles believers into the church of Christ. The foundational value of the gift of tongues there is easy to see. Might not that foundational aspect be applied to those other spiritual gifts as well?

We have also noted that Paul's list of spiritual gifts in Romans 12 does not include those just mentioned. Could it be that, in writing Romans 12, Paul is looking beyond the days of the foundation of the Church to subsequent days, during which those gifts would not have the same value?

BUT WHAT ABOUT JOHN 20:31?

There may be some who, after reading the above material, would call our attention to the verses found at the end of John, chapter 20:

> Therefore. many other signs Jesus also performed in the presence of the disciples, which are not written in this book; but these have been written so that you may believe that Jesus is the Christ, the Son of God, and that believing you may have life in His name" (John 20:30-31).

We speak now with regard to various Christian groups, the people of which sincerely believe that miracles are important for our day as an aid to evangelism. Their ministries are very much centered in miracles such as healing, exorcism, and prophetic revelations. John H. Armstrong, writing about the views of the Vineyard movement, says, "*The signs and wonders present in Jesus' ministry are to be regarded as power encounters and as normative.*"[86] He quotes from a book entitled *Power Evangelism*, by John Wimber and Paul Cain Springer. "Wimber calls signs and wonders 'the calling cards of the kingdom,'" and writes in reference to the inauguration

---

[86] John H. Armstrong, "In Search of Spiritual Power," Power Religion, *The Selling Out of The Evangelical Church*, Ed. Michael Scott Horton, (Chicago: Moody Press, 1992), p. 68.

and the consummation of the kingdom of God: 'This explains the twofold pattern of Christ's ministry, repeated wherever he went: first proclamation, then demonstration. First, he preached repentance and the good news of the kingdom of God. Then he cast out demons, healed the sick, raised the dead —which proves he was the presence of the kingdom, the Anointed One.'"[87]

In response to this kind of thinking, James M. Boice has written an essay entitled,

"A Better way: The Power of the Word and Spirit." He writes:

> Let me reiterate that I believe in miracles. I believe that God answers prayer in healing the sick. I believe that there is such a thing as demon possession and exorcisms, particularly in areas of the world saturated with paganism, such as those targeted by pioneer missionaries. But if I believed that casting out demons and performing healings was the way to do evangelism, what would I do? I would go around looking for a lot of demons to cast out, or I would begin to interpret demonism to include a lot of other things I encountered.[88]

Let us now bring John 20:30-31 into the argument. Do not these two verses lend support to the view of some that signs and wonders are an aide to evangelism -- "… these (signs) have been written so that you may believe that Jesus is the Christ, the Son of God; and that believing you may have life in His name" (John 20:3131)?

The answer to that question is found in the wording of the text itself. John says, "…these things are written…" His purpose in writing is that the reader may respond to his account of the life and ministry of Jesus, which included many signs. We have, in the forgoing pages, noted that with the exception of a small minority, people did not respond in a positive way to the miracles performed by Jesus. It was important for Him to do those

---

[87] Ibid., p. 68.

[88] James M. Boice, "A Better Way: "The Power of The Word and Spirit," Power Religion, The Selling Out of The evangelical Church, ed. Michael Scott Horton, (Chicago: Moody Press, 1992), p. 128.

miracles, on the one hand to authenticate His claims and on the other hand to minister in compassion to those who were hurting. With respect to those of us living in the twenty first century, we respond to what is written about Christ. We read of His miracles. We do not witness them first hand. We believe because of the power of the preaching of the Word, as executed by the Holy Spirit.

Paul writes:

> For the word of the cross is foolishness to those who are perishing, But to us who are being saved it is the power of God. ... For indeed Jews ask for signs and Greeks search for wisdom; but we preach Christ crucified, to Jews a stumbling block and to Gentiles foolishness, But to those who are the called, both Jews and Greeks, Christ the Power of God and the wisdom of God (I Corinthians 1:18-24).

GREATER THINGS

There is a problematic verse of scripture that, nevertheless, has been something of a standard proof text for many in the Vineyard movement and for many others through the years. In John chapter 14 Jesus says, "Truly, truly, I say unto you, he who believes in Me, the works that I do, he will do also; and greater *works* than these he will do; because I go to the Father" (John 14:12). To be noticed is the fact that the word "works" which follows the word "greater," is in italics, indicating that it is not in the Greek text. Perhaps it should be translated "greater things."

Many interpreters of Scripture have found this verse difficult to explain. When we think of all the signs and wonders that Jesus performed, such as stilling the storm, walking on water, feeding five thousand people from the food in a boy's lunch and bringing back to life a man who had been in the grave four days, it is difficult to imagine how anything the followers of Jesus might do could even equal, let alone, exceed the magnitude of what He did. What then does Jesus mean by "greater things?"

Adam Clarke, in his commentary, notes that some account for the greater works by referring to some of the events that we read of in the book of Acts. We read there that on one occasion the very shadow of Peter healed the diseased (Acts 5:15). According to a verse in chapter 19 "diseases were cured, and demons cast out, by applying to the persons handkerchiefs and aprons that had before touched the body of Paul" (Acts 19:12).[89] By the word of Peter, Ananias and Sapphira were struck dead. Elymas the sorcerer was struck blind by the word of Paul. After thus referring to what some have said Clark suggests the following:

> Christ only preached in Judea, and in the language only of that country; but the apostles preached through the most of the then known world, and in all the languages of all countries. But let it be remarked that all this was done by the power of Christ; and I think it still more natural to attribute the greater works to the greater number of conversions made under the apostles' ministry.[90]

Albert Barnes writes in a similar vein:

> Interpreters have been at a loss in what way to understand this. The most probable meaning of the passage is the following: The word "greater" cannot refer to the miracles themselves, for the works of the apostles did not exceed those of Jesus in power. ... But, though not greater in themselves considered, yet they were greater in their effects. They made a deeper impression on mankind. They were attended with more extensive results. They were the means of the conversion of more sinners. The works of Jesus were confined to Judea. They were seen by few. The works of the Apostles were witnessed by many nations, and the effect of their miracles and preaching was that thousands from among the Jews and the Gentiles were converted to the Christian faith. The word "greater" here is used, therefore, not to denote the absolute exertion of

---

[89] Adam Clarke, *Adam Clarke's Commentary on the Bible*, (e-Sword, Rich Meyers, 2008).
[90] Ibid., e-Sword.

power, but the effect which the miracles would have on mankind. The word "works" here probably denotes not merely miracles, but all things that the apostles did that made an impression on mankind, including their travels, their labors, their doctrine, etc.[91]

The most common suggestion of the commentators seems to be the one represented in John Gill's commentary. He writes that the word "greater" does not mean, "greater in nature and kind, but more in number; for the apostles, in a long series of time, and course of years, went about preaching the Gospel, not in Judea only, but in all the world; 'God also bearing them witness with signs and wonders, and divers miracles and gifts of the Holy Ghost', Heb.2:4, wherever they went...."[92]

D.A. Carson, on the other hand, declares that it can't mean more in number. He writes, "it cannot simply mean more works: the church will do more things than Jesus did. There are perfectly good ways to say that sort of thing in Greek, and John did not choose any of them."[93]

BECAUSE I GO TO THE FATHER

These are the words found at the end of John 14:12. They convey to us the reason why Jesus uses the word "greater." That clause, or its equivalent, is found several times in the verses and chapters which follow in this, the Lord's Upper Room Discourse. We find it at verse 28 of John 14: "You have heard that I said to you, 'I go away, and I will come to you.' If you loved Me you would have rejoiced *because I go to the Father*, for the Father is greater than I" [Emphasis mine].

Verse 7 of John chapter 16 is very helpful to an understanding of that which is implied in the clause: "But I tell you the truth, it is to your advantage that I go away; for if I do not go away, the Helper will not come to you; but if I go, I will send Him to you."

The significant context of Jesus departure is that of the advent of the

---

[91] Albert Barnes, *Albert Barns' Notes on The Bible*, (e-Sword, Rick Meyers, 2008).
[92] John Gill, *John Gill's Exposition of the Entire Bible, (e-Sword, Rich Meyers, 2008)*.
[93] Carson, p. 108.

Holy Spirit to indwell the Church and the individual believer. We read in verse 8 that when the Helper comes He will "convict the world concerning sin and righteousness and judgment" (John 16:8). We find the clause again in John 16:10, "and concerning righteousness, *because I go to the Father* and you no longer see Me;" [Italics mine].

All of this is to say that when Jesus speaks in this discourse of going to the Father, He has in mind that which comes next, the coming of the Holy Spirit.

MARY MAGDALENE

This sequence of events can be seen also, I believe, in the post-resurrection appearance of Jesus to Mary Magdalene on that first Easter morning. There stands Mary, standing outside the tomb and weeping. Her focus is that of the dead body of Jesus. She says to the one she supposes to be a gardener, "Sir, if you have carried Him away, tell me where you have laid Him, and I will take Him away" (John 20:15). When Jesus reveals Himself to her by the sound of His voice speaking her name, she immediately begins to cling to Him.

Jesus says, "Stop clinging to Me, for I have not yet ascended to the Father; but go to My brethren and say to them, 'I ascend to My Father and your Father, and My God and your God" (John 20:17).

The Apostle John records these words, making a connection, I believe, to what we have just considered in the Upper Room Discourse. The words, "because I go to the Father" (John 14:28) seem say in effect that He hasn't ascended yet, but soon will. Mary is told to go and tell the others that what He had spoken of is about to happen. Mary has been very much occupied with the physical. But when He goes to the Father the Holy Spirit will come and by means of the indwelling Spirit the relationship will be spiritual, not physical. So, she is to stop clinging to His physical body. She is to go and tell the disciples that the era of the Spirit is soon to begin."

THE PRIMARY WORK OF THE SPIRIT

When Jesus begins to teach his disciples concerning the coming of the Holy Spirit, He refers to Him as, "the Spirit of truth" (John 14:17). Just before this He has said, "I am the way, the truth and the life" (John 14:6). It would seem that verses 12-15 of John chapter sixteen speak of the primary work of the Holy Spirit:

> I have many more things to say to you, but you cannot bear *them* now. But when He, the Spirit of truth, comes, He will guide you into all truth; for He will not speak on His own initiative, but whatever He hears, He will speak; and He will disclose to you what is to come. He will glorify Me, for He will take of Mine and disclose *it* to you. All things that the Father has are Mine; therefore, I said that He takes of Mine and will disclose *it* to you. (John 16:12-15)

Jesus says, "He will glorify Me." That, I believe is the primary work of the Spirit of God. Of interest, also, are the words of John 16:25-26: "These things I have spoken to you in figurative language; an hour is coming when I will no longer speak to you in figurative language, but will tell you plainly of the Father. In that day you will ask in My Name, and I do not say to you that I will request of the Father on your behalf."

To what future hour does He refer? In that day they will be praying to the Father in His Name. He must be referring to the forthcoming teaching ministry of the Holy Spirit. After He goes to the Father, the Holy Spirit will come. The Holy Spirit, operating in the hearts and minds of believers will be teaching truth and, most importantly, glorifying Jesus Christ. Those believers will be praying and accomplishing things in His name, that is to say, in the realm of the Spirit. There is a miracle performed by Peter, as found in Acts chapter three. It is the healing of the lame beggar. Peter said to this man, "I do not possess silver and gold, but what I do have I give to you: In the name of Jesus Christ the Nazarene – walk" (Acts 3:6).

GREATER IN CLARITY

What then is the greatness that Jesus speaks of when He says, "Greater things will you do?" I am indebted to D.A. Carson on this point and submit to the reader that it has to do with the Spirit's glorification of Christ with a greater clarity than was realized before the coming of that Spirit. Carson has put it this way:

> But in the wake of Jesus' glorification and the descent of the Spirit (themes that dominate chaps. 14-17), the words and deeds of Jesus followers, empowered by the Spirit of truth, the Paraclete, will take on a clarity, and thus a "greatness," that necessarily eluded some of Jesus' words and deeds in the period before the Cross. The words and signs of Jesus could not be as effective before the cross as they become after, when they are reported, in the wake of Jesus' exaltation and His gift of the Spirit. In the same way, Jesus' followers perform "greater things" (the expression is ambiguous enough to include more than miracles), precisely because they belong to the period of greater clarity, of less ambiguous witness to Jesus.[94]

The reader may recall that this same standard of greatness was discussed in reference to the ministry of John the Baptist and those who are little in the kingdom of God (Matthew 11:9-11). It has to do with the matter of pointing to and lifting up our Savior in a way that was not possible before the cross.

So then, the words of John 14:12 do not speak of the exercise of spectacular miracles that are greater than those performed by Jesus. It has to do with the world-wide work of the Spirit whereby believers are enabled to glorify Jesus, whether in word or deed, in a way that was not possible before the ascension of the Savior and the advent of that Spirit to His Church.

---

[94] Carson, p. 109.

SIXTEEN WEEKS AT MADISON SQUARE GARDEN

Not long ago I watched and listened to George Beverly Shea as he was being interviewed on a television program. Ninety-eight years old at the time of the interview he made reference to a Billy Graham crusade that had taken place back in the 1950's. Night after night, for sixteen weeks, crowds of people poured into Madison Square Garden to attend a Gospel-preaching service. I had forgotten just how phenomenal those days were. I was there for one of those meetings and listened as Mr. Shea sang, "I'd Rather Have Jesus." I watched as Billy Graham preached the Gospel. I watched and prayed as hundreds of people went forward in response to the invitation.

There were no signs and wonders in evidence. It was not a healing service. But it seemed obvious, not only to myself, but to many others that the Holy Spirit was moving in an extraordinary way. Again, I point out that this went on night after night for *sixteen weeks* in the heart of New York city. The message was clear. "The Bible says." And it was all about Jesus. The Holy Spirit was doing "greater things" as the name of Jesus was lifted up with great clarity.

ONCE AGAIN, IT'S NOT THERE

With regard to the New Testament epistles, with regard to the letters that Paul, Peter, John, Jude, James, and the writer of the book of Hebrews wrote to the churches, there is no encouragement to look for *signs and wonders* in Christian life and service. There is no exhortation to seek the performance of miracles as an aide to evangelism. That is the *bottom line* of all that has been considered in this chapter. Yes, the *effecting of miracles* is listed as a spiritual gift by Paul in I Corinthians 12:10. And yes, the Corinthian church is exhorted to desire the "greater gifts" (I Cor. 12:31), with the emphasis being upon the gift of prophecy as opposed to the gift of tongues (I Cor. 14:1). We have in these pages expressed our opinion that the gift of *miracles* is one of those we can call *foundational gifts*, gifts which had a definite purpose for the infant church, but are not included among those listed by Paul in Romans 12:6-8. Whatever view might be taken in the controversy surrounding spiritual gifts, whether one agrees with us or not, the fact remains that the subject of *signs and wonders* are not a matter of emphasis in the Epistles or encouraged at all.

Again, we are not saying that miracles do not happen. We would not limit what God is doing around the world or will do in the future. Rather, we seek to draw a contrast between what seems to be all-important to some and that which is found in the Letters to the Churches. While it may be a matter of great interest to some, the practice of *signs and wonders* is not exhorted or encouraged in that body of Scripture known as the Epistles. Especially to be noted, with regard to this chapter, is the fact that nowhere in those last twenty- two books of the New Testament are we enjoined to regard signs and wonders as the power required for effective evangelism.

CHAPTER THIRTEEN

END TIME TEACHING

We Are Not Paranoid

On a page entitled, "TO THE READER," Charles C. Ryrie writes the following by way of introduction to his Study Bible: "The Bible is the greatest of all books; to study it is the noblest of all pursuits; to understand it, the highest of all goals."[95] That statement is certainly true with regard to the study of the Prophetic Word.

A NOBLE PURSUIT INDEED

To study the book of Revelation and do so in connection with the material found in Daniel, Ezekiel, Isaiah, Zechariah, Matthew 24-25, I-II Thessalonians, II Peter 3, and a number of other passages, is to be involved in the consideration of a large body of Scripture. Many Bible students -- and that includes this writer -- study these Scriptures because we enjoy seeing how it all fits together. We are edified in the faith as we see what a great system of truth it is. We are not necessarily trying to figure out if the Anti-Christ is alive and active today. We are not trying to align Scripture with every geo-political crisis that dominates the news.

---

[95] Charles Caldwell Ryrie, *The Ryrie Study Bible,* (Chicago: Moody Press, 1976), p. v.

A PRESENT PARANOIA?

On the other hand, there are some evangelical leaders who, it seems, are inclined to portray us in a negative light. They imply that those who show real interest in Eschatology (last things) are guilty of perverting or abusing good Christian doctrine. In their writings reference is usually made to all of the abuses of the past and of those who have tried to predict when the Second Coming of Christ will take place.

One writer takes a different approach. Kim Riddlebarger has written an essay entitled, "This Present Paranoia." According to Riddlebarger, those who focus on Bible prophecy are part of an evangelical sub-culture; that subculture, according to the essay, includes the writings or teachings on end times, conspiracy theories, spiritual warfare, and the New Age Movement. The common denominator for all of this subculture is a kind of paranoia. We read:

> "This world is not my home, I'm just a passing through," goes the refrain of a popular American hymn. The world is understood to be a very evil place …. The goal held out to the weary faithful is survival as unwelcome pilgrims in a world and culture that is not thought of as "home," but merely as a place to endure, to just "pass through" while awaiting the return of Christ. In the middle of all this tension many American evangelicals, not surprisingly, reflect a good degree of fear and suspicion of the world around them, a kind of paranoia if you will.[96]

May the reader be assured that the above certainly does not apply to this writer; I do not see myself as paranoid with respect to the world around me. Rather, I am fascinated by the profound nature of the Word of God as I await the coming of my Savior.

In the writing of this book we have referred to matters of emphasis which are not supported by way of exhortation or encouragement in the New Testament epistles. People write books, speak at conferences and

---

[96] Kim Riddlebarger, "This Present Paranoia," *Power Religion*, ed. Michael Scott Horton, (Chicago: Moody Press, 1992),p. 265.

counsel on subjects of Christian life and service which are not supported in the Letters to the Churches. And yet, when it comes to the study of prophecy, we are labeled as those who distort doctrine by means of over-emphasis. They imply that we give too much attention to it. This is maintained in spite of the fact that the Epistles contain a great deal by way of exhortation and encouragement with regard to the study of Eschatology.

In the section of this book that follows, Appendix II, I have listed the number of exhortations in this category as 32. Those verses contain specific exhortation or encouragement with regard to prophetic truth. The total number of verses is much greater, however, when the supporting context is taken into consideration.

THE RESURRECTED BODY

In verse 58 of I Corinthians 15 Paul says, "Therefore, my beloved brethren, be steadfast, immovable, always abounding in the work of the Lord, knowing that your toil is not *in* vain in the Lord." The first word of this specific exhortation, "therefore," comes at the end of a lengthy discourse in which the apostle writes about the fact of Christ's resurrection and the nature of the resurrected body that will be ours. That is a pattern that we see in a number of passages, whether in the epistles of Paul or Peter. First there is a presentation of prophetic truth and then follows the word, "therefore."

Over the space of 57 verses Paul speaks about the truth of Christ's resurrection and the victory that will be ours when we too will be resurrected. He includes in his discourse the revelation of a "mystery:"

> Behold, I tell you a mystery; we will not all sleep, but we will all be changed, in a moment, in the twinkling of an eye, at the last trumpet; for the trumpet will sound, and the dead will be raised imperishable, and we will be changed. For this perishable must put on the imperishable, and this mortal must put on immortality. (I Corinthians 15:51-53)

After Paul delivers a long and detailed discourse on our victory in

Christ, he gives us this specific exhortation: "...be steadfast, immovable, always abounding in the work of the Lord, knowing that your toil is not *in* vain in the Lord" (I Corinthians 15:58).

MORE ABOUT THE RAPTURE

We see again the same pattern of presentation in I Thessalonians 4. In verse 18 Paul says, "Therefore comfort one another with these words." Leading up to the word, "therefore," we find more details concerning the "mystery" that he spoke of in I Corinthians 15:51, "Behold, I tell you a mystery; we will not all sleep, but we will all be changed."

> For this we say to you by the word of the Lord, that we who are alive and remain until the coming of the Lord, will not precede those who have fallen asleep. For the Lord Himself will descend from heaven with a shout, with the voice of the archangel and with the trumpet of God, and the dead in Christ will rise first. Then we who are alive and remain will be caught up [raptured] together with them in the clouds to meet the Lord in the air, and so we shall always be with the Lord. (I Thessalonians 4:15-17)

This precious truth concerning the rapture of the church is designed to bring comfort to those who have seen loved ones go to sleep in Christ.

STAY AWAKE FOR YOUR OWN SAKE

Once again, the pattern is the same in I Thessalonians 5. The word "therefore" comes at the end of a discourse on prophetic truth. We read, "Therefore encourage one another and build up one another, just as you also are doing" (I Thessalonians 5:11). There is one difference, however, in this chapter. In the middle of his discussion about the forthcoming "day of the Lord," Paul exhorts, "so then let us not sleep as others do, "But since we are of the day, let us be sober, having put on the breastplate of faith and love, and as a helmet, the hope of salvation" (I Thessalonians 5:6,8). Paul is repetitive for the sake of emphasis.

Here we have very specific exhortation on remaining alert to the times in which we live. He says that we should be alert, and sober. We are to stay awake so that the day does not "overtake" us "like a thief in the night" (I Thess. 5:4). Again, in I Thess. 5:8 we read, "let us be sober." This passage would seem to be strong encouragement with regard to a focus on Bible prophecy.

ABOUT THE ANTICHRIST

Rather than another "therefore" we have in II Thessalonians 2 the words, "so then." "So then brethren, stand firm and hold to the traditions which you were taught, whether by word of mouth or by letter from us" (II Thessalonians 2:15). After a discourse occupying 24 verses, the apostle exhorts, "so then."

With regard to the persecution that they were experiencing, the apostle speaks about God's judgment in "dealing out retribution to those who do not know God and to those who do not obey the gospel of our Lord Jesus Christ ... when He comes to be glorified in His saints on that day ...." (II Thessalonians l: 8-10). With regard to some misinformation that had come their way Paul speaks to clarify details as to "the day of the Lord" and the manifestation of "the man of lawlessness" (II Thessalonians 2:2-4).

With a view to the affliction that they were experiencing and with a view to their confusion about certain details pertaining to end-time events, Paul writes:

> Now we request you, brethren, with regard to the coming of our Lord Jesus Christ and our gathering together to Him, that you not be quickly shaken from your composure or be disturbed either by a spirit or a message or a letter as if from us, to the effect that the day of the Lord has come. (II Thessalonians 2:1-2)

Rather than accusing them of being "paranoid," Paul calls their attention to some of the details of Bible prophecy. During my trips to the former Soviet Union I gained the impression that most Christians there, many of who had suffered real persecution, were very much interested in the subject of prophecy. I would not accuse them of being "paranoid." They had endured a good deal of *worldly* hostility.

THE COMING DAY OF THE LORD

The apostle Peter follows the same pattern in his second letter. The word "therefore" is found at verse 14: "Therefore, beloved, since you look for these things, be diligent to be found by Him in peace, spotless and blameless, and regard the patience of our Lord as salvation; …." (II Peter 3:14-15). His teaching regarding the "day of the Lord" begins at verse 3 of II Thess. chapter 3. He refers to the "mockers" who are saying, "Where is the promise of His coming?" Peter exhorts in verse 8, "Do not let this one *fact* escape your notice, beloved, that with the Lord one day is like a thousand years, and a thousand years like one day" (II Peter 3:8).

Peter's words of verses 11 and 12 of II Peter 3 would seem to be important with respect to the matter of our interest in Eschatology (last things). He asks, "… what sort of people ought you to be in holy conduct and godliness, *looking for and hastening the coming of the day of God* [emphasis mine] because of which the heavens will be destroyed by burning, and the elements will melt with intense heat" (II Peter 3:11,12)! Again, we note the words of verse 14 of II Peter 3, "Therefore, beloved, since you look for these things …." That's what we do as students of the Prophetic Word. We are looking "for these things." Our occupation with these scriptures, as stated before, helps us maintain an awareness that, indeed, our Savior will return soon.

AN APOSTOLIC BEAUTITUDE

In the first chapter of the book of Revelation we find an encouragement to study Bible prophecy, one that has in view that entire book. We read in Revelation 3:1,

Blessed is he who reads and those who hear the words of the prophecy, and heed the things which are written in it; for the time is near.

Two opinions prevail as to how we should interpret these words. John Walvoord writes on Revelation 1:3:

The prologue concludes with a blessing on each individual who reads the book as well as on those who hear it and take to heart what is written in it. The implication is that a reader will read this message aloud to an audience. Not only is there a blessing for the reader and the hearer, but there is also a blessing for those who respond in obedience.[97]

Albert Barnes, on the other hand, suggests that the blessing extends to anyone who reads and studies the book for himself in a spirit of obedience. He writes:

That is, it is to be regarded as a privilege attended with many blessings, to be permitted to mark the disclosures to be made in the book; the important revelations respecting future times. Prof. Stuart supposes that this refers to a public reading, and that the phrase "those who hear the words of the prophecy" refers to those who listened to the public reader, and that both the reader and the hearer should regard themselves as highly favored…but as this book was sent abroad to be read by Christians, and not merely to be in the hands of the ministers of religion to be read by them to others, it is more natural to interpret the words in the usual sense.[98]

It would seem that both perspectives on the promise hold true. Highly

---

[97] John F. Walvoord, "Revelation," *The Bible Knowledge Commentary*, ed. By John F. Walvoord and Roy B. Zuck, (Wheaton, Illinois: Victor Books, 1983), p. 928.
[98] Albert Barnes, *Albert Barnes' Notes on the Bible*, (e-Sword, Rick Meyers).

favored or blessed are those believers who focus on the content of the book. We find here strong encouragement to give attention to the content of "The Revelation of Jesus Christ."

A FINAL EXAM

At this point I suggest to the serious Bible student that our ability to understand a particular passage in the book of Revelation depends to a great degree upon how much and how well we remember what is set forth in the Old Testament. Much of what we find in the book should refer us back to some event, some person, or some prophecy found on the earlier pages of the Bible. In a sense then, reading the book of Revelation is like taking a final exam.

SEVEN TRUMPETS

Here is an exam question: Why does the apostle speak of "seven trumpets" in chapters 8 and 9 of Revelation? Does that terminology just come out of "the blue," so to speak, or does it come out of the Old Testament? It should only take a moment or two of reflection for most Bible students to remember that when Joshua fought the battle of Jericho, the people of Israel marched around the city seven times on the seventh day and the priests, carrying seven trumpets, blew those trumpets just before the walls came tumbling down (Joshua 6:15-16).

The Old Testament story contains some additional details which correspond to that which we find in the book of Revelation. We note first the words of Moses found in Deuteronomy 11:24, "Every place on which *the sole of your foot treads* shall be yours; your border will be from the wilderness to Lebanon, and from the river, the river Euphrates, as far as the western sea [emphasis mine]."

This promise is repeated in the first few verses of the book of Joshua. We read that the Lord instructed Joshua saying:

> "Moses My servant is dead; now therefore arise, cross this Jordan, you and all this people, to the land which I am

giving to them, to the sons of Israel. Every place on which *the sole of your foot treads*, I have given it to you, …. No man will be able to stand before you all the days of your life. Just as I have been with Moses, I will be with you; I will not fail you or forsake you. Be strong and courageous, for you shall give this people possession of the land which I swore to their fathers to give them [emphasis mine]" (Joshua 1:2-6).

The next reference to "the soles of the feet" occurs in chapter 3 as the priests lead the way to the waters of the Jordan. Joshua instructs the people of Israel concerning the crossing into the land of promise:

It shall come to pass that when *the soles of the feet* of the priests who carry the ark of the LORD, the Lord of all the earth, rest in the waters of the Jordan, the waters of the Jordan will be cut off, and the waters which are flowing down from above will stand in one heap [emphasis mine]. (Joshua 3:13)

All of this, I believe, provides us with insight as to what happened at the battle of Jericho. Why were the people of Israel commanded to march around Jericho? They did it once each day for seven days and on the seventh day, they marched around the city seven times. The priests blew their seven trumpets, the people shouted and the walls came tumbling down. It would seem that during each trip around Jericho, the people of Israel are echoing the promise given through Moses and then through Joshua. "Every place that the sole of your foot shall tread upon, that I have given to you." By marching around Jericho, Israel is laying claim to the promise. They are declaring by treading on that ground that "Jericho belongs to us. Jericho will fall to Joshua."

Before returning to the book of Revelation we mark another significant detail. The word "Joshua" corresponds to the word "Jesus." The Old Testament Hebrew word means *Jehovah is Salvation*. The word "Jesus" signifies Savior. The English word is a transliteration of the Greek word for Jesus which corresponds to the Hebrew word translated Joshua. The phenomenon is illustrated by a mistranslation of Acts 7:45 in the King

James Version. According to the New American Standard Bible, Stephen says, "And having received it in their turn, our fathers brought it in with Joshua upon dispossessing the nations whom God drove out before our fathers, until the time of David" (Acts 7 :25).

It is obvious from the context that the above translation is correct. However, the King James Version translates the Greek word as "Jesus" instead of Joshua. We suggest at this point that the equivalency of the two terms is not simply a matter of coincidence. The victory accomplished by Joshua as the captain of the Israelites is analogous to that accomplished by Jesus who is the captain of our salvation and Who is coming to take possession of planet earth.

IT LOOKS LIKE JESUS

It happens between the sounding of the sixth and seventh trumpets. According to Revelation 10:1 the apostle John sees a "strong angel coming down out of heaven, clothed with a cloud; and the rainbow was upon his head, and his face was like the sun, and his feet like pillars of fire." Commentators differ as to the identity of this great angel. Some say it is a representation of Jesus because of the description given; "his face was like the sun, and his feet like pillars of fire; …." The description resembles somewhat that of Jesus as presented in Revelation 1:12-17. Again, we might take into account the Old Testament appearances of the pre-incarnate Son of God where He is referred to as "the Angel of Jehovah."

Other commentators prefer to interpret Revelation 10:1 as describing a great angel, but not the second person of the Trinity. Whether the words designate Jesus Himself or one who represents Him, the important things to mark is what He does. Having in His hand "a little book which was open" (perhaps a reference to the seven sealed scroll of Revelation chapter 6 which is now almost completely unrolled; I take it to be the title deed to this earth), He places "his right foot on the sea and his left on the land; and he cried out…and swore by Him who lives forever and ever, WHO CREATED HEAVEN AND THE THINGS IN IT, AND THE EARTH AND THE THINGS IN IT, AND THE SEA AND THE THINGS IN IT, that there should be delay no longer" (Revelation 10: 2-6), ….

Just as Joshua led the people of Israel in conquering the land of promise by treading upon it with the "soles of their feet," so Jesus will take possession of planet earth by placing one foot on the land and one foot on the sea and declaring that "there will be delay no longer" (Revelation 10:6). After that, the seventh trumpet sounds and the walls begin to tumble.

> Then the seventh angel sounded; and there were loud voices in heaven saying, "The kingdom of the world has become *the kingdom* of our Lord and of His Christ; and He will reign forever and ever" (Rev. 10:15-16).

I submit to the reader that this is the dominant theme of the book of Revelation, Jesus Christ coming to take possession of that which He has redeemed. All this is to say that when we come to the mention of "seven trumpets" in the last book of the Bible, we should ask, "Where in the Old Testament do we find the sounding of seven trumpets?" The profound nature of the Prophetic Word can be realized in study that involves comparing the imagery found in the Apocalypse (the book of Revelation) with corresponding events and persons set forth in the Old Testament.

ELEGANT APPARELL

We present to the reader another exam question, "Who is the woman of Revelation 12:1 described as clothed with the sun, moon and twelve stars?" When we read the words, "sun, moon, and twelve stars," does that ring a bell? "Where did I read something like that?"

In Genesis chapter 37 we read of a seventeen- year old boy who had a dream. Actually, he had more than one dream. But here is the one that connects with Revelation 12:

> Now he had still another dream, and related it to his brothers, and said, "Lo, I have had still another dream; and behold, the sun and the moon and eleven stars were bowing down to me." And he related it to his father and to his brothers; and his father rebuked him and said to him, "What is this dream you have had? Shall I and your

mother and your brothers actually come to bow ourselves
down before you to the ground" (Genesis 37:9-10)?

The story in this part of Genesis—and it is a long one—is that of
Jacob and his 12 sons. Jacob, who is also called Israel, was the father of the
twelve tribes of Israel. The woman, therefore, of Revelation 12 is a symbolic
representation of the nation Israel enduring Satanic persecution in the time
of the Great Tribulation.

ANOTHER EXAM QUESTION—A DIFFICULT ONE

In the fifth chapter of Revelation we read of a special book, so special
that no one was worthy to open it except the Lion of the tribe of Judah
who is also the Lamb that was slain (Revelation 5:3-6). It is not a codex,
or a book as we think of it; it is actually a scroll that has been rolled up and
sealed seven times with some sort of a wax seal each time. Furthermore,
we read that it is "a book written inside and on the back" (Revelation 5:1).

As each seal is broken and a portion of the scroll is unrolled we read
of a great event taking place on earth. In Revelation 6:8 and following we
read of conquest, war, famine and death. Then we read about martyrdom
and great events terrorizing the earth. Our exam question is this: Is this a
scroll of judgment? Are the events that are revealed as falling upon earth
manifestations of God's judgment? In verses 16-17 of Revelation 6 we find
men crying out that a time of wrath has come:

> and they said to the mountains and to the rocks, "Fall on
> us and hide us from the presence of Him who sits on the
> throne, and from the wrath of the Lamb; for the great
> day of their wrath has come, and who is able to stand."
> (Revelation 6:16-17)

It would certainly seem that what takes place as the sixth seal is broken
is a manifestation of God's wrath, but what about the first five seals? Those
who hold to a mid-tribulation rapture position, as well as those who hold
to a pre-wrath tribulation position are inclined to say "no." The time of
God's wrath does not begin as the first seal is opened. It is not necessary,

they maintain, to hold to a position that views the rapture of the church (being caught up to meet Him in the air) as taking place before the time of the tribulation begins.

I am not inclined to pursue further the various arguments pertaining to the time of the rapture, whether it occurs before the tribulation, in the middle of it, at some point during the second half of that fearsome time, or at the end of that time. Rather, the exam question is: Are the seal judgments really judgments? Are they manifestations of God's wrath upon the people of this earth? Or, are they simply revelations of great and dire events that will take place upon this earth leading up to His Second Coming?

THE FLYING SCROLL

Our point in these pages is to suggest that the book of Revelation is a like a final exam. Our ability to answers its questions is somewhat dependent upon how much we remember about certain matters found in the Old Testament.

In the fifth chapter of Zechariah we read about a flying scroll:

> Then I lifted up my eyes again and looked, and behold, *there was* a flying scroll. And he said to me, "What do you see?" And I answered, "I see a flying scroll; its length is twenty cubits and its width ten cubits." Then he said to me, "This is the curse that is going forth over the face of the whole land; surely everyone who steals will be purged away according to the writing on one side, and everyone who swears will be purged away according to the writing on the other side. I will make it go forth," declares the LORD of hosts, "and it will enter the house of the thief and the house of the one who swears falsely by My name; and it will spend the night within that house and consume it with its timber and stones (Zechariah 5:1-4).

Important to our discussion is the fact that it is seen to be a large scroll that is going forth over the whole land, a scroll that has writing on both sides. A scroll that has writing on its two sides would seem to point ahead to the seven-sealed scroll of Revelation that has writing on both its sides (Revelation 5:1). Most important to be noted is the obvious fact that it is an instrument of judgment sent by the LORD of hosts (Zechariah 5:44). The scroll of Revelation five would seem, then, to correspond to the scroll of Zechariah five. This would seem to lend support to the thought that the seal judgments of Revelation are indeed judgments.

Our purpose in this chapter has not been to pursue all the details of Bible prophecy, but rather to suggest that the prophetic Word is a profound body of truth, worthy of our great interest and study.

WHAT ABOUT NINE ELEVEN?

After our country was attacked on September 11, 2001, people asked me about its significance relevant to the details of Bible prophecy. They asked questions like: "Is this predicted in the Bible?" "Is this the beginning of the great tribulation?" "What do you think it means?" I replied, "I don't know." I cannot connect it with any specific detail of Bible prophecy."

However, I did say something like this: "I do not believe that we were attacked principally because of our way of life or the freedom we enjoy. Rather, America is hated because America has been the best friend that Israel has in this world. They hate us because they hate Israel. They hate Israel because they hate Jesus Christ, the King of the Jews."

We noted above the woman of Revelation 12:1,2. She is there seen to be dressed with the sun, moon and the stars. Symbolically, she represents the nation Israel. We read in Rev. 12:3 of a great red dragon who "stood before the woman who was about to give birth, so that when she gave birth he might devour her child." Then we read in verse 5, of Revelation chapter 12. "And she gave birth to a son, a male child, who is to rule all the nations with a rod of iron; and her child was caught up to God and to His throne" (Revelation 12:5). But the persecution of the woman (Israel) has continued. In verse 12 of Rev.12, the dragon is identified as "the devil." In verses 14 and 15 of Rev. 12 he is "the serpent." What we saw portrayed on our television screens, over and over again, was the face of evil.

But then again, perhaps I am just paranoid. Of course, I am being facetious. I don't think I am paranoid We have noted in this chapter that by means of many verses of Scripture we are exhorted and encouraged to study the prophetic Word of God.

Matthew Henry has commented on Revelation 1:3 with these words:

> More generally, to all who either read or hear the words of the prophecy, this blessing seems to be pronounced with a design to encourage us to study this book, and not be weary of looking into it upon account of the obscurity of many things in it; it will repay the labor of the careful and attentive reader.[99]

On the subject of last things there are many exhortations for us today to be considered, in contrast to the forgoing chapters dealing with issues about which there is little or no exhortation

---

[99] Matthew Henry, *Matthew Henry's Commentary on The Whole Bible*, (e-Sword, Rick Meyers, 2008).

CHAPTER FOURTEEN

CONCLUSION

What does it all come down to?

THE BOTTOM LINE IN REVIEW

We began our consideration by asking the question, "Why Not?" If Jesus raised the dead, if Peter and Paul were used of God to raise the dead, why shouldn't we attempt to do the same? We then expanded the question so as to include other matters of the Bible narrative such as exorcism, fasting, speaking in tongues, etc. If Jesus fasted for forty days in the wilderness, should we try to do the same? We could also ask, if Jesus manifested a righteous indignation by overturning the tables of the money changers in the temple, should we consider taking similar action when it seems appropriate to do so?

The main question presented in this writing is, how do we delineate? How do we know what examples of Scripture, what commandments, instructions and admonitions are meant for us in our day? Years ago Francis Schaeffer wrote a book entitled, "How Should We Then Live?"[100] Perhaps more appropriate to our question is the title that Charles *Colson* and Nancy Pearcey gave to a more recent work, "How Now Shall We Live?"[101] After we have read all the history that is presented to us in the

---

[100] Francis A. Schaeffer, *How Should We Then Live?* 1955, (now available from Crossway Books,) title page.
[101] Charles Colson and Nancy Pearcey, *How Now Shall We Live*, Tyndale House Publishing, Inc. 1999, title page.

Old Testament, after the Gospel accounts, after the record of that time of transition found in the book of Acts, "How *Now* Shall We Live as disciples of the Lord Jesus Christ?" What exhortations and instructions are meant for God's people living in the twenty first century? What is normative for us today? The answer, we believe, is to be found in a consideration of The Bottom Line, the exhortations and instructions found in the New Testament epistles.

SOME THINGS NEVER CHANGE

Chapter two of this writing is entitled, *Some Things Never Change, But Some Things Do.* Because some things never change there is a great deal of correspondence between that which is found in the Epistles and that which is found in the rest of the Bible. The eternal moral law of God as reflected in the content of the Ten Commandments and further interpreted in "The Sermon on The Mount" does not change. Timeless truths concerning faith, humility, love, etc. are found throughout the Bible. The testing of Abraham's faith, for example, as found in the book of Genesis is worthy of much study and reflection and is very relevant to the challenges of our day. We do not want to diminish to any degree the value of any part of the Bible with respect to insights for Christian living. But we do want to recognize that while some things never change, some things do. There is sometimes a change in God's program for His people and, furthermore, some events in the Bible's narrative are not meant to be repeated in any time frame. So, how do we know what admonitions, exhortations or examples are to be applied to our lives today? We have suggested that answers are to found in a consideration of what is found in the Letters to The Churches (Romans through Revelation). The New Testament epistles present to us *The Bottom Line.* After all that has been said before, what does it all come down to?

OUR FOCUS

Again, we want to emphasize that the focus of this writing has been upon a number of subjects or issues that have been held up by some as being of central importance for Christian life and service. Books are written and sermons are delivered on matters that find no support in the writings of Paul, Peter, James or John. How is it possible, for example, that Paul, writing in some cases to Gentiles, who know very little about the Old Testament and who do not as yet have the Gospels in writing, *completely ignores* subjects that seem to some people to be of supreme importance? Our focus has been upon major points of interest as seen in Christendom today. We have not tried to deal with every issue whether great or small, but those that are a major source of distraction and confusion, some indeed being harmful to the cause of Christ.

As stated in my introductory chapter, it is my hope that this writing will be helpful to new believers who find themselves somewhat bewildered by the plethora of beliefs and practices of modern- day Christendom as well as help for Christians further along the way who desire clarification on certain issues, or help with certain seemingly awkward passages of Scripture.

THE FACTS PRESENTED

Looking into the content of the New Testament Epistles with regard to specific instructions for Christian life and service we have found the following:

1. Some matters or subjects previously found in the Scripture are not even mentioned in the Epistles.
2. Some matters are mentioned, but not exhorted.
3. One particular subject we have considered is given priority, but seemingly has changed with regard to its function.

NOT EVEN MENTIONED

First of all, the subject of *exorcism* is not even mentioned in the Epistles. It is not found among the spiritual gifts listed in Romans 12, I Corinthians 12-14, or Ephesians 4. The truth of this observation is remarkable considering the fact that the matter is so important in the ministry of Jesus. Some suggest that the gift of casting out demons is included either in the category of "gifts of healings" (I Corinthians 12:18) or that of "the effecting of miracles" (I Corinthians 12:10). I do not exclude that possibility, but it seems significant to me that something so much in evidence in the Gospel accounts is not mentioned by name in the Epistles.

Perhaps God in His foreknowledge saw a future abuse of such a gift and in His wisdom saw fit to exclude mention of it among the spiritual gifts, lest some be encouraged in that abuse. Nevertheless, the practice is not presented as normative in the Epistles.

Likewise, *fasting* as a spiritual discipline is not mentioned in any of the Epistles. The word is found in the King James rendering of I Corinthians 7:5. The NASB and NIV translations exclude the word "fasting" because its inclusion in the text is not supported by the earlier Greek manuscripts. Even if the reading of the King James Bible is accepted as valid (and some do accept it as such), verse 5 of I Corinthians 7 does not constitute an exhortation or encouragement to practice it as a spiritual discipline.

We also pointed out that the word as found in II Corinthians 12:27 simply means being hungry or going without food, though the King James translates it "fastings."

With regard to the fourth Commandment we noted that it is the only one of the ten not included as such by the writers of the Epistles. There is no exhortation or command to keep the Sabbath Day in the Letters to the Churches. We suggested that the antitype of the Old Testament type is to be realized in the spiritual Sabbath of which the author of Hebrews writes. He exhorts us in Hebrews 4:11 to "be diligent to enter into that rest." We are to rest heart and mind completely in God's provision for us at Calvary. The "works" of the believer are not to be added to that which must be realized by faith.

MENTIONED, BUT NOT EXHORTED

Secondly, we have considered some matters that are mentioned in one particular section of Scripture (I Corinthians 12-14), but are not exhorted or encouraged elsewhere in the Epistles.

In I Corinthians 12-14 the gift of *speaking in tongues* is discussed relative to the other gifts listed. It is presented as being least in value. Comparing it to the gift of *prophecy* Paul declares, "I thank God, I speak in tongues more than you all; however, in the church I desire to speak five words with my mind so that I may instruct others also, rather than ten thousand words in a tongue" (I Corinthians 14:18-19). In these chapters we find no encouragement or exhortation to seek or practice the gift.

There is no mention of it in any of the other Epistles. We do not find reference to the gift of *tongues* in places where we might expect to – in passages where the spiritual life is highlighted, such as Galatians 5:16-26 or Ephesians 5:18-21. However, we do find this exhortation about the gift of tongues: In I Corinthians 14:39 Paul says, "...forbid not to speak in tongues." However, we are not exhorted to speak in tongues.

The gifts of *effecting miracles* and *gifts of healings* are also found mentioned in that one section of Scripture, I Corinthians 12, but are not exhorted or enjoined elsewhere in the Epistles. The passage in James chapter 5 might be the one exception with regard to the *gift of healing.* It should be noted, however, that it is the elders of the local church who are to be called that they might pray for the sick. It cannot be assumed that they all had or anyone one of them had the *gift of healing.* It would seem that our statement remains true; there is no mention of the gift outside of the I Corinthian passage.

The cluster of gifts found in I Corinthians 12 – tongues, healings, effecting of miracles and others – are sometimes referred to as *foundational gifts.* They fulfilled a purpose with regard to the establishment of the early Church, before the canon of Scripture was completed. Of significance is fact that they are not mentioned among the spiritual gifts listed by Paul in Romans 12:6-8.

PROPHECY FOR TODAY

The gift of prophecy is listed in Romans 12 and I Corinthians 12 and is also one of the prominent gifts mentioned in Ephesians 4. We read:

> And he gave some as apostles, and some as prophets, and some as evangelists, and some as pastors and teachers, for the equipping of the saints for the work of service, to the building up of the body of Christ; until we all attain to the unity of the faith, and of the knowledge of the Son of

God, to a mature man, to the measure of the stature which
belongs to the fullness of Christ (Ephesians 4:11-13).

It seems quite clear that there were two kinds of prophets who served
God in Bible times. There were men like Isaiah, Daniel, Ezekiel, Peter and
Paul who received Special Revelation from God (prophets in the classic
sense). Having received such revelation they spoke before men for God and
sometimes authored books of the Bible. As many have said, it involved both
foretelling (predicting the future) and *forthtelling* (preaching the messages
they had received from God).

In the book of Acts we read of a second class of prophets, men like
Agabus (Acts 11:28) and the four daughters of Phillip (Acts 21:9) the
evangelist. They apparently served a purpose with regard to the needs of
the early church.

We asked the question, if there were two classes of prophets referred
to in Scripture, why not a third? If a man stands up before people today,
completed Bible in hand, and preaches forth the Word, can he be called
a prophet? I believe so. Paul's inclusion of the gift of prophecy in Romans
12 would seem to support that thought.

A HOPE FOR FREEDOM

It is my sincere hope that a degree of freedom will be realized by those
who read these pages. Much of what has been written might seem to be
negative. Chapters have been devoted to areas of Christian life and service
which do not find emphasis (and sometimes even mention) in the New
Testament Epistles. My prayer, however, is that there will be a positive
effect.

I pray that God's people will find freedom to feel normal in their
devotion to God. While having knowledge of the many exhortations
that are found in the Epistles (see the 54 categories of exhortation in
the appendix), they will not feel intimidated by some book or some
motivational speaker who suggests that they are missing something in
their Christian life because they are not, for example, fasting or speaking
in tongues.

Furthermore, God's people should be able to rest in a realization of the profound nature of the Word of God. For this reason, we have endeavored to explain several passages of Scripture. Why are certain matters not found in the Epistles? Why did Jesus fast for 40 days? Why was the Lord God so strict with regard to keeping the Jewish Sabbath? We suggested that Jesus fasted in the wilderness so as to mourn the forthcoming separation from a loved One. As the sins of the world were laid on Him at Calvary, He cried out, "My God, My God, why have you forsaken me" (Matthew 27:46)? He fasted in anticipation of that dreadful moment.

Finally, as the writer of Hebrews puts it, "So there remains a Sabbath rest for the people of God" (Hebrews 4:9). As God gave the fourth commandment to the people of Israel in the days of Moses, He strictly prohibited the occurrence of any kind of work taking place on that day. His people were to completely rely on His provision for them. This anticipated what God would do for us on that Cross. His Son was to perfectly atone for our sins. This work of Christ accomplished for us at Calvary a spiritual rest. It is a Sabbath rest that we should all learn to enjoy.

THE STRANGE CASE OF SAINT ANTHONY

A book entitled "The 100 Most Important Events in Christian History" tells the story of a man who was one of the first Christian hermits. He was born in Egypt of well-to-do parents around 250 A.D. They died when was he was about twenty, leaving him all their possessions. He took very seriously the words of Jesus given to the rich young ruler. "If you would be perfect, go and sell all that you have...(Luke 18:22). As the writers of the book tell us, that changed his life. He sold everything and gave the money to the poor." The above –mentioned book goes on to say that an elderly Christian taught him the joys of self-denial. "He lived on one meal a day of bread and water and slept on the bare ground."

With the conversion of Emperor Constantine life became easier for believers in Christ when he recognized and legalized Christianity. With that, many started to compromise on their life-style. Not Anthony, he chose to fight back against such behavior by choosing to withdraw from the world even further. He decided to live in a cave. After twelve years there, struggling, as Athanasius, his biographer says, "with demons who took the shapes of various strange beasts,' he finally emerged victorious.

CONCLUSION

Desiring to withdraw further from the world he moved into an abandoned fort. He lived there for twenty years without ever seeing a human face, while people threw to him food over the walls. As time passed, numbers of people heard of his great self-denial and were drawn to him. Finally, during the days when Emperor Maximian was persecuting Christian for their faith, Anthony left his home to minister to believers who were condemned to work in the imperial mines. Later in 350 A.D. he again left home to defend orthodoxy against the Arian heresy. He died at the age of one hundred five.

Saint Anthony was regarded and remembered by many as a wonderful godly man. "Before long the idea that a real spiritual warrior became a monk and denied himself took hold within the church."

The life of Saint Anthony was remarkable and his story is very interesting. But I wonder if he would have lived a little differently if he had considered the normal Christian life as taught by Peter, Paul, John and other writers of the New Testament Epistles. 105

APPENDIX I

Additional Thoughts on Hebrews Six and Ten

It might seem to be a strange expression. Why is it said of those who had left the fellowship of believers that they "again crucify to themselves the Son of God and put Him to open shame" (Hebrews 6:6)? Most would agree, I believe, that one does not normally think of it in that way. When someone turns away from the Faith we do not say that they have or are crucifying the Son of God. As we see it they simply choose not to believe in Christ or refuse to acknowledge the value of Calvary as applied to their lives.

We suggest that the answer to the above question can be found in a careful study of Acts two and three. A quotation from the NIV Study Bible reminds us concerning the recipients of the letter to the Hebrews:

> The letter was addressed primarily to Jewish converts who were familiar with the OT and who were being tempted to revert to Judaism or to Judaize the gospel (cf. Gal. 2:14). Sone have suggested that these professing Jewish Christians were thinking of merging with a Jewish sect, such as the one at Qumran near the Dead Sea. It has been suggested that the recipients were from the "large number of priests who became obedient to the faith" (Acts 6:7).

A PERVERSE GENERTION

As the writer of Hebrews speaks of some who were leaving the fellowship of believers in Christ, he may have had in mind also the recipients of Peter's sermon as found in Acts 2. Peter refers to them as "perverse generation" (Acts 2:40).

Peter's words are direct and forceful. He declares, "You nailed Him to a cross. You put Him to death. But God raised Him up" (my paraphrase). You put Him on a cross. God put Him on a throne. You crucified Him. God has glorified Him" (paraphrase of verses 23, 24, and 36 of Acts 2.

> Therefore, let all the house of Israel know assuredly that God has made this Jesus, whom you crucified, both Lord and Christ....And with many other words he testified and exhorted them saying, "Be saved from this perverse generation." (Acts 2:36-40)

We remember that on that first Psalm Sunday the crowds in Jerusalem were praising Him, shouting out, "HOSANNA! BLESSED IS HE WHO COMES IN THE NAME OF THE LORD; Blessed is the coming kingdom of our father David; Hosanna in the highest" (Mark 11:9-10)! Five days later it'd a very different scene. "But they cried out, 'Away with *Him,* away with *Him*! Crucify Him'! Pilate said to them, 'Shall I crucify your king'? The chief priests answered, 'We have no king but Caesar'"! (John 19:15) In five short days that generation of Jews in Jerusalem went from acknowledging Him as their king to demanding that He be crucified.

THE ANALOGY

Likewise, it appears that some individual Jews, of whom the writer of Hebrews speaks, had tasted of the Heavenly gift and professed to worship Jesus as Lord and King, but then had left the fellowship of the church after a brief period of time. By way of analogy the writer refers to apostasy as "crucifying with respect to themselves" (literal meaning) the Son of God. As individuals they were doing what that generation of Jews had done. Although they had not literally crucified Christ, they had identified themselves with the "perverse generation" to whom Peter spoke on the Day of Pentecost. First there was acknowledgement and acceptance of the Christ. A short time later it was a story of complete and dramatic rejection.

REPENTANCE STILL POSSIBLE

Peter's message to nation at Pentecost centered on repentance:

> Now when they heard this, they were cut to the heart, and said to Peter and the Rest of the apostles, 'Men and brethren, what shall we do?' Peter said to them, 'Repent, and let every one of you be baptized in the name of Jesus Christ for the Remission of sins; and you shall receive the gift of the Holy Spirit' (Acts 2:37-39)

Likewise, I believe, repentance was still possible for the people of whom the writer of Hebrews spoke, although the translation of the text seems to declare otherwise. We suggested in a previous chapter that the word "crucify" found in Hebrews 6:6 is a temporal participle which can be translated "while" or "as long as," The tense of the participle is present, which tense in Biblical Greek depicts continuing action. We can then translate the clause as, "It is impossible to renew them to repentance as long as they continue to crucify for themselves the Son of God…" I think the writer is saying, "We can't do much for these people as long as they continue to reject Christ, except pray for them." They are crucifying for themselves (in a sense), rejecting Him as the nation did while He was on earth.

SUPPORT FROM CHAPTER TEN

Verse 26 of chapter ten of Hebrews seems to present the same thought:

> For if we go on sinning willfully after receiving the knowledge of the truth, there no longer remains a sacrifice for sins, but a terrifying expectation of judgment and

the fury of a fire which will consume the adversaries. (Hebrews 10:26)

We notice once again the reference is to a *continuing* action. The NASB reads, "if we go on sinning"(Hebrews 6:6),- that is if we continue to reject Him as our Savior.

> How much severer punishment do you think he will deserve who has trampled under foot the Son of God, and has regarded as unclean the blood of the covenant by which he was sanctified, and has insulted the Spirit of grace? (Hebrews 10:29)

> \Indeed, chapter ten does seem to parallel chapter six. The words of Hebrews 10:26 add the aspect of warning to that of explanation. In chapter six the writer endeavors to explain to his readers concerning the matter of so many who had left their fellowship. In chapter ten there is the word of warning to any who might be in a state of rejection. "If we sin willfully (go on sinning) after receiving the knowledge of the truth, there no longer remains a sacrifice for sins..." (Hebrews 10:26)

BETTER THINGS OF YOU

Another point of parallel can be found with respect to an assurance of salvation. The content of chapters six and ten seems to be quite similar in this regard. In chapter 6 of Hebrews, verses 9-12 we read:

> But beloved we are confident of better things concerning you, yes, things that accompany salvation, though we speak in this manner, For God is not unjust to forget your work and labor of love which you have shown toward His name, in that you have ministered to the saints, and do minister. And we desire that each one of you show the same diligence to the full assurance of salvation of hope

until the end that you do not become sluggish, but imitate those who through faith and patience inherit the promise. (Hebrews 6:9-12)

The passage in chapter ten also testifies to the genuine faith of his readers:

> But recall the former days in which, after you were illumined, you endured a great struggle with sufferings: partly while you were made a spectacle both by reproaches and tribulations, and partly while you became companions of those who were so treated; for you had compassion on me in my chains, and joyfully accepted the plundering of your goods, knowing that you have a a better and enduring possession for yourselves in heaven. (Hebrews 10:32-34)

All of this was to the writer, evidence of a heart condition quite different than that of those who were "crucifying to themselves" the Son of God. (Hebrew 6:6).

APPENDIX II

The Epistles Categorized -- Exhortations

FIFTY-FOUR CATEGORIES

In the pages that follow the reader will find the exhortations of the Epistles divided into 54 categories.

The book of Philemon has been omitted because it does not contain specific exhortation for the Church. It is a personal letter from Paul to Philemon concerning a run-away slave, Onesimus. Paul's plea that the man be forgiven and accepted back does give us an example of Christian graciousness. Because there is no specific exhortation in the letter, that example has not been included in the category of *personal reconciliation.*

AN IMPRECISE METHOD

Because it would seem to be very difficult to accomplish the task otherwise, the unscientific method of determining emphasis by the number of verses has been used. According to our count, the category of *false doctrine / teachers* occupies 149 verses in the Epistles. That of *personal reconciliation* is presented in 121 verses and *Christian Liberty,* 108 verses.

Adding to the challenge of sorting it all out is the question regarding supporting context. How many verses does the writer use to support a specific exhortation that may occupy only one verse? Please note: The total number of verses indicated for each category may be more than the number of verses listed. This is because supporting verses have been added to the specific exhortation. Furthermore, there is obviously an over-lapping of categories. We might ask, do we make those two verses into a separate category or do we include them in with verses that make up another category? This is all to say that there has been a degree of subjectivity in this endeavor.

THE FORMAT

The verses set forth in the sections are presented in a variety of ways. A verse may be found complete, quoted as such from a particular version, or a portion of a verse out of that out of that translation may be used. The variety of presentation relates to the available space afforded. The purpose of this project was to display the great panorama of exhortations that are found in the Epistles – to show what is there, what is emphasized and what, by implication, is not there.

To my knowledge, every category of exhortation has been included, although not every verse in each category has been listed.

IN THE BOOK OF ROMANS <u>seven categories of exhortation</u>

<u>Dedication</u> – Rom. 6:11-13, 12:12   5 verses in the whole passage

"Likewise reckon ye also yourselves to be dead indeed unto sin, but alive unto God through Jesus Christ our Lord." (Rom.6:11 /KJV)

"Neither yield ye your members as instruments of unrighteousness unto sin: but yield yourselves unto God, as those that are alive from the dead, and your members as instruments of righteousness unto God." (Rom. 6:13 /KJV)

"I beseech you therefore, brethren, by the mercies of God, that ye present your bodies a living sacrifice, holy, acceptable unto God, which is your reasonable service." (Rom.12:1 /KJV)

<u>Spiritual gifts</u> – Rom.12:3, 6-8   4 verses in the whole passage

"Having then gifts differing according to the grace that is given to us, whether prophecy, let us prophesy according to the proportion of faith;" (Rom.12:6 /KJV)

<u>Love</u> – Rom.12:9, 12-13, 14-21,   22 verses in the whole passage"
13:8-14, 16:16

"Be kindly affectioned one to another with brotherly love; in honour preferring one another;" (Rom.2:10 /KJV)

<u>Submission to government</u> --   7 verses in the whole passage
Rom.13 :1,3-7

"Let every soul be subject unto the higher powers. For there is no power but of God: the powers that be are ordained of God." (Rom.13:1 /KJV)

<u>Christian liberty</u> – Rom. 14:1,13,20,   35 verses in the whole passage
22, 15:2,7

Prayer -- Rom.15:30-32   3 verses in the whole passage

"Now I beseech you, brethren, for the Lord Jesus Christ's sake, and for the love of the Spirit, that ye strive together with me in your prayers to God for me;" (Rom.13:30 /KJV)

False Teachers -- Rom.16:17-20   4 verses in the whole passage

"⁷Now I beseech you, brethren, mark them which cause divisions and offences contrary to the doctrine which ye have learned; and avoid them." (Rom.16:17 /KJV)

EXHORTATIONS IN FIRST CORINTHIANS   twelve categories

Unity -- I Cor. 1:10, 3:15, 17,21, 4:5,6   91 verses in the whole passage

"Now I beseech you, brethren, by the name of our Lord Jesus Christ, that ye all speak the same thing, and that there be no divisions among you; but that ye be perfectly joined together in the same mind and in the same judgment" (I Cor.1:10 /KJV).

Discipline -- I Cor. 5:7,11,13   13 verses in the whole passage

"Purge out therefore the old leaven, that ye may be a new lump, as ye are unleavened. For even Christ our passover is sacrificed for us:" I Cor. (5:7 /KJV)

But them that are without God judgeth. Therefore, put away from among yourselves that wicked person." (I Cor.5:13 /KJV)

Litigation -- I Cor. 6:1-8   8 verses in the passage

"Know ye not that the unrighteous shall not inherit the kingdom of God? Be not deceived: neither fornicators, nor idolaters, nor adulterers, nor effeminate, nor abusers of themselves with mankind, …shall inherit the kingdom of God. (I Cor.6:9-20 /KJV)

"Now therefore there is utterly a fault among you, because ye go to law one with another. Why do ye not rather take wrong? why do ye not rather suffer yourselves to be defrauded?..." (I Cor.6:7 /KJV)

<u>Sexual immorality</u> – I Cor. 6:15-20   6 verses in the passage

"Flee fornication. Every sin that a man doeth is without the body; but he that committeth fornication sinneth against his own body." (I Cor.6:19 /KJV)

<u>Marriage</u> – I Cor.   40 verses in the whole long chapter
7:3,5,9,10,13,15,20,24

"Defraud ye not one the other, except it be with consent for a time, that ye may give yourselves to fasting and prayer; and come together again, that Satan tempt you not for your incontinency." (I Cor.7:5 /KJV)

The NASB reads "…fulfill your marital duty…stop depriving one another…"(ICor.7:5)

<u>Christian Liberty</u> I Cor. 8:9, 9:1-   73 verses over two chapters

"But take heed lest by any means this liberty of yours become a stumblingblock to them that are weak." I Cor. (8:9 /KJV)

<u>Public worship</u> – I Cor.11:1,7,10,12   16 verses in the passage

"For a man indeed ought not to cover his head, forasmuch as he is the image and glory of God: but the woman is the glory of the man." (I Cor.11:7 /KJV)

"But every woman that prayeth or prophesieth with her head uncovered dishonoureth her head: for that is even all one as if she were shaven." (I Cor.11:5 /KJV)

Communion -- I Cor. 11:28, 33, 34   34 verses in the passage

"But let a man examine himself, and so let him eat of that bread, and drink of that cup." (I Cor.11:28 /KJV)

Spiritual gifts – I Cor.12:31,   40 verses in the whole chapter
14:1,13,20,40

(Note: This chapter extends from chapter 12 through 14. Thirteen is the love chapter which contains no exhortations)

"Pursue love, yet desire earnestly spiritual gifts, but especially that you may prohesy," (I Cor.14:1 /NASB)

"Wherefore, brethren, covet to prophesy, and forbid not to speak with tongues." (ICor.14:29 /KJV)

Faithfulness – I Cor.15:33,34,58   58 verses in the whole section

"Awake to righteousness, and sin not; for some have not the knowledge of God: I speak this to your shame." (I Cor.15:34 /KJV)

Stewardship –   4 verses in the passage

"Upon the first day of the week let every one of you lay by him in store, as God hath prospered him, that there be no gatherings when I come." (I Cor.16:2 /KJV)

Respect for leaders – I Cor.16:10,13,14,16,18   9 verses in the passage

---

EXHORTATIONS IN SECOND   six categories in the book
CORINTHIANS

Church discipline -- II Cor. 2:6-8   7 verses in the passage

"Sufficient for such a one is this punishment which was inflicted by the majority…you should rather forgive and comfort him …" (II Cor. 2:6)

Separation – II Cor. 6:14,27, 7:1   6 verses in the passage

"Do not be bound together with unbelievers; for what partnership have righteousness and lawlessness, or fellowship has light with darkness?" (II Cor.6:14)

Love -- II Cor.13:12   1 verse

"Greet one another with a holy kiss" (II Cor.13:12)

Reconciliation -- II Cor. 7:2, 10:1,   21 verses in this whole section
11:1, 12:1

"Make room for us in your hearts; we wronged no one, we took advantage of no one" (II Cor.7:2)

"Now I, Paul, myself urge you by the meekness and gentleness of Christ – I who am meek when face to face with you, but bold toward you when absent." (II Cor.7:2)

Stewardship – II Cor.8:7,11,24, 9:7   39 verses in the whole section

"Let each of you do just as he has purposed in his heart; not grudgingly or under compulsion; for God loves a cheerful giver." (II Cor.9:7)

Christian living -- II Cor.13:11   1 verse

"…rejoice, be made complete, be comforted, be like-minded, live in peace…"

(II Cor.13:11)

Doctrinal Purity – Gal. 1:6-9,   129 verses in two separate chapters
3:3, 4:9, 4:12-20, 5:1-4

"I marvel that ye are so soon removed from him that called you into the grace of Christ unto another gospel: which is not another; but there be some that trouble you, and would pervert the gospel of Christ. But though we, or an angel from heaven, preach any other gospel unto you than that which we have preached unto you, let him be accursed. As we said before, so say I now again, If any man preach any other gospel unto you than that ye have received, let him be accursed. (Gal.1:6-9 /KJV)

"Are ye so foolish? having begun in the Spirit, are ye now made perfect by the flesh?" (Gal. 3:3 /KJV)

"Open your hearts to what we once had together."   Gal. 4:12-20

Love – Gal. 5:13-15, 6:1,2   5 verses in two chapters

"For, brethren, ye have been called unto liberty; only use not liberty for an occasion to the flesh, but by love serve one another." (Gal. 5:13 / KJV)

"For all the law is fulfilled in one word, even in this; Thou shalt love thy neighbour as thyself." . (Gal. 5:14 /KJV)

The spiritual life -- Gal. 5:16, 22,25,26, 6:3,4 14 verses in the whole passage

"This I say then, Walk in the Spirit, and ye shall not fulfil the lust of the flesh. For the flesh lusteth against the Spirit, and the Spirit against the flesh: and these are contrary the one to the other: so that ye cannot do the things that ye would." (Gal. 5:16,17 /KJV)

Stewardship – Gal. 6:6,7,9,10   5 verses in the passage

"As we have therefore opportunity, let us do good unto all men, especially unto them who are of the household of faith." (Gal. 6:10 /KJV)

EPHESIANS   four categories

Christian unity –Eph. 2:11-4:16 49 verses in chapters 1,2 and 4 of Ephesians

"with all lowliness and meekness, with longsuffering, forbearing one another in love; 3 endeavoring to keep the unity of the Spirit in the bond of peace."

(Eph.4:2-3 KJV)

"Find and exercise your spiritual gift until we all attain to the unity of the faith...for the building up of the body of Christ." (Eph.4:1-3)

The New Life – Eph.4:17-5:21   36 verses in the section

"that ye put off concerning the former conversation the old man, which is corrupt according to the deceitful lusts; and be renewed in the spirit of your mind; and that ye put on the new man, ..." (Eph.4:17 KJV)

"and be ye kind one to another, tenderhearted, forgiving one another, even as God for Christ's sake hath forgiven you." (Eph.4:32 /KJV)

The Spiritual Life   5 verses

"And be not drunk with wine, wherein is excess; but be filled with the Spirit; speaking to yourselves in psalms and hymns and spiritual songs, singing and making melody in your heart to the Lord; 20 giving thanks always for all things unto God and the Father in the name of our Lord Jesus Christ; 21 submitting yourselves one to another in the fear of God." (Eph.5:18-22 /KJV)

"If we live in the Spirit, let us also walk in the Spirit. 26 Let us not

be desirous of vain glory, provoking one another, envying one another."
(Eph.5:25-26 /KJV)

"As we have therefore opportunity, let us do good unto all men, especially unto them who are of the household of faith." (Eph.6:10 /KJV)

At Home and Work – Eph. 5:22-69   68 verses in the section

"Wives, submit yourselves unto your own husbands, as unto the Lord. 23 For the husband is the head of the wife, even as Christ is the head of the church: and he is the saviour of the body." (Eph.5:22,23 /KJV)

"Husbands, love your wives, even as Christ also loved the church, and gave himself for it; 26 that he might sanctify and cleanse it with the washing of water by the word, 27 that he might present it to himself a glorious church, not having spot, or wrinkle, or any such thing; but that it should be holy and without blemish. (Eph.5:25-27)

"Children, obey your parents in the Lord: for this is right. Honor thy father and mother; (which is the first commandment with promise;…)" (Eph.5:1-2 /KJV)

"Servants, be obedient to them that are your masters according to the flesh, with fear and trembling, in singleness of your heart, as unto Christ; not with eyeservice, as men-pleasers; but as the servants of Christ, doing the will of God from the heart;

(Eph.6:5,6 /KJV)

Spiritual Warfare – Eph.6:1-20   7 verses in the passage

"Finally, my brethren, be strong in the Lord, and in the power of his might. Put on the whole armour of God, that ye may be able to stand against the wiles of the devil."

(Eph.6:10,11 /KJV)

"...with all prayer and petition, pray at all times in the Spirit...be on the alert with all perseverance and petition." (Eph.6:18)

PHILIPPIANS   Seven Categories

Unity – Phil. 1:27-30   10 verses

"Only let your conversation be as it becometh the gospel of Christ: that whether I come and see you, or else be absent, I may hear of your affairs, that ye stand fast in one spirit, with one mind striving together for the faith of the gospel;..." (Phil.1:27 /KJV)

"...fulfil ye my joy, that ye be likeminded, having the same love, being of one accord, of one mind. Let nothing be done through strife or vainglory; but in lowliness of mind let each esteem other better than themselves. Look not every man on his own things, but every man also on the things of others. Let this mind be in you, which was also in Christ Jesus: who, being in the form of God, thought it not robbery to be equal with God:" (Phil.2:2-6 /KJV)

"Receive him therefore in the Lord with all gladness; and hold such in good reputation: because for the work of Christ he was nigh unto death, not regarding his life,..." (Phil.2:29,30 /KJV)

The Humility of Love – Phil.2:3-18   18 verses

"Let nothing be done through strife or vainglory; but in lowliness of mind let each esteem other better than themselves." (Phil.2:3 /KJV)

"Do not merely look out for your own personal interests." (Phil. 2:4)

Hospitality for godly men --   12 verses

"Receive him therefore in the Lord with all gladness; and hold such in reputation:" (Phil.2:29 /KJV)

"Beware of dogs, beware of evil workers, beware of the circumcision." (Phil.3:2 /KJV)

"Therefore, my brethren dearly beloved and longed for, my joy and crown, so stand fast in the Lord, my dearly beloved." (Phil. 4:1 /KJV)

Trust in God – Phil.4:6-7   2 verses

"Be careful for nothing; but in everything by prayer and supplication with thanksgiving let your requests be made known unto God. And the peace of God, which passeth all understanding, shall keep your hearts and minds through Christ Jesus.

(4:6-7 /KJV)

Thought Life – Phil.4:8-9   2 verses

"Finally, brethren, whatsoever things are true, whatsoever things are honest, whatsoever things are just, whatsoever things are pure, whatsoever things are lovely, whatsoever things are of good report; if there be any virtue, and if there be any praise, think on these things." (Phil. 4:8 /KJV)

Rejoicing – Phil. 2:12,18,29, 31: 4:4   5 verses

"Rejoice in the Lord alway: and again I say, Rejoice. Let your moderation be known unto all men. The Lord is at hand." (Phil. 4:4 /KJV)

"For the same cause also do ye joy, and rejoice with me." (Phil. 2:18 /KJV)

"Rejoice in the Lord alway: and again I say, Rejoice." (Phil. 4:4 /KJV)

COLOSSIANS   Four Categories

<u>False Doctrine</u> – Col. 2:6-23   18 verses

"Beware lest any man spoil you through philosophy and vain deceit, after the tradition of men, after the rudiments of the world, and not after Christ." (Col.2:8 /KJV)

<u>At Home and Work</u> – Col.3:18-41   9 verses

"Wives, submit yourselves unto your own husbands, as it is fit in the Lord. Husbands, love your wives, and be not bitter against them. Children, obey your parents in all things: for this is well pleasing unto the Lord. Fathers, provoke not your children to anger, lest they be discouraged. Servants, obey in all things your masters according to the flesh; not with eyeservice, as men-pleasers; but in singleness of heart, fearing God: and whatsoever ye do, do it heartily, as to the Lord, and not unto men; knowing that of the Lord ye shall receive the reward of the inheritance: for ye serve the Lord Christ." (Col. 3:18-24 /KJV)

"Masters, give unto your servants that which is just and equal; knowing that ye also have a Master in heaven. (Col.4:1 /KJV)

<u>The New Life</u> – Col.3:1-17   19 verses

"If ye then be risen with Christ, seek those things which are above, where Christ sitteth on the right hand of God." (Col.3:1 /KJV)

"Set your affection on things above, not on things on the earth." (Col.3:2 /KJV)

"Lie not one to another, seeing that ye have put off the old man with his deeds." (Col.3:9 /KJV)

"And let the peace of God rule in your hearts, to the which also ye are called in one body; and be ye thankful. Let the word of Christ dwell in you richly in all wisdom; teaching and admonishing one another in psalms and hymns and spiritual songs, singing with grace in your hearts to the Lord. And whatsoever ye do in word or deed, do all in the name of the Lord." ((Col.3:15-17 /KJV)

Prayer – Col.4:1-2   2 verses

"Continue in prayer, and watch in the same with thanksgiving; withal praying also for us, that God would open unto us a door of utterance, to speak the mystery of Christ, for which I am also in bonds:" (Col.4:2 /KJV)

I THESSALONIANS   Six Categories

Sexual Immorality

                                                                     6 verses

"For this is the will of God, even your sanctification, that ye should abstain from fornication: that every one of you should know how to possess his vessel in sanctification and honour; not in the lust of concupiscence," (I Thess. 4:3.4/KJV)

Love – I Thess. 4:9-10   2 verses

"But as touching brotherly love ye need not that I write unto you: for ye yourselves are taught of God to love one another." (I Thess. 4:10 /KJV)

Orderly Living – I Thess. 4:11   2 verses

"and that ye study to be quiet, and to do your own business, and to work with your own hands, as we commanded you; that ye may walk honestly toward them that are without, and that ye may have lack of nothing." (I Thess. 4:11.12 /KJV)

Last Things – I Thess. 4:13-5:11   17 verses

"Therefore, let us not sleep, as do others; but let us watch and be sober." (I Thess. 5:5 /KJV)

"Wherefore comfort one another with these words." I Thess. 4:18 /KJV)

Miscellaneous – I Thess. 5:14-22,25,27   12 verses

"Now we exhort you, brethren, warn them that are unruly, comfort the feebleminded, support the weak, be patient toward all men. See that none render evil for evil unto any man; but ever follow that which is good, both among yourselves…(I Thess. 5:14,15/KJV)

"Rejoice evermore. Pray without ceasing. In every- thing give thanks: for this is the will of God in Christ Jesus concerning you. Quench not the Spirit. Despise not prophesyings. Prove all things; hold fast that which is good. Abstain from all appearance of evil." (I Thess. 5:17-22 /KJV)

II THESSALONIANS   three categories

Last Things – II Thess. 2:1-15   15 verses

"Now we beseech you, brethren, by the coming of our Lord Jesus Christ, and by our gathering together unto him, that ye be not soon shaken in mind, or be troubled, neither by spirit, nor by word, nor by letter as from us, as that the day of Christ is at hand." (II Thess.2:1-3 /KJV)

"Let no man deceive you by any means: for that day shall not come, except there come a falling away first, and that man of sin be revealed, the son of perdition; who opposeth and exalteth himself above all that is called God, or that is worshipped; so that he as God" (II Thess.2:2-4 /KJV)

"Therefore, brethren, stand fast, and hold the traditions which ye have been taught, whether by word, or our epistle." (II Thess. 2:15 /KJV)

<u>Prayer</u> – 3:1-2   2 verses

"Finally, brethren, pray for us, that the word of the Lord may have free course, and be glorified, even as it is with you: and that we may be delivered from unreasonable and wicked men: for all men have not faith." (II Thess.3:1,2 /KJV)

<u>Orderly Living</u> – II Thess. 3:6-15   10 verses

"Now we command you brethren, in the name of our Lord Jesus Christ, that you keep away from every brother who leads an unruly life and not according to the tradition which you received from us." (II Thess.3:6)

'But ye, brethren, be not weary in well doing. And if any man obey not our word by this epistle, note that man, and have no company with him, that he may be ashamed. Yet count him not as an enemy, but admonish him as a brother."

(II Thess.3:13-15 /KJV)

"But ye, brethren, be not weary in well doing. And if any man obey not our word by this epistle, note that man, and have no company with him, that he may be ashamed. Yet count him not as an enemy, but admonish him as a brother."

(II Thess. 3:14-15 /KJV)

FIRST TIMOTHY   Ten categories

<u>False Teaching</u> I Tim. 1:3,4,6,7; 6:20   21 verses

"As I besought thee to abide still at Ephesus, when I went into Macedonia, that thou mightest charge some that they teach no other doctrine, neither give heed to fables and endless genealogies, which minister questions, rather than godly edifying which is in faith: so do." (I Tim.1:3-4 /KJV)

"neither give heed to fables and endless genealogies, which minister questions, rather than godly edifying which is in faith: (I Tim.4:7 /KJV)

<u>Prayer</u> – I Tim. 2:1-8   8 verses

"I exhort therefore, that, first of all, supplications, prayers, intercessions, and giving of thanks, be made for all men; 2 for kings, and for all that are in authority; that we may lead a quiet and peaceable life in all godliness and honesty. 3 For this is good and acceptable in the sight of God." (I Tim.2:1-3 /KJV)

<u>Women</u> –I Tim. 2:9-12   7 verses

"I will therefore that men pray everywhere, lifting up holy hands, without wrath and doubting. In like manner also, that women adorn themselves in modest apparel, with shamefacedness and sobriety; not with broided hair, or gold, or pearls, or costly array; but (which becometh women professing godliness) with good works."

(I Tim.2:8-10 /KJV)

<u>Church Officers</u> – I Tim.3:2-12   13 verses

"This is a true saying, If a man desire the office of a bishop, he desireth a good work. A bishop then must be blameless, the husband of one wife, vigilant, sober, of good behaviour, given to hospitality, apt to teach; ...."
(I Tim.2:1-2 /KJV)

"Even so must their wives be grave, not slanderers, sober, faithful in all things."

(I Tim.3:11 /KJV)

<u>Miscellaneous</u> – I Tim.4:7-12   6 verses

"Let no man despise thy youth; but be thou an example of the believers, in word, in conversation, in charity, in spirit, in faith, in purity."
(I Tim.4:12 /KJV)

<u>Pastoral Relationships</u>-- I Tim.5:1-16   16 verses

"Rebuke not an elder, but intreat him as a father; and the younger men as brethren; the elder women as mothers; the younger as sisters, with all purity."

(I Tim.5:1,2 /KJV)

Elders – I Tim. 5:17-24   9 verses

"Let the elders that rule well be counted worthy of double honour, especially they who labour in the word and doctrine. For the scripture saith, Thou shalt not muzzle the ox that treadeth out the corn. And, the labourer is worthy of his reward."

(I Tim. 5:17-19 /KJV)

Slaves – I Tim 6:1-2   2 verses

"Those who have believers as masters must not be disrespectful to them because they are brothers, but must serve them all the more." (I Tim. 6:2)

Teaching the Word – I Tim. 4:3-13   4 verses

"Till I come, give attendance to reading, to exhortation, to doctrine. Neglect not the gift that is in thee, which was given thee by prophecy, with the laying on of the hands of the presbytery. [1] Meditate upon these things;" (I Tim. 4:14,15 /KJV)

Love of Money – I Tim. 6:10-19   14 verses

"Charge them that are rich in this world, that they be not high-minded, nor trust in uncertain riches, but in the living God, who giveth us richly all things to enjoy; that they do good, that they be rich in good works, ready to distribute, willing to communicate; 19 laying up in store for themselves a good foundation..." (I Tim. 6:10-19 /KJV)

(In this epistle as in several others, the total number of verses listed includes the context. Sometimes Paul writes several sentences so as to back up what he wants to exhort or command.)

Suffering – II Tim.1:8-2:9   21 verses

"Be not thou therefore ashamed of the testimony of our Lord, nor of me his prisoner: but be thou partaker of the afflictions of the gospel according to the power of God;" (II Tim.1:8 /KJV)

"Thou therefore, my son, be strong in the grace that is in Christ Jesus." (II Tim.2:1 /KJV)

Doctrine – Teachers – II Tim.2:14-2:25   13 verses

Study to shew thyself approved unto God, a workman that needeth not to be ashamed, rightly dividing the word of truth. But shun profane and vain babblings: for they will increase unto more ungodliness. And their word will eat as doth a canker: of whom is Hymenaeus and Philetus; who concerning the truth have erred, saying that the resurrection is past already; and overthrow the faith of many." (II Tim.2:14-18 /KJV)

"In meekness instructing those that oppose themselves; if God peradventure will give them repentance to the acknowledging of the truth;" (II Tim.2:25 /KJV) Heb.

Teaching the Word – II Tim.3:4- 4:5 9 verses

Preach the word; be instant in season, out of season; reprove, rebuke, exhort with all long suffering and doctrine." (II Tim.4:1,2 /KJV)

"But watch thou in all things, endure afflictions, do the work of an evangelist, make full proof of thy ministry." (II Tim.4:5 /KJV)

Personal – II Tim. 4:9-22   5 verses

"Of whom be thou ware also; for he hath greatly withstood our words." (II Tim.4:15 /KJV)

"Salute Prisca and Aquila, and the household of Onesiphorus." (II Tim.4:19 /KJV)

TITUS   Four Categories

Church Officers – Titus 1:5-9   5 verses

"For this cause left I thee in Crete, that thou shouldest set in order the things that are wanting, and ordain elders in every city, as I had appointed thee:" (Titus1:5 /KJV)

"Holding fast the faithful word as he hath been taught, that he may be able by sound doctrine both to exhort and to convince the gainsayers." (Titus 1:9 /KJV)

False Teaching – Titus1:10-16   10 verses

"For there are many unruly and vain talkers and deceivers, specially they of the circumcision:" (Titus 1:10 /KJV)

"Whose mouths must be stopped, who subvert whole houses, teaching things which they ought not, for filthy lucre's sake." (Titus 1:10 /KJV)

"Wherefore rebuke them sharply, that they may be sound in the faith; not giving heed to Jewish fables, and commandments of men, that turn from the truth."

(Titus1:13,14 /KJV)

"But speak thou the things that become sound doctrine." (Titus 2:2 /KJV)

"The aged women likewise, that they be in behaviour as becometh holiness, not false accusers, not given to much wine, teachers of good things;" (Titus 2:3 /KJV)

HEBREWS   seven categories

Spiritual Growth --   24 verses in various places

"Therefore we ought to give the more earnest heed to the things which we have heard, lest at any time we should let them slip." (Heb.2:1 /KJV)

"Therefore leaving the principles of the doctrine of Christ, let us go on unto perfection; not laying again the foundation of repentance from dead works, and of faith toward God,…" (Heb.6:1 /KJV)

"And we desire that every one of you do shew the same diligence to the full assurance of hope unto the end:' (Heb.6:11 /KJV)

Consider Jesus --   72 verses in various places

(*In fact, all of Hebrews was written that we might consider Him.*)

"Wherefore, holy brethren, partakers of the heavenly calling, consider the Apostle and High Priest of our profession, Christ Jesus;" (Heb.3:1 /KJV)

"Now observe how great this man was to whom Abraham, the patriarch, gave a tenth of the choicest spoils. (Heb.7:4)

Apostasy --   29 verses

"Harden not your hearts, as in the provocation, in the day of temptation in the wilderness: When your fathers tempted me, proved me, and saw my works forty years.

(Heb.3:8,9 /KJV)

"Let us therefore fear, lest, a promise being left us of entering into his rest, any of you should seem to come short of it." (Heb.4:1 /KJV)

<u>Prayer</u> --   7 verses

"Let us therefore come boldly unto the throne of grace, that we may obtain mercy, and find grace to help in time of need." (Heb.4:16 /KJV)

"Let us draw near with a true heart in full assurance of faith, having our hearts sprinkled from an evil conscience, and our bodies washed with pure water. Let us hold fast the profession of our faith without wavering; (for he is faithful that promised;)

And let us consider one another to provoke unto love and to good works:" (Heb.10:22-24 /KJV)

<u>Endurance</u> – Heb.10:25-12:15   38 verses in the section

"But call to remembrance the former days, in which, after ye were illuminated, ye endured a great fight of afflictions;" (Heb.10:32 /KJV)

"Let us hold fast the profession of our faith without wavering; (for he is faithful that promised;)" (Heb.10:23 /KJV)

"Cast not away therefore your confidence, which hath great recompence of reward." (Heb.10:35 /KJV)

<u>Love</u> – Heb.13:1-3   3 verses

"Let brotherly love continue. Be not forgetful to entertain strangers: for thereby some have entertained angels unawares." (Heb.13:1,2 /KJV)

"Remember them that are in bonds, as bound with them; and them which suffer adversity, as being yourselves also in the body." (Heb.13:3 /KJV)

– Heb.10:24-25   3 verses

"And let us consider one another to provoke unto love and to good works: Not forsaking the assembling of ourselves together, as the manner of some is; but exhorting one another: and so much the more, as ye see the day approaching. (Heb.10:24,25 /KJV)

Christian Living --   17 verses in this section

"Let your conversation be without covetousness; and be content with such things as ye have: for he hath said, I will never leave thee, nor forsake thee." (Heb.13:5 /KJV)

"Remember them which have the rule over you, who have spoken unto you the word of God: whose faith follow, considering the end of their conversation." (Heb.13:7 /KJV)

"Be not carried about with divers and strange doctrines. For it is a good thing that the heart be established with grace; not with meats, which have not profited them that have been occupied therein." (Heb.13:9 /KJV)

"Marriage is honourable in all, and the bed undefiled: but whoremongers and adulterers God will judge." (Heb.13:4 /KJV)

"By him therefore let us offer the sacrifice of praise to God continually, that is, the fruit of our lips giving thanks to his name." (Heb.13:14 /KJV)

THE BOOK OF JAMES   Six Categories

Trials – James1:12-16   16 verses including context

"My brethren, count it all joy when ye fall into divers temptations;" (James 1:2 /KJV)

"But let patience have her perfect work, that ye may be perfect and entire, wanting nothing." (James 2:4 /KJV

"If any of you lack wisdom, let him ask of God, that giveth to all men liberally, and upbraideth not;" (James1:5 /KJV)

Love – James 1:19-22; 2:1,12; 3:1,13   54 verses including context

"Wherefore, my beloved brethren, let every man be swift to hear, slow to speak, slow to wrath:" (James 1:19 /KJV)

"My brethren, have not the faith of our Lord Jesus Christ, the Lord of glory, with respect of persons." (James 2:1 /KJV)

Worldliness – James 4:7-5:1   23 verses

"Submit yourselves therefore to God. Resist the devil, and he will flee from you. Draw nigh to God, and he will draw nigh to you. Cleanse your hands, ye sinners; and purify your hearts, ye double minded." (James 4:7,8 /KJV)

"Humble yourselves in the sight of the Lord, and he shall lift you up." (James 4:10 /KJV)

Endurance – James 5:7-5:13   7 verses

"Be patient therefore, brethren, unto the coming of the Lord. Behold, the husbandman waiteth for the precious fruit of the earth, and hath long patience for it, until he receive the early and latter rain. (James 5:7 /KJV)

"Be ye also patient; stablish your hearts: for the coming of the Lord draweth nigh." (James 5:8 /KJV)

"Grudge not one against another, brethren, lest ye be condemned: behold, the judge standeth before the door." (James 5:9 /KJV)

Healing and Prayer – James 5:14-16   5 verses

"Is any among you afflicted? let him pray. Is any merry? let him sing psalms. Is any sick among you? let him call for the elders of the church;

and let them pray over him, anointing him with oil in the name of the Lord:" (James 5:13,14 /KJV)

"Confess your faults one to another, and pray one for another, that ye may be healed. The effectual fervent prayer of a righteous man availeth much." (James 5:16 /KJV)

5
Conversion of the Erring – James 5:19-20   2 verses

"Brethren, if any of you do err from the truth, and one convert him; Let him know, that he which converteth the sinner from the error of his way shall save a soul from death, and shall hide a multitude of sins." (James 5:19,20 /KJV)

THE BOOK OF FIRST PETER   Nine Categories of Exhortation

Spirtual Sobriety   5 verses

"Wherefore gird up the loins of your mind, be sober, and hope to the end for the grace that is to be brought unto you at the revelation of Jesus Christ;" (I Peter 1:13 /KJV)

"Be sober, be vigilant; because your adversary the devil, as a roaring lion, walketh about, seeking whom he may devour:" (I Peter 5:8 /KJV)

Holy Living – I Peter 1:14-16; 2:11-12   11 verses

"Dearly beloved, I beseech you as I Peter strangers and pilgrims, abstain from fleshly lusts, which war against the soul;" (I Peter 2:11 /KJV)

"...but as he who called you is holy, you also be holy because it is written, 'Be Holy for I am holy.'" (I Peter 1:15-16)

Love – I Peter 1:22-23; 4:8-9; 5:14   6 verses

"Seeing ye have purified your souls in obeying the truth through the Spirit unto unfeigned love of the brethren, see that ye love one another with a pure heart fervently." (I Peter 1:22 /KJV)

"And above all things have fervent charity among yourselves: for charity shall cover the multitude of sins." (I Peter 4:8 /KJV)

Greet ye one another with a kiss of charity. Peace be with you all that are in Christ Jesus. Amen." I Peter (5:14 /KJV)

The Word – I Peter 2:1-3   3 verses

"Wherefore laying aside all malice, and all guile, and hypocrisies, and envies, and all evil speakings, As newborn babes, desire the sincere milk of the word, that ye may grow thereby:" (I Peter 2:1,2 /KJV)

Submission --   20 verses the section

"Submit yourselves to every ordinance of man for the Lord's sake: whether it be to the king, as supreme; Or unto governors, as unto them that are sent by him for the punishment of evildoers, and for the praise of them." (I Peter 2:13,14 /KJV)

"Servants, be subject to your masters with all fear; not only to the good and gentle, but also to the froward." (I Peter 1:18 /KJV)

"Likewise, ye wives, be in subjection to your own husbands; that, if any obey not the word, they also may without the word be won by the conversation of the wives; (I Peter 3:1 /KJV)

Grace in Suffering – I Peter 3:8-12; 3:15-16   13 verses

"Finally, be ye all of one mind, having compassion one of another, love as brethren, be pitiful, be courteous: Not rendering evil for evil, or railing for railing: but contrariwise blessing; knowing that ye are thereunto called, that ye should inherit a blessing." (I Peter 1:8,9 /KJV)

"But sanctify the Lord God in your hearts: and be ready always to give an answer to every man tha I Peter t asketh you a reason of the hope that is in you with meekness and fear:" (I Peter 3:15 /KJV)

Suffering – I Peter 4:12-19   8 verses

"Beloved, think it not strange concerning the fiery trial which is to try you, as though some strange thing happened unto you:" (I Peter 4:12 /KJV)

"But rejoice, inasmuch as ye are partakers of Christ's sufferings; that, when his glory shall be revealed, ye may be glad also with exceeding joy." (I Peter 4:13 /KJV)

Elders – I Peter 5:1-3   4 verses

"The elders which are among you I exhort, who am also an elder, and a witness of the sufferings of Christ, and also a partaker of the glory that shall be revealed: Feed the flock of God which is among you, taking the oversight thereof, not by constraint, but willingly; not for filthy lucre, but of a ready mind;" (I Peter 5:!-2 /KJV)

"Neither as being lords over God's heritage, but being examples to the flock." (I Peter 5:3 /KJV)

"Likewise, ye younger, submit yourselves unto the elder. Yea, all of you be subject one to another, and be clothed with humility: for God resisteth the proud, and giveth grace to the humble." (I Peter 5:5 /KJV)

Humility – I Peter 5:5-7   3 verses

"Humble yourselves therefore under the mighty hand of God, that he may exalt you in due time: Casting all your care upon him; for He careth for you." (I Peter 5:6,7 /KJV)

THE BOOK OF II PETER   four categories

Christian Qualities – II Peter 1:5-10   6 verses

"And beside this, giving all diligence, add to your faith virtue; and to virtue knowledge; and to knowledge temperance; and to temperance patience; and to patience godliness; and to godliness brotherly kindness; and to brotherly kindness charity." (II Peter 1:5-7 /KJV)

The Word –II:Peter 19-21   6 verses

"We have also a more sure word of prophecy; whereunto ye do well that ye take heed, as unto a light that shineth in a dark place, until the day dawn, and the day star arise in your hearts:" (II Peter 1:19 /KJV)

3

The Second Coming – II Peter 3:8-15   9 verses

"But, beloved, be not ignorant of this one thing, that one day is with the Lord as a thousand years, and a thousand years as one day.: (II Peter 3:8 /KJV)

"Wherefore, beloved, seeing that ye look for such things, be diligent that ye may be found of him in peace, without spot, and blameless." (II Peter 3:14 /KJV)

False Teachers – II Peter 3;2-18   31 verses

"Knowing this first, that there shall come in the last days scoffers, walking after their own lusts, and saying, Where is the promise of his coming? for since the fathers fell asleep, all things continue as they were from the beginning of the creation." (II Peter (3:3,4 /KJV)

Ye therefore, beloved, seeing ye know these things before, beware lest ye also, being led away with the error of the wicked, fall from your own stedfastness." (II Peter 3:17 /KJV)

"But grow in grace, and in the knowledge of our Lord and Saviour Jesus Christ. To him be glory both now and for. (II Peter 3:18 /KJV)

THE BOOK OF FIRST JOHN   Four categories

<u>Fellowship with God</u> – I John1:6-9:2:1-3   26 verses

["If we confess our sins, he is faithful and just to forgive us our sins, and to cleanse us from all unrighteousness."] (I John 1:9 /KJV)

"And now, little children, abide in him; that, when he shall appear, we may have confidence, and not be ashamed before him at his coming." (I John 2:28 /KJV)

<u>Love</u> – I John 2;8; 2:10; 3:13; 3:17; 3:18; 4:7; 4:11; 4:21   35 verses

["Brethren, I write no new commandment unto you, but an old commandment which ye had from the beginning. The old commandment is the word which ye have heard from the beginning. Again, a new commandment I write unto you, which thing is true in him and in you: because the darkness is past, and the true light now shineth."] (I John 2:7,8 /KJV)

"Little children, let no man deceive you: he that doeth righteousness is righteous, even as he is righteous." (I John 3:7 /KJV

"My little children, let us not love in word, neither in tongue; but in deed and in truth." (I John 3:18 /KJV)

"And this is his commandment, that we should believe on the name of his Son Jesus Christ, and love one another, as he gave us commandment." (I John 3:23 /KJV)

<u>Idolatry</u> – I John 2:15-16; 5:20-21   8 verses

"Love not the world, neither the things that are in the world. If any man love the world, the love of the Father is not in him." (I John 2:15 /KJV)

Prayer -- I John 5:4-16   4 verses

"And this is the confidence that we have in him, that, if we ask any thing according to his will, he heareth us:" (I John 5:14 /KJV)

"If any man see his brother sin a sin which is not unto death, he shall ask, and he shall give him life for them that sin not unto death. There is a sin unto death: I do not say that he shall pray for it." (I John 5:16 /KJV)

False Prophets – I John 2:24; 2:26; 4:1; 4;6   16 verses

"Beloved, believe not every spirit, but try the spirits whether they are of God: because many false prophets are gone out into the world." (I John 4:1 /KJV)

"Let that therefore abide in you, which ye have heard from the beginning. If that which ye have heard from the beginning shall remain in you, ye also shall continue in the Son, and in the Father." (I John 2:24 /KJV)

(Note: Brackets enclosing a verse indicates that the exhortation is implied rather than explicit.)

THE BOOKS OF II AND III JOHN   Three categories

II JOHN

Love – II John verses 5-6   2 verses

"And now I beseech thee, lady, not as though I wrote a new commandment unto thee, but that which we had from the beginning, that we love one another." (II John v. 5 /KJV)

"And this is love, that we walk after his commandments. This is the commandment, That, as ye have heard from the beginning, ye should walk in it." (II John v. 6 /KJV)

False Teachers – II John vs. 7-11   5 verses

"Look to yourselves, that we lose not those things which we have wrought, but that we receive a full reward." II John. v.8 /KJV)

If there come any unto you, and bring not this doctrine, receive him not into your house, neither bid him God speed:" (II John vs.10 /KJV)

III. JOHN   One category

Christian Hospitality –III John vv.5-12   7 verses

"Beloved, thou doest faithfully whatsoever thou doest to the brethren, and to strangers; which have borne witness of thy charity before the church: whom if thou bring forward on their journey after a godly sort, thou shalt do well:" (III John vv. 5-8 /KJV)

"Beloved, follow not that which is evil, but that which is good. He that doeth good is of God: but he that doeth evil hath not seen God." (III John vs. 11 /KJV)

THE BOOK OF JUDE   one category

False Teachers – Jude vv.3-23   20 verses

"Beloved, follow not that which is evil, but that which is good. He that doeth good is of God: but he that doeth evil hath not seen God." (Jude v. 3 /KJV)

"But, beloved, remember ye the words which were spoken before of the apostles of our Lord Jesus Christ; How that they told you there should be mockers in the last time, who should walk after their own ungodly lusts." (Jude vv. 17,18 /KJV)

"But ye, beloved, building up yourselves on your most holy faith, praying in the Holy Ghost, keep yourselves in the love of God, looking for the mercy of our Lord Jesus Christ." (Jude vv. 20,21 /KJV)

"And others save with fear, pulling them out of the fire; hating even the garment spotted by the flesh." (Jude v. 23 /KJV)

(NOTE: In these pages I have included every category that I could find in the Epistles. For the sake of space, I have not included every verse, but, to my knowledge, I have included every category of exhortation.

As I have noted before, I have included the number of verses in the context, the supporting argument when calculating the number of verses devoted to each category. I know that that can be a little subjective.

Adding them all up, I have found that more space in the Epistles is devoted to the matter of false teaching or false teachers than to any other category. The entire, though small, writing of JUDE contributes to that category.)

THE BOOK OF REVELATION   Seven Categories

Last Things - Rev. 1:1-3   3 verses

"Blessed is he that readeth, and they that hear the words of this prophecy, and keep those things which are written therein: for the time is at hand." (Rev.1:3 /KJV)

Love for God   4 verses

"Nevertheless, I have somewhat against thee, because thou hast left thy first love." (Rev.2:4 /KJV)

"Remember therefore from whence thou art fallen, and repent, and do the first works; or else I will come unto thee quickly, and will remove thy candlestick out of his place, except thou repent." (Rev.2:5 /KJV)

"He that hath an ear, let him hear what the Spirit saith unto the churches; To him that overcometh will I give to eat of the tree of life, which is in the midst of the paradise of God." (Rev. 2:7 /KJV)

(NOTE: This admonition occurs also in: Rev. 2:11, 2:17; 2:29; 3:6; 3:13 and 3:22).

.Suffering   3 verses

"Fear none of those things which thou shalt suffer: behold, the devil shall cast some of you into prison, that ye may be tried; and ye shall have tribulation ten days: be thou faithful unto death, and I will give thee a crown of life." (Rev.2:10 /KJV)

False Teaching   11 verses

"Repent; or else I will come unto thee quickly, and will fight against them with the sword of my mouth." (Rev.2:16 /KJV) *(Concerning false doctrines)*

Revival -- Rev. 1-3   3 verses

"Be watchful, and strengthen the things which remain, that are ready to die: for I have not found thy works perfect before God." Rev. (3:2 /KJV)

"Remember therefore how thou hast received and heard, and hold fast, and repent. If therefore thou shalt not watch, I will come on thee as a thief, and thou shalt not know what hour I will come upon thee." (Rev.3:3 /KJV)

Perseverance   3 verses

"Behold, I come quickly: hold that fast which thou hast, that no man take thy crown." (Rev. 3:11 /KJV)

<u>Salvation</u>   9 verses

"I counsel thee to buy of me gold tried in the fire, that thou mayest be rich; and white raiment, that thou mayest be clothed, and that the shame of thy nakedness do not appear; and anoint thine eyes with eye salve, that thou mayest see." (Rev. 3:18 /KJV)

"Behold, I stand at the door, and knock: if any man hear my voice, and open the door, I will come in to him, and will sup with him, and he with me." (Rev.3:20 /KJV)

"And the Spirit and the bride say, Come. And let him that heareth say, Come. And let him that is athirst come. And whosoever will, let him take the water of life freely." (Rev.22:17)

END NOTES

One -Why Not

1 The NIV Study Bible, (Grand Rapids, Michigan: Zondervan Bible Publishers, 1985) p. 1662

2 James M. Boice, "A Better Way: The Power of the Word and Spirit," Power Religion, *The Selling of the Evangelical Church,* Ed. Michael Scott, (Chicago: Moody Press, 1982). P. 128

Three --Exorcism- case in point

3 Fenton John Anthony Hort, and Brooke Foss Westott, *The New Testament in the Original Greek,* Vol. 1., (New York: Macmillan Co. 1881.

Four -- To Fast of Not to Fast

4 Patrick Morley, *A Man's guide to The Spiritual Disciplines,* (Chicago: Moody Press), 125.

5 Ibid p 125

6 Ibid., p. 118

7 Ibid., p. 118

8 The NIV Study Bible, (Grand Rapids, Michigan: Zondervan Corporation,) p.1455

9 NSIN OUM, Helene, *Prayer and Fasting for Evangelism,* online article, (Lausanne World Pulse,) p. all.

10 Jentezen Franklin, *Fasting,* (Lake Marky, FL. Charisma House, 2006) cover Ibid., page 112.

11 Ibid., p. 11

12 Ibid., p. 14

13 Ibid., page 16

Five -- Critical Fast

14 *The Analytical Greek Lexicon,* (Grand Rapids, Michigan: Zondervan Publishing House, 1970) p. 65
15 Ibid., p. 65
16 Abbott-Smith, G., *A Manuel Greek Lexicon of the New Testament,* T.&T. Clark, Edinburg, 1956. P.74
17 John G. Mitchell, *The Gospel of John,* (Dallas Texas: Lecture series delivered at Dallas Theological Seminary,) 1961.
18 Merrill F. Unger, *Unger's Bible Dictionary,* (Chicago: Moody press, 1957, p. 236

Six --The Baptism of the Spirit

19 A.T. Robertson, *Word Pictures in the New Testament,* (From CD-ROM, E-Sword, Rick Meyers, 2008)
20 The American Standard Bible, 1901

Seven --The Primacy of Prophecy

21 Marvin R. Vincent, *Vincent's Word Studies,* (taken from E-Sword, CD-Rom, Rick Meyers, 2000)
22 Merrill Unger, *Unger's Bible Dictionary,* (Chicago: Moody Press, 1957), p.890
23 Vincent Op. Cit.
24 Graham Houston, Prophecy, a Gift for Today, (Downers Grove, Illinois: Inter Varsity Press, 1989) p.110
25 Ibid., p. 110
26 Ibid., p. 111
27 Andrew L. Blackwood, "I and II Corinthians," *The Communicators Commentary,* Ed. Lloyd J. Ogilvie, (Waco, Texas: Word Books, Publishers, 1985), p. 153
28 *The NIV Study Bible,* New International Version, (Grand Rapids, Mi; 1985), p. 1846
29 *Vincent's Word Studies,* (from E-Sword, CD-Rom, Rich Meyers, 2000).
30 Ibid., E-Sword
31 Vincent's Word Studies, op., cit.

32 Frederick L. Godet, *Commentary on the Epistle to the Romans*, translated from the French by Rev. A. Cusin and Talbot W. Chambers, (Grand Raids, Mi.: Zondervan Publishing House, American ed., 1956), p. 431

33 Joel C. Rosenberg, Inside the Revolution, (Carol Stream, Illinois: Tyndale house Publications Inc. 2009), p. 379

34 Ibid., p. 387

35 Ibid., p. 387

36 Stanley D. Toussaint, "Acts," *The Bible Knowledge Commentary*, editors; John F. Walvoord and Roy B. Zuck, (Wheaton, Illinois: Victor Books, Scripture Press Publications, 1983), p. 358.

Eight --The Question of Healing (part one)

37 Albert Barnes, *Commentary on I Timothy*, (E-Sword, CD Rom by Rick Meyers).

38 Ibid., on I Timothy 5:23.

39 A.T. Robertson, *Word Pictures*, (E-Sword) on 1 Timothy 5:23

40 Spiros Zodhiates, The Patience of Hope, (Grand Rapids, Mi.: WM. B. Eerdmans Publishing Company, 1960) o. 117

41 Zodhiates, p. 122

42 Ibid., p 123\

43 Ibid., p. 125

44 Ibid., p. 126

45 Ibid., 127 Zodhiates devotes about three chapters in his commentary to this subject. I recommend these chapters to anyone wishing to pursue the matter.

46 Ibid., p. 129

47 Marvin R. Vincent, *Vincent's Word Studies in the New Testament*, (CD Rom E-Sword on I Corinthians 11L29

48 Ibid., on I Corinthians 11:29

Nine --The Question of Healing (part two)

49 Albert Barnes, *Albert Barnes' Notes on the Bible*, (CD Rom E-Sword, Rich Meyers), on James 5:16.

50 Jay P. Green St., *Literal Translation of the Holy Bible*, (CD Rom, E-Sword, Rick Meyers).

51 Marvin R. Vincent, *Word Studies in the New Testament*, (CD Rom, E Sword, Rick Meyers)

52 Ibid., on James 5:16

53 Green, (E-Sword).

54 Spiros Zodhiates, *The Patience of Hope*, (Grand Rapids Mi: WM Eerdmans Publishing Company, 1960) p. 195

55 Ibid., p. 195

56 The NIV Study Bible, (Grand Rapids Michigan: Zondervan Bible Publishers, 1985) p. 1718

57 John A. Witmer, "Romans", *The Bible Knowledge Commentary*, ed. John F. Walvoord and Roy B. Zuck (Wheaton. Illinois: Victor Books, a division of SP publications, Inc. 1983), p 473

58 Ibid., p. 473

Ten --The Sabbath Day Controversy

59 Lewis Sperry Chaffer, *Systematic Theology*, vol. four, Grand Rapids, Mi: Kregel Publications, 1948). p. 101

60 Ibid., p. 104

61 Ibid., p. 103

62 Ibid., p.103

63 Ibid., p. 102

64 Ibid., p. 1-3

65 Ibid., p. 107

66 Merrill Unger, *Unger's Bible Dictionary*, (Chicago: Moody Bible Institute, 1957, p. 1050

67 Chafer, p. 119

68 Unger, p. 1050

69 Chafer, p 120

70 Unger. P. 1050

71 Chafer, pp. 120-121

72 NIV Bible Study Bible, (Grand Rapids Mi: Zondervan Bible Publishers, 1985), p 1727

73 Albert Barnes, *Albert Barnes' Notes on the Bible*, (computer program, E-Sword, version 7.9.5., Rich Meyers, 2001)

Eleven --Search for The True Sabbath

74 Merrill Unger, *Unger's Bible Dictionary*, (Chicago: Moody Bible Institute) p. 941

75 NIV Study Bible, (Grand Rapids, Mi: Zondervan Bible Publishers, 1985), p. 1815

76 Norman Geisler, "Colossians,", The Bible Knowledge Commentary, editors John F. Walvoord and Roy B. Zuck, (Wheaton, Ill; Victor Books, 1983) p. 678

77 Lewis Sperry Chafer, *Systematic Theology*, vo.4 (Grand Rapids Mi: Kregel Publications, 1948), p. 110.
78 NIV Study Bible, 2879. Ibid., p. 28
79 See Appendix for "More Thoughts on Hebrews 6 and 10

Twelve Looking for Signs and Wonders

80 NIV Study Bible, (Grand Rapids, Michigan: Zondervan, 1995), p 1504
81 John Wesley, *John Wesley's Explanatory Notes on the Whole Bible.* (E-Sword, Rick Meyers).
82 D.A. Carson, "The Purpose of Signs and Wonders in the New Testament," *Power Religion, The Selling Out of the Evangelical Church*, ed. Michael Scott Horton, (Chicago: Moody Press 1992), p. 106
83 A.T. Robertson, *Word Pictures in the New Testament*, (E-Sword, Rich Meyers)
84 Carson, p. 107
85 Ibid., p. 107
86 Carson, pp. 107-108
87 John H. Armstrong, "In Search of Spiritual Power," *Power Religion, The Selling out of The Evangelical Church*, Ed. Michael Scott Horton, Chicago: Moody Press, 1992, p. 68
88 Ibid., p. 68
89 James M. Boice, "A Better way, The Power of The Word and Spirit," *Power Religion, The Selling Out of the Evangelical Church*, ed. Machel Scott Horton, (Chicago: Moody Press, 1992) p. 128
90 Adam Clarke, Adam Clark's Commentary on the Bible, (E-Sword, Rich Meyers, 2008).
91 Ibid., E-Sword.
92 Albert Barnes, *Albert Barn's Notes on The Bible*, (E-Sword, Rick Meyers, 200
93 John Gill, *John Gill's Exposition of the Entire Bible*, (E-Sword, Rich Meyers, 2008)
94 Carson, p. 108
95 Ibid, p. 109

Thirteen -End Time Teaching

96 Charles Caldwell Ryrie, *The Ryrie Study Bible*, (Chicago, Moody Press, 1976)
97 Kim Riddlebarger, "This Present Paranoia," *Power Religion the, The Selling of The Evangelical Church*, ed. Michael Scott Horton, (Chicago: Moody Press, 1992) p 265

98 John F. Walvoord, "Revelation," *The Bible Knowledge Commentary*, ed. By John F. Walvoord and Roy B. Zuck, (Wheaton, Illinois; Victor Books, 1983), p 928

99 Albert Barnes, *Albert Barns' Notes on The Bible*, (E-Sword, Rich Meyers).

100 Matthew Henry, Matthew Henry's Commentary on The Whole Bible, (E-Sword, Rich Meyers, 2008).

Fourteen --Conclusion

101 Francis A. Schaeffer, *How should We Then Live?* 1955, (now available from Crossway Books) title page.

102 Charles Colson and Nancy Pearcey, *How Now Shall We live?* (Tyndale House Publishing, Inc. 1999), title page.

103 A. Kenneth Curtis, J. Stephen Lang, Randy Petersen. *The 100 Most Important Events in Christian History*, (Fleming H. Revell, 1991,) pp.30 and 31

104 NIV Study Bible (Grand Rapids, Michigan: Zondervan Bible Publishing, 1985) p.1857.